# How Sports Betting Works

LIU, CHIEN C.

# Introduction

# Online Sportsbook

# Agent

## Player

# Other Characters

# Concept

# Conclusion

# Letters from readers

# Appendix

# Introduction

This book was published many years ago in Taiwan, with the title "The Game Rules Not Told by Sports Betting and Lottery Bookmakers," issued by Business Weekly Publishing. As a memento of my departure from the sports betting industry, I penned down this book, hoping to enlighten people on the lesser-known rules within the industry, and to offer a fresh perspective on how operators of sports betting manage this game to make money. Currently, there are numerous articles teaching people how to win money on online sportsbooks, yet few discuss how these platforms win money from the public.

The response to the publication was stronger than I had anticipated. Over the years, many readers have written to me, expressing their love for the book and raising various questions hoping for answers. As time has passed, the physical copies of this book have sold out in bookstores, making it difficult for interested readers to find a copy.

Fortunately, with the rise of e-books, I have been able to re-list the electronic version of this book in online stores. Additionally, I have updated some sections and included discussions from letters exchanged with readers over the years, hoping to provide further insight.

This book specifically delves into sports betting, simply put, gambling related to sports, such as the Taiwan Sports Lottery issued by the government, legally permitted online sportsbooks, or illegal underground betting websites, etc. Some might think of common sports betting apps on smartphones, which are essentially extensions of online platforms, and thus we regard apps and websites as the same. Many might also think of placing bets over the phone, which essentially is having someone place bets on a website on your behalf. Hence, when we talk about sports betting here, in real-life terms, it refers to sports lotteries you see on the streets, betting sites, a variety of online sportsbooks, mobile apps, etc.

However, this book isn't about teaching you how to bet on websites, how to place a bet, there are plenty of books like that everywhere. On the contrary, we discuss how online sportsbooks are established, how do they make money? What are the economic rules behind? Who are the players involved? And how do they grow and flourish, enticing batch after batch of players to continuously invest time and money in this game, eventually losing everything.

In other words, I want to tell you some things that online sportsbooks won't tell you, and hope that after reading, you'll realize that betting should only be for entertainment. The phrase "a little gambling is amusing" holds, treating it as spending money on watching a movie is fine, but considering gambling as a profession, or hoping to get rich from it is mere fantasy. In the game of betting, the ones making money will never be the players, so for the sake of you and your family, please stay away from illegal betting, and treat legal betting with a leisurely attitude, without hoping to make money from this game.

If you have close friends or family obsessed with online gambling, you can give them this book to read. As long as they understand how online sportsbooks operate behind the scenes, they naturally won't gamble again. The best way to quit something is to first understand what it essentially is. They think they can win only because they are unaware of the rules behind these platforms, once they know, no one would want to keep losing, handing over money to online sportsbooks for nothing.

## Who Am I?

I am a systems engineer, specialized in constructing massive software systems line by line of code. Over a decade ago, through a fortuitous opportunity, I was commissioned to delve into online and sports betting, eventually planning and designing the betting transaction system used behind online sportsbooks, thus entering this circle.

What everyone recognizes as online sportsbooks, is actually a complete computer software transaction system. In the online gambling industry, a high degree of computerization is required to ensure smooth operation of daily business. Hence, operators need to encode their ideas, rules, profit models, and risk control into the system. For this reason, a systems engineer has the chance to see what operators are truly contemplating. So, I understand the mindset of online sportsbooks.

However, I don't want to narrate this industry in a textbook manner. Online sportsbooks are a colorful and thrilling sector. Moving forward, I will take you on a cursory tour in a simplistic manner, elaborating more on interesting aspects, while sparing you the serious statistics and mathematics. The aim is not to be rigorously detailed, but to ensure the conveyed concepts are accurate.

## I Would Like to First Talk to Everyone About a Common Misconception

The game of betting on sports, known as "Sports Betting" in English, differs from lottery games that solely rely on luck for winning. It possesses a technical aspect. Many people will tell you that as long as you understand the teams and the game well enough, predicting the outcome is quite probable, six out of ten times. Thus, by diligently following the sports section in various newspapers, you can steadily make money.

**But is this really the case?**

Of course not. In fact, the reality is the opposite. Those who visit online sportsbooks will only end up losing money steadily. Do you know the real reason why? However, there's an intriguing aspect to this game – it allows a small portion of people to consistently make money, creating an illusion that sports betting can be profitable.

That's why we want to discuss online sportsbooks, as while everyone is familiar with sports events, "Sports Betting" is different. Specifically concerning online sportsbooks and apps, they encompass the game represented by the words "bet" and "game", so those who wish to participate, besides being familiar with the sports events or being "game-savvy", must also understand the rules of gambling and placing bets. That is, we need to understand what the "bet" in this game is about, and this book aims to make you "bet-savvy".

In this book, we won't discuss sports or games, and certainly, we won't tell you which team to bet on. I assume that you are a sports fan, have a good understanding of games, and are intrigued by online sportsbooks, but just don't know how to engage.

Yet, this is not a beginner's textbook. Regarding how to engage in sports betting, major betting sites on the market have tutorials, and the rules are simple, making it easy to get started. Thus, that's not our focus here.

So, what is the focus of this book?

**Anecdote One:**

"You wake up feeling good in the morning, skim through the sports section of the newspaper, and find that your favorite team has a game today. So, on your way to work, you grab a Starbucks coffee and place a bet on a betting site, thinking that if the team wins, you could earn some extra money." Is this how you bet? Then we categorize you as an average player. But did you know? In this game, average players are always destined to lose money.

**Anecdote Two:**

In the game of betting, apart from average players, there are numerous roles involved, like the so-called websites, agents, shrewd players, and opportunistic passersby. But did you know? Only the average players are gambling, the others are not; they have their means to make money safely.

**Anecdote Three:**

"In a recent election, an underground website opened a betting line, where a certain candidate was given a 500,000 vote handicap, with odds as high as one to eight." Do you realize how illogical this betting line is? In our calculations, it's a complete loss, the underground website loses $60 for every $100 they take. Yes, regardless of the outcome or which candidate wins, they are bound to lose that much.

**Anecdote Four:**

Regardless of the country or type of game, we always hear rumors about a team deliberately losing, or news about fixed games. Match-fixing is detested by all. From a gambling perspective, when match-fixing occurs, uninformed players easily lose money. But do you understand the logic behind it?

**Anecdote Five:**

The debate around the legalization of sports betting has never ceased. Many believe that legalizing sports betting cannot eradicate underground betting, while others think that post-legalization, tax revenue can benefit public welfare. But do you know why underground betting cannot be stopped? Why is benefiting public welfare and eliminating underground betting mutually conflicting? And why should we support the legalization of sports betting?

## What Do We Want To Discuss?

Sports betting is a remarkable invention with a unique operational principle for its betting lines, which makes the game appear less like gambling, and players may find it hard to realize they're losing money. Yet under conditions prioritizing the interests of the online sportsbook, it creates a scenario where astute players can always find an edge. Therefore, this is a game of money, and only those who are clueless are actually gambling.

This book starts with standard game rules, discussing what online sportsbooks will tell everyone about sports betting, but we'll delve directly into their thoughts behind the scenes, their means of making money. We will discuss all roles attached to this game, including astute players, agents, and explore what their survival principles are?

Moreover, we'll discuss their unique tactics, which are ways of making money not dependent on the outcomes of the games, sharing insights on how these tactics are profitable and where the risks lie.

Furthermore, we'll examine this industry from a systemic perspective, exploring unique features within the sports betting industry like the "Three-level Agent System," "Betting Line Commission System," and "Betting Line Classification System," and how these systems contribute to the incessant nature of this game. Hence, various governments towards underground betting can only prohibit but not eradicate it.

Without playing the game of sports betting, it's hard to understand its intricacies. The design of this game ensures that online sportsbooks make money in the long run, subtly, making many who understand the axiom of "the house always wins" still puzzled about why they can't win money. Many might attribute their losses to bad luck or inadequate understanding of the games.

Yet, one would notice that there are people making money in this game. So, you might end up searching the internet for insider tips or believe in some superstitions, hence the vicious cycle, losing more and more until you lose it all, perhaps still clueless about how you lost.

The reality is, the nature of this game allows a small portion of people to always win money, while the majority always lose money. The math and logic behind this can be explained, and once laid out, the mysteries will be unraveled.

Regrettably, such information is not shared by online sportsbooks, and astute players are too indifferent to teach, leaving sports betting shrouded in mystery and misconceptions, not only in countries where sports betting is illegal but also in many where it is legal.

Hence, the necessity for this book. We aim to base our discussions on mathematics, explain using market economics concepts to debunk common myths or superstitions. I will also share the perspectives and interests of online sportsbooks, why they devise various complex play methods, and what secrets lie behind these methods? I will also share insights into the industry's ecosystem and the internal organization of online sportsbooks, enabling a deep understanding of how an online sportsbook is structured, what kind of systems they have, how many people are involved in operations, what roles they play, and what their daily operations look like?

## Who Is This Book for?

For the average player. Losing money in sports betting isn't the scary part; what's frightening is continually losing money over time without realizing it. Therefore, this book aims to teach you how to calculate your return on investment and help you understand how normal it is to lose money. Once you know, you can decide what to do next.

For those aspiring to run online sportsbooks. It's not easy to run an online sportsbook, and one can't simply copy others. Seeing other sportsbooks offering low odds and deciding to offer higher odds to appear more generous or to attract more bets could lead to ridicule. However, being laughed at is a minor issue compared to the risks of not managing odds well. Then, the loser might not be the average player, but you, the bookmaker.

For those interested in this industry. The industry has risk management experts with annual salaries in the millions, and nearly priceless software trading systems. In this book, we will discuss what exactly they do?

For those interested in the regulatory systems of sports betting. We will also discuss the game from various systemic perspectives to understand why it's vibrant enough to form an industry of its own and whether we can develop it into an emerging industry.

Before we delve into explaining this game, you must understand several terms, the jargon of this game.

**Player** - If you plan on opening an account on an online sportsbook or buying a betting ticket from a sports betting station by the roadside, then you are the player.

**Online Sportsbook** - Run by main bookmaking companies offering specific odds for players to bet on. Players primarily participate via websites, but also through mobile apps and telephone betting. Common online sportsbooks include Bet365, William Hill, DraftKings, and FanDuel, offering a variety of sports events ranging from football and basketball to less popular sports.

**Betting** - To participate in sports betting, you first need to bet on which team will win on an online sportsbook. The act of putting your money on a team is called "betting" or "placing a bet," abbreviated as "buying." We can also ask, "Which team did you buy?" meaning, which team did you bet on?

**Bet** - The term "bet" refers to the money you've placed. In layman's terms, it's your money.

**Accepting Bets** - When the online sportsbook takes your money, it's called "accepting bets," also referred to as "online sportsbook accepting bets" or "online sportsbook taking in goods." In sports betting, the money players bet is considered a type of goods, traded often between online sportsbooks.

**Payout** — If you win your bet, the online sportsbook owes you money. This action, from the sportsbook's perspective, is called a "payout" or also referred to as "paying out." Traditionally, you could collect your winnings with your betting ticket, but modern online sportsbooks encourage players to create accounts, with all transactions recorded within these accounts, eliminating the need for physical tickets. The sportsbook reflects your winnings in your account immediately after the game ends.

**Winnings** — The aforementioned "winnings" refers to the money you can retrieve from the sportsbook after winning a bet.

**Point Spread (also known as the spread or margin)** — This is a common gameplay in sports betting used to balance the strength difference between competing teams. Simply put, it's like giving the underdog a head start to make the betting more appealing and challenging. For example, if Team A is significantly stronger than Team B, the bookmaker might set a "point spread" of 2 points in favor of Team B. This means if you bet on Team A to win, they must win by more than 2 points for you to win the bet. It's akin to a race where the slower runner gets a head start; the faster runner not only needs to catch up but also surpass by a certain distance to win. Through the point spread, the bookmaker makes the game more balanced and enticing for betting, reducing the likelihood of a one-sided victory, making the gameplay more thrilling and unpredictable.

**Betting Sites** — Much like a 'supermarket' or 'store' for gambling, providing various betting events and odds for customers to choose and place bets. These betting sites could be physical storefronts, online websites, or mobile applications.

**Direct Customers** — Customers who register and interact with the sportsbook directly without going through any agents, different from those brought in by agents.

**Wise Guy** — A slang term for a professional or highly skilled gambler. They usually have a deep understanding of the events and often find value in the odds, earning long-term profits. They typically have their own sources of information and research methods, giving them a certain edge in betting.

**Patriotic Book** — A special type of betting book usually seen in sports events involving national or regional honor, mostly used in Asian gambling culture. The setup of this book intentionally favors the side supported by the locals or nationals, attracting more bets.

**Juice** — Also known as vigorish, commission, or simply "the vig." It is a common term in the gambling world, especially in sports betting, representing the profit or commission taken by the bookmaker or casino from each bet. It's like envisioning a large pool as the casino, with each bet being a small whirlpool from which the casino takes a bit of "water" as their reward for providing the betting service.

**Arbitrage** — A term in sports betting referring to a technique where a player buys two tickets, betting on both teams, and regardless of which team wins, the player secures a profit. This technique relies on mathematical principles and the ever-changing nature of betting odds, allowing players to profit as long as the timing of their bets is right.

**Trader** — Also known as a trading manager, is the person in the bookmaker responsible for controlling the betting lines.

**Betting Balance Sheet** — Also known as the balance sheet, is a tool or method of recording all betting activities, odds changes, and potential payouts. It's like the accounting book of a company, recording who bet how much on which team or player, and how much payout may be needed based on current odds. Bookmakers adjust the odds based on this balance sheet.

**Betting Ticket** — Refers to the Taiwan Sports Lottery, the government-approved sports betting operation in Taiwan. Going to a betting site and placing a bet is akin to buying a lottery ticket, although it is essentially a bet. The ticket indicates the betting amount, the team bet on, the odds, and how much money can be retrieved if you win.

Feeling overwhelmed by the terminology? This is just the beginning. More terms will come up later on, and these terms are essentially the jargon of this industry. To understand the game, you must grasp what people in this field are talking about. But worry not about memorizing them; these terms are so commonly used that we will keep using and explaining them throughout, making it hard for you to forget.

Furthermore, every region has its own specific terminology. In this book, we will use the terms and jargon common in Taiwan. Once you understand the concepts, you'll find it easy to transition to the terminology used in other regions or countries since the underlying concepts of sports betting are globally consistent. Different online sportsbooks might tweak some minor details, but the core principles remain unchanged and align with the concepts laid out in this book.

How to play sports betting? What's the allure that keeps you coming back? In simple terms, you place bets and win money.

Note that I used the word "win," not "hit the jackpot" like in lottery gaming. Hitting the jackpot means you're relying on luck, sitting at home waiting for money to fall from the sky. In sports betting, we use the word "win" because you rely on your judgment, your knowledge, and of course, your cash to earn those crisp bills from the sportsbook. Effort is required. The more money you bet, the more you win, and vice versa. This is what we call "no pain, no gain"

## First, Check the Betting Line and Then Place a Bet

Now let's dive into the topic at hand: how to "play" sports betting? Suppose you wake up feeling good one morning, wanting to join in on the fun. So, you take your beloved $100, head to the betting site to buy a betting ticket. At the betting site, you'll first encounter something like the following:

| Football League | |
|---|---|
| Team A | Odds 1.78 |
| Team B | Odds 1.82 |

This is what we call a "betting line." The sportsbook offers dozens of betting lines every day for everyone to choose from, and the above is an example of a betting line. It indicates that Team A will face off against Team B tonight, and we can bet on which team will come out victorious.

So how should we bet after seeing the betting line? According to this betting line, we have two options:

The first option is to place $100 on Team A to win. If Team A indeed wins, we can collect $178. The calculation is as follows:

**Principal $100 x Team A odds 1.78 = $178**

The second option is to place $100 on Team B to win. If Team B wins, we can collect $182. The calculation is:

**Principal $100 x Team B odds 1.82 = $182**

The rules above are straightforward, and I believe everyone can understand them. To play sports betting, first look at the betting line, then choose a team to bet on. If you win, the payout is the principal multiplied by the odds. But perhaps someone might ask, what if I bet on Team A, and they end up losing?

The answer is simple: if Team A loses, you lose. When you lose, you lose, and you won't be able to get a single cent back from the sportsbook. Discard your betting ticket, and consider it a donation to charity. (This is true, as most governments mandate that a portion of the profits from sports betting must go to charity, so maybe $10 of your $100 will go to the government for charitable causes.) Or consider it as pure entertainment (this is also true, as the remaining profit goes to the company hosting the sports betting, so maybe the other $90 goes to entertaining others).

## Odds Including the Principal

Here, it's necessary to clarify that, taking Team B as an example, although the sportsbook pays out $182, since we previously placed $100 when buying the betting ticket, although we receive $182, after deducting the principal, we actually only win $82.

Hence, this odds of 1.82 is also known as "odds inclusive of the principal," where the 1 in the odds represents our principal.

**1.00 X Principal = Our Principal, which means we first retrieve our principal.**

And 0.82 represents the extra money you won.

**0.82 X Our Principal = Actual winnings**

It needs to be emphasized that some sportsbooks use "odds exclusive of the principal," indicating only 0.82, with the intention of making it easier for players to see at a glance how much they won. In this book, we use "odds inclusive of the principal," that is 1.82, to make it easier to see how much money can be retrieved in total, because such odds display a larger figure, making it look like you win more, which is also the international norm.

Let's revisit the concept of odds. Expanding the term "odds," it refers to the "payout ratio." In layman's terms, it's how much of the money collected by the sportsbook is paid out to players as winnings?

So, in the game of sports betting, there are two characteristics of odds:

First, the odds you bet on cannot exceed 3.00.

Second, the odds you bet on cannot be less than 1.00.

Speaking of the second point first, if the odds we bet on are less than 1.00, for example, 0.90, this means if we bet $100, if we win, we could only retrieve $90, which results in a loss of $10. Winning yet losing money, no one would buy such foolish odds, hence odds cannot be less than 1.00.

Next, about the odds not exceeding 3.00, this might be puzzling to most. Traditionally, when it comes to betting lines, there seems to be no upper limit. We've heard of 2-to-1, 5-to-1, 8-to-1, or even 100-to-1 odds. Why is there this limitation of 3.00, which is essentially a maximum of 3-to-1?

The detailed explanation will be provided later in this book, but a brief mention here is that in the game of sports betting, most people are playing bets with a ½ probability of winning. In such bets, the odds absolutely cannot exceed 3-to-1. However, in bets with a winning probability of less than ½, the odds can indeed exceed 3-to-1.

**Why is it so appealing?**

The introduction above outlines the most basic way to play sports betting, and from here, we can see why this game is so enticing. It has four major attractions:

- High probability of winning, compared to lottery games where you draw numbered balls, the chance of winning the lottery is one in a million or even one in ten million. Frankly speaking, you have a better chance of getting struck by lightning than winning the lottery. However, in sports betting, if you buy a soccer ticket or place a bet on a sportsbook, even if you close your eyes and pick, there's a fifty-fifty chance since either Team A or Team B will win.

- Typically, on a regular sportsbook, as long as you win your bet, there won't be anyone else sharing the winnings with you. Whatever you bet, you win. For instance, with odds of 1.82, if you bet $100, you can retrieve $182, if you bet $1 million, you can retrieve $1.82 million.

- In contrast to the number ball lottery, after the draw, we have to check how many others have won to know how much we can get (though I guess, if you really hit the jackpot, you probably wouldn't care much about sharing).

- Information regarding sports events is open and transparent. Which team is strong? Which team is weak? Many newspapers have special sections discussing this, and there are experts on media platforms teaching us how to analyze games, making predictions before games. Their accuracy is much higher compared to stock market pundits. Predicting game outcomes, you could say six out of ten predictions could be correct.

We can have second thoughts. This means after buying into sports betting, if you realize the team you picked isn't performing well or think they will lose, or suddenly remember you need to pay rent at the end of the month and can't afford to lose, you can still retrieve most of your principal and quit betting!

Of course, this doesn't mean you can return your betting ticket at the betting site for a refund. They won't refund you, but you can achieve the goal of quitting by "hedging." This will be discussed in detail later, and it will also teach you how to make a quick escape when you realize halfway through the game that the situation isn't favorable and the team you bet on is bound to lose, so you decide to quit betting and retrieve some of your principal.

By the way, there's no way to hedge in number ball lottery games, the more you try to hedge, the bigger the hole you dig for yourself. If you pick the wrong numbers, just accept your fate and don't buy more.

These four characteristics differentiate sports betting completely from traditional lottery tickets, contributing to its widespread popularity and an increasing number of players. Therefore, most governments allow the issuance of two different types of lottery games simultaneously, one being the number ball lottery, and the other being sports lottery.

So, after understanding the gameplay, can we go buy lottery tickets or play on sportsbooks in this manner?

Indeed, the above-mentioned rules are public, and playing according to them is fine. Although the gameplay may slightly differ from country to country, the basic principles remain the same. You may also realize all sportsbooks operate similarly, just bet according to the odds. For those who don't care much about winning or losing and just want to bet for fun, knowing this much is sufficient.

Because we've discerned a key factor, that is the betting line's odds. From the example above, we have a vague sense that how much you can win depends on the odds. And how do sportsbooks make money? Probably from setting the odds. So, at first glance, this seems like a fairly fair game where everyone wants to win money based on their own abilities. It's all about how accurately you can predict the outcomes of games.

## Key Odds

Unfortunately, this game is not as "fair" as everyone imagines. In fact, the term "fair" in this game has always had two meanings: one is fairness to the players, and the other is fairness to the online sportsbook, and these two meanings have never been the same concept.

There is also unfairness among players. For instance, in the example of Team A versus Team B above, perhaps when you bet on Team A, the odds you get are 1.78, but someone else might get 1.88, and someone less fortunate might even get 1.50. These discrepancies are unpredictable. This goes to say that the fairness of this game is quite peculiar.

The concept of "odds" is much more important than everyone imagines. Firstly, it determines that ordinary players are destined to lose money. Players who guess accurately break even, and only those who guess very accurately can make money. What does this mean?

- Ordinary Players: They are the ones who, at most, can get five out of ten bets right, which is the chance you get when you close your eyes and pick, a fifty-fifty chance.

- Accurate Guessers: They nearly get six out of ten bets right, which is typical for people who follow the games. The probability of guessing correctly should be close to this number.

- Very Accurate Guessers: They get more than seven out of ten bets right, which definitely leads to making money, but almost no one can achieve this.

Therefore, we need to discuss more on the most crucial aspect of this game, which is the "odds." And there is a common misconception about it, which is, who sets the odds?

## Who Sets the Odds?

The term "odds" traditionally seems to be determined by various sports publications or experts. It's common knowledge that stronger teams have lower odds while weaker teams have higher odds, so it seems logical that the odds are set based on experts' opinions on which team is stronger or weaker.

If that were the case, our previous assumptions would be incorrect, as this would imply that the game is absolutely fair. Since sports experts are objective, all roles in this game, amongst each other, should be fair. And whether players can make money would solely depend on how accurately they can predict the game outcomes.

However, our assumptions are actually correct, as odds are not set by experts. We could say that the common perception about this is slightly correct, or even completely wrong. We need to look at this from an economic perspective:

- Who hosts the sports betting game? The answer is simple, the various online sportsbooks/companies.

- Why do online sportsbooks host these games? This answer is also simple: to make money.

- How do online sportsbooks make money? As everyone has sensed, it's through the odds.

- What's crucial for online sportsbooks to make money? Regardless of the game outcome, they need to profit.

So, deducing from these points, since online sportsbooks profit from odds and not from game outcomes, it's evident that odds have nothing to do with who wins or loses the game. Hence, no matter how accurate sports experts are, their opinions are irrelevant to online sportsbooks.

**Fairness of the Game**

Here, we can summarize the three basic elements of this game:

- It's a game between the online sportsbook and players, and there will always be betting lines and odds.

- If players want to win money, they must look at game outcomes and rely on odds to win the prize money.

- For online sportsbooks to profit, they must rely on odds for earnings, regardless of game outcomes.

These characteristics form the uniqueness of sports betting. Its fairness is quite peculiar.

Some might argue that there should be a fourth element: that the betting is always on sports events. Indeed, since we're discussing sports betting, sports events should be a basic element. However, what we're about to delve into—the principles of betting lines and online sportsbooks—can be applied not just to sports events. Whether it's baseball, basketball, horse racing, car racing, or even predicting the next President or the winners of the next Oscars, these principles apply.

Thus, this is essentially a book discussing "betting." Starting from the next chapter, we'll explore how online sportsbooks in sports betting actually make money, what measures they employ, and what actions they undertake to ensure profits.

# Online Sportsbook

## Introducing Online Sportsbooks

In the chapter "Online Sportsbooks," we are going to introduce the most crucial player in sports betting—the "House," commonly referred to as "online sportsbooks," betting companies, or big casinos. Due to advancements in modern technology, they have transitioned into online platforms, usually appearing as websites. Hence, for ease of understanding, we'll call them online sportsbooks.

Online sportsbooks essentially host these betting games, and the rules they adopt, along with their operation of betting lines, deeply impact everyone involved.

Whether we are discussing how average players lose money, how savvy players make money, how agents earn commissions, or even the so-called "indifferent" money-making tactics, we first need to understand how online sportsbooks profit. This is because their earnings are independent of the outcomes of the games—regardless of who wins or loses a game, they must make money. Therefore, when others also wish to make money in this manner, they would need to emulate all the methods employed by online sportsbooks.

So now, let's delve into the ways online sportsbooks make money. Before we can fully grasp how they operate, we must first understand where this "money" comes from. In other words, what exactly is the "profit" for online sportsbooks?

### The Profit of Online Sportsbooks: "Juice"

The profit of online sportsbooks has a specific term, called "Juice," also referred to as "Vig" or "Vigorish" in English. In the news, it's often termed as

"Payout Commission" or "Online Commission." Despite the variety in terminology, they all point to the money earned by the online sportsbook. This term is common in the gambling arena, especially in sports betting. Essentially, it's the profit or commission that the house or bookmaker earns from each betting event. You can visualize it this way: the betting house is a large pool, and each betting event is like a small whirlpool within this large pool. No matter which side you bet on, the house will scoop a little "water" from this small whirlpool as compensation for providing gambling services.

For instance, if the odds for a particular event are 1.95 to 1.95, theoretically, these odds should be 2 to 2 to ensure fairness. However, the house takes a small portion, altering the odds to 1.95, so that no matter which side wins, the house will earn the difference, which is the "Juice."

This model ensures that the house or bookmaker earns a stable profit regardless of the outcome of the betting event. If you are a gambler, understanding the concept of "Juice" is important as it directly affects the profitability of your long-term betting. Simply put, "Juice" is the bread and butter of the betting house, a necessity for their operations.

So how do online sportsbooks make money? It's quite straightforward, just a matter of a mathematical formula. The rule is set at the beginning of the game. Regardless of the amount of bets collected, the online sportsbook takes a certain percentage of it, and that's it.

The actual percentage could be 5%, 10%, or even higher; it varies from one online sportsbook to another. However, hardly ever is it below 5% since too low a profit is not sustainable, a point we will discuss later.

In Taiwan, the Securities Transaction Tax is well-known to be 0.3%. For instance, if we buy stocks worth $10,000, the tax amount is merely $30, which is considered a small amount. However, when it comes to the "Juice"? Even at a minimum of 5%, for a $10,000 bet, one would have to give away $500. If you encounter a more ruthless online sportsbook, it could even be $1,000, which certainly isn't a small amount.

Due to the hefty "Juice" collection, it's not easy for online sportsbooks to collect this money. Imagine a scenario where a betting event is opened with odds of 1 to 1, you bet $10,000 and win. But then the online sportsbook comes asking for $1,000 as "Juice." Would you be willing to pay?

People risk losing everything when they buy betting tickets, and the winnings are often marginal. If every time you win, the online sportsbook comes to collect 10%, isn't that too harsh? Especially considering that bank deposit interest rates are far below this percentage. Thus, contrary to the traditional belief that online sportsbooks take a cut from the winners, i.e., the "Juice" from the winners, this notion is incorrect in sports betting.

If online sportsbooks indeed took a direct cut, soon nobody would play. Or at the very least, you'd want to negotiate with the online sportsbook to reduce the "Juice," which would be troublesome for the online sportsbook. So, the biggest difference between "Juice" and tax is that it cannot be collected openly.

Nevertheless, online sportsbooks must make money. Fairly speaking, who would run a business that doesn't profit? Who could manage that? Especially after online sportsbooks have invested heavily in this business. Besides setting up websites, betting companies might need to spend money on betting stations, printing betting tickets for people to fill out, and hiring counter staff to tirelessly handle the money transactions. So, earning this "Juice" is absolutely necessary for them.

## The Invisible Juice

Therefore, the "Juice" needs to be collected, but the online sportsbook has to package it carefully. It can't be collected too obviously, nor can players feel its presence; otherwise, the game loses its charm. In fact, in sports betting, the "Juice" is as omnipresent as air, yet often invisible to most, and though it's substantial, it's not easily perceived. If you have a sports lottery ticket in hand, check if there's any phrase like "Charging you Juice $13.5" printed on it. I can assure you there won't be. At most, it might say "Bet with hope, share love" or "Charitable Sports Lottery for a joyful life."

So, how is the Juice packaged? This packaging has already established a perception in traditional thinking, which is to hide the Juice within the odds. Everyone would tell you that the online sportsbook just needs to change the original 1 to 1 odds to 1 to 0.9, and then tell you that the game is unfair, the online sportsbook will take a lot from the winners.

But this explanation has its flaws. Let's take a look at the table below.

|  | odds | bet | prize money |
|---|---|---|---|
| For a fair scenario (**1:1**) | 2.00 | 100 | 200 |
| For an unfair scenario (**1:0.9**) | 1.90 | 100 | 190 |

In a fair scenario, meaning when the online sportsbook doesn't collect Juice, if we place a bet of $100, we can get back $200. After deducting the principal, we essentially win $100. Using $100 to win $100, this is a 1 to 1 odds, which is fair.

But what about in an unfair scenario? We bet $100, but can only get back $190, with a payout of $190, we win $90. After deducting the principal, we only win $90. Using $100 to win $90, this is a 1 to 0.9 odds, which is unfair.

By this logic, every time the online sportsbook sets the odds, as long as the odds are lower than 1 to 1, they will naturally earn money. But here lies the problem, this is quite obvious and players would notice!

If a website always offers 1.90 odds, it's no different from taxing. Players would easily understand that to be a winner, they would be taxed 10%, which would significantly dampen their enthusiasm for betting. So, isn't this Juice just as obvious as it was before hiding?

Therefore, hiding the Juice in the odds requires tact. In reality, except for a few special circumstances, there's absolutely no online sportsbook that would stick to 1.90 odds all the way. This method is too naive, and online sportsbooks don't use it. The highest guiding principle for online sportsbooks in hiding the Juice is to make it "invisible" to you.

**Example of Collecting Juice**

Why do we say that the Juice is invisible? Please take a look below, this is a betting line with collected Juice.

| Football League | |
| --- | --- |
| Team A | Odds 2.00 |
| Team B | Odds 1.60 |

Suppose you bet $100 on Team A, and in the end, Team A wins. Then you really can get back a payout of $200, bet $100 to win $200, for you it's a 1 to 1 odds, which seems very fair. Moreover, you don't have to pay any additional tax.

(Please note, although the payout is $200, as mentioned earlier, $100 out of the $200 is the principal of the original bet, so you actually only win back $100.)

Examples like the above are common in reality, so we can't say that the online sportsbook is taking a cut from the winner, or taking extra money from the winner. Furthermore, sometimes the odds on the betting line might even exceed 2.00. Suppose the odds today are 2.50, then if we bet $100, we can get back $250. Looking at it this way, the online sportsbook is not just being fair to us, it's practically a blowout sale, greatly favoring us.

But in reality, the online sportsbook also collects the Juice, otherwise, you could have won even more, or perhaps we can say, it's the losing party that paid this Juice for you. Has everyone spotted the problem now? Those who are more sensitive to numbers should have a vague feeling that there's something not quite right with these odds, right? Indeed, the problem lies in these odds.

Now let's talk some math. In an ideal situation, that is when the online sportsbook doesn't take any Juice, no matter which team we bet on, the odds should be 2.00, or to be precise, the sum of the odds for both teams in the betting line should be 4.00.

So, in the above betting line, if the online sportsbook didn't take any Juice, it should look like this:

| Football League | |
| --- | --- |
| Team A | Odds 2.00 |
| Team B | Odds 2.00 |

Why say this? Because only in such a betting line, no matter which team wins in the end, those who bet can all get a 1 to 1 payout, meaning if you bet $100, you can get back $200. From this betting line, it's evident at a glance, betting on Team A can get a 1 to 1 payout, and betting on Team B can also get a 1 to 1 payout, ensuring fairness to all bettors.

However, the previous betting line with Juice doesn't work the same way. Although Team A can get a 1 to 1 payout, Team B is left with a 1 to 0.6 payout. This creates a scenario where those betting on Team A are treated fairly, but those betting on Team B are at a disadvantage.

But we can't say the online sportsbook isn't fair, they are fair, but their definition of fairness isn't the same as yours, which will be discussed more later on. Here, the fairness from the sportsbook's perspective means, they want to earn a 10% Juice, and they've told you upfront, and you're aware of it, so it's a fair deal with no deception.

If Team A wins in the end, actually, the losing party has nothing much to say. After all, they lost, and there's no way to get the money back. The winners have no complaints either, as it's a 1 to 1 payout, and they get what they deserve. Of course, the online sportsbook, having taken its 10% Juice, is satisfied as well, making this a happy scenario for all.

So, Juice does exist, and it's hidden within the odds, but if everyone doesn't know how to look for it, it's not easy to realize its existence. Despite all the discussion, you might still not understand how this "Juice" is hidden within the odds by the online sportsbooks.

## Juice and Total Odds

The online sportsbooks approach the issue of "Juice" from a different perspective than us. They are business entities, and they see things in terms of revenue and expenses.

The money bet by players is the revenue for the online sportsbook. The money that needs to be paid out to the players is the expense. So the principle is, as long as expenses are less than revenue, the remaining money naturally is the profit for the online sportsbook.

Suppose today someone bets $100 on Team A, and someone else bets $100 on Team B, then the total revenue for the sportsbook today is $200. So if the sportsbook wants to earn a 10% Juice, the basic practice is to hold back $20, and just find a way to pay out $180. This means the payout ratio is 90% of the revenue.

With this benchmark, things become easier. The only expense for the sportsbook is the payout, and the payout ratio is precisely the odds. So, if the sportsbook wants to collect Juice, they need to tweak the odds, not the odds for a single team, but the total odds of both teams.

As discussed earlier, in a situation without Juice, the odds offered by the sportsbook for both teams should be 2.00 each, adding up to a total odds of 4.00.

| Football League | |
|---|---|
| Team B | Odds 2.00 |
| Team B | Odds 2.00 |
| | |
| | Total Odds 4.00 |

Having deduced earlier that in order to collect a 10% Juice, the online sportsbook needs to control its expenses, now if the total odds are 4.00, it represents a total payout of 4. So, to collect Juice, the payout needs to be reduced by 10%, making it 3.6. This reflects a payout which is 90% of the revenue, translating to a total odds of 3.60.

Hence, the "Juice" is not hidden within a particular team or a particular odd; to identify this aspect, one must look at the total odds. Simply looking at the odds of one team won't reveal it, which is why it's hard for people to feel its existence. (Also, the betting ticket only shows the odds of the team you bet on, so just by looking at the ticket, you cannot spot the Juice either).

Let's explore a few more examples.

| Football League | |
|---|---|
| Team A | Odds 2.40 |
| Team B | Odds 1.20 |
| | Total Odds 3.60 |
| | The online sportsbook can take 10% of the revenue |

| Football League | |
|---|---|
| Team A | Odds 1.50 |
| Team B | Odds 2.30 |
| | |
| | Total Odds 3.60 |
| | The online sportsbook can take 10% of the revenue |

By using this simple concept of income and expenditure, online sportsbooks can hide the "juice" within the total odds, and bettors, who usually look at the odds of a single team, naturally find it hard to realize they are being heavily taxed.

From the examples above, we can also see that as long as the online sportsbook is earning juice, the total odds must be less than 4.00. If they earn 10%, the total odds must be 3.60. If they earn 5%, the total odds must be 3.80.

By controlling the total odds, the principle of income and expenditure for the online sportsbook is established, which puts the juice into perspective without causing resentment from the players. Additionally, the juice is not fixed; the sportsbook may take 10% in one game and 5% in the next.

This can be adjusted. The details will be discussed later, but here's a hint: have you ever heard of "end of season sales"? Online sportsbooks also have promotions, and juice is the perfect discount tool. Savvy players will definitely pay attention to these promotional activities.

And when an online sportsbook earns 10% from you, in the industry, it's called "earning 10 points of juice" or "taking 10 points of juice", abbreviated as "10 points juice". This "point juice" refers to how many cents the sportsbook earns from every dollar, as in earning a few cents of juice money. Of course, the sportsbook doesn't always earn 10 points of juice; 10% is just an example for ease of explanation. In reality, it might be more, like 12 points of juice, or 12%, or less, like 5 points of juice, or 5%.

**Hard-Earned Juice**

We need to clarify once again that the aforementioned 10% is purely for explanatory convenience, and not a standard in the industry. If you want to know the official market rates, you can check the odds provided by various major betting companies and online sportsbooks to get an idea. Generally, private online sportsbooks have about 5% juice, while state-run sports lotteries like those in Hong Kong or Singapore have juice ranging from 10% to 12%.

Now, we are concerned about something else: is it necessary for the sportsbook to take so much juice? With a minimum of about 5% to a maximum of 12%, and knowing that a moderately scaled online sportsbook has a daily turnover of around a hundred million, this means that the "juice" equates to tens of millions in profit for the sportsbook every day.

Such a ferocious sportsbook, you might think. However, don't jump to conclusions just yet; this is only a theoretical value and in reality, it's absolutely impossible to earn that much. This doesn't mean the estimated betting amount is inaccurate, nor does it mean the sportsbook won't make money.

Because the juice is actually an expected value. Even if the turnover is a hundred million and the juice is set at 10%, no one can earn that figure. In fact, if a sportsbook sets the juice at 5% and manages to achieve half of it, i.e., 2.5%, then this sportsbook is already considered to be doing quite well.

Therefore, the juice must be set high, and earning money for the sportsbook is very hard. It's not as everyone imagines that by just setting the mathematical formula right, the money will roll in steadily. There's a key to profitability involved in this. Please see the next chapter, "The Key to Profitability".

## The Key to Profitability

We generally have a concept about online sportsbooks. What they do every day is open betting lines, accept bets from players, provide a betting ticket after a bet is placed, and finally, payout winnings to the winners according to the odds on the ticket. In the last section, we introduced the basic elements of a betting line, that is, the total odds must be less than 4.00. As long as the odds on the betting line are within this number, essentially, the sportsbook has the conditions to make money.

It seems, therefore, that setting up an online sportsbook is not difficult, and it appears that anyone could do it. Everyone can hang up a betting line, accept bets from players, and then start making money. For instance, here is a betting line with total odds of 3.60, a very simple betting line that anyone can open. So, it looks like anyone can do it, right?

But is this really the case?

Yes, on the surface, it indeed seems so. The task of bookmaking in sports betting is simple in essence. Once the aforementioned betting line is posted, the sportsbook can start accepting bets. When betting is closed and the game is over, everything falls into place. After paying out the winnings, the sportsbook has the opportunity to find that they have retained 10% of the total income.

We have discussed the reason—this betting line with a total odds of 3.60 ensures that the expenditure is only 90% of the income, so naturally, the sportsbook can keep 10%. If the sportsbook collects $100, they have the chance to keep $10; if they collect $1 million, they have the chance to keep $100,000.

However, please note that this is merely a "chance." And this chance is probably as small as you winning the lottery or being struck by lightning. To understand the key, one must first comprehend the principle of making money from betting lines. So in this section, we will explore under what circumstances can a betting line be profitable?

| Football League | |
|---|---|
| Team A | Odds 1.80 |
| Team B | Odds 1.80 |

## Betting Balance Sheet

To understand how online sportsbooks make money, it's crucial to first understand how they determine their profits. One common tool they use is the "Betting Balance Sheet." With this chart, they can immediately know whether a betting line is profitable once it's posted. Below is an example:

| | Team A | | | Team B | |
| --- | --- | --- | --- | --- | --- |
| Bets | Odds | Payout | Bets | Odds | Payout |
| 100 | 1.8 | 180 | 100 | 1.8 | 180 |
| 200 | 1.8 | 360 | 200 | 1.8 | 360 |
| 小計 | | | | | |
| 300 | | 540 | 300 | | 540 |
| | | | | | |
| Total Bets | | Projected profit | | | Projected profit |
| 600 | | 60 | | | 60 |

The method for this chart is straightforward. Once a betting line is posted, players will place bets and purchase betting tickets. When they place bets, the sportsbook records the betting tickets on this chart. For example, if a player bets $100 on Team A, then a record of a $100 bet is made next to Team A, with odds of 1.80 (the odds are provided by the sportsbook, so whatever the odds are at that time, that's what is recorded). Then a calculation is made to determine how much would be paid out if this player wins; this is the purpose of the "Projected Payout" column, where we can calculate it as $180.

Projected Payout = Bet x Odds

After recording all the betting tickets from players in this manner, the sportsbook can perform statistical analysis when the betting line is closed. The analysis mainly looks at three things:

- What is the total amount of bets? In this example, the total amount collected from players for both teams is $600.

- If Team A wins, how much needs to be paid out? Here it's $540, and since the total amount of bets is $600, the profit at this point is $60.

- If Team B wins, how much needs to be paid out? Here it's also $540, and since the total amount of bets is $600, the profit at this point is also $60.

**The concept of income and expenditure is useful**

The above is a standard Betting Balance Sheet. From this chart, we can also see that the mathematical formula regarding income and expenditure we discussed earlier is perfectly validated.

The initial betting line had a total odds of 3.60, which is 90% of the total expenditure of 4.00, indicating the sportsbook aims to earn 10%. In the Betting Balance Sheet, we can see that the actual total amount of bets is $600, and no matter which team wins, the sportsbook only needs to pay out $540, earning $60.

And this earned $60 is exactly 10% of $600. Theory and practice align perfectly, which is ideal, and that's why we said earlier that bookmaking is simple. As long as the sportsbook sets the total odds correctly, the "juice" will naturally fall into place.

This Betting Balance Sheet, which can instantly show the profits of the sportsbook, is a very useful tool that we will use often. Not only is it commonly used in this book, but in reality, sportsbooks use it even more frequently. Basically, as soon as a betting line is posted and players start buying betting tickets, the sportsbook will keep a close eye on this chart, always monitoring their betting situation.

There's even a position within the sportsbook called "Risk Management Trader (TRADER)" specifically responsible for monitoring this kind of report. Perhaps you've heard of these individuals in the news, and heard about their value with annual salaries in the millions. We will have a dedicated section later on to introduce this job.

## The Risks of Bookmaking

Indeed, one may have already noticed a problem: the act of purchasing betting tickets by a player is voluntary. How much to bet? Which team to bet on? These decisions are all up to the individual. It's highly unlikely that players will obediently comply with the sportsbook's setup when buying tickets. Therefore, the earlier Betting Balance Sheet, where the bets on both teams are identical, represents a situation that is quite improbable in reality.

This is true, which is why we mentioned at the beginning of the article that after setting up the income and expenditure formula, the sportsbook merely has a "chance" of making money. Encountering such a perfect Betting Balance Sheet is highly unlikely.

Let's now look at another example.

| Team A | | | Team B | | |
|---|---|---|---|---|---|
| Bets | Odds | Payout | Bets | Odds | Payout |
| 200 | 1.8 | 360 | 400 | 1.8 | 720 |
| | | | | | |
| Subtotal | | | | | |
| 200 | | 360 | 400 | | 720 |
| | | | | | |
| Total Bets | | Projected profit | | | Projected profit |
| 600 | | 240 | | | -120 |

In this scenario, we assume there are only two betting tickets, one for $200 and the other for $400. This kind of imbalance is actually quite common.

Looking at this table, the total revenue is still $600. If Team A wins, it's good for the bookmaker; they only need to pay out $360, making a profit of $240. However, if Team B wins, it's bad news since the payout will be $720.

This means, apart from paying out the total bet amount of $600, the bookmaker will have to dip into their own pocket for an extra $120. This is a substantial loss for the bookmaker, making it a losing deal.

We call this situation the bookmaker betting against the players. At this point, whether the bookmaker can make money depends on whether Team A wins, similar to how players need their team to win to make money. And just like the players, the bookmaker doesn't know the outcome of the game; there's no assurance that Team A will win.

But what if they really have to pay out? It's not a small amount. In this case, with a collection of $600, they have to pay an extra $120. If it were $600,000, it would be $120,000. And if it were $300 million? That's $60 million. This is only for one game on one day, and for one betting line.

We know that bookmakers run dozens of games and hundreds of betting lines each day. And we also know that the betting balance sheet is supposed to be imbalanced; achieving the perfect balance like in the first table is impossible. So, if a bookmaker starts losing, it could be endless.

This is the risk of bookmaking. As long as there's "betting," there's a possibility of losing, and bookmakers might lose money. From the betting balance sheet, even with the revenue and expense formula, even if theoretically, the bookmaker declares to make a 10% "juice", there's no guarantee against losing money.

So, the basic premise of bookmaking in sports betting is simple, but not everyone can do it. If you let players bet and rely solely on luck to make a living, you're bound to lose big. In essence, bookmaking is easy, but the risks are high.

Yet, everyone wants to run these online sportsbooks in sports betting, as we've seen from numerous news reports. Whenever there's a sports betting contract up for grabs, competitors from all over the world swarm in.

We all know that no one runs a business to make losses! So now there's a question, given the high risk and substantial chance of losing money in bookmaking, why is everyone eager to take on this role?

Here lies a key point, and for better understanding, let's compare the two betting balance sheets from the examples above.

**Making money**

| | Team A | | Team B | |
|---|---|---|---|---|
| | | | | |
| | Total Bets | 600 | | |
| | | | | |
| Bets | Payout | Bets | Payout |
| 300 | 540 | 300 | 540 |
| | | | | |
| | Projected profit | | Projected profit | |
| | 60 | | 60 |

## Losing money

| | Team A | | Team B | |
|---|---|---|---|---|
| | | | | |
| | Total Bets | 600 | | |
| | | | | |
| Bets | Payout | Bets | Payout | |
| 200 | 360 | 400 | 720 | |
| | | | | |
| | Projected profit | | Projected profit | |
| | 240 | | -120 | |

This time, we have juxtaposed the two tables and made a slight modification to the betting balance sheet by pulling out the total section separately and removing the details of each betting ticket. This has turned into a simplified version of the betting balance sheet. In reality, this simplified version is what online sportsbooks actually look at in real-time because it's concise and the profit situation can be seen at a glance.

Now we can make a comparison. Both tables have the same total bets of $600, but the outcomes are vastly different. The "profitable" table allows the bookmaker to earn $60 regardless of the game's outcome. However, the "loss-making" table could potentially lead to a loss of $120.

Upon careful examination, a key factor can be identified, which is "balance." What is balance? It's the "Projected Payout" column in the table. If the projected payouts for both teams are equal, the bookmaker can make money. If they are not equal, there's a potential for loss.

- In the profitable table, Team A's projected payout is $540, and Team B's is $540. They are equal, so the bookmaker can make money either way.

- In the loss-making table, Team A's projected payout is $360, and Team B's is $720. The difference is too large, hence the bookmaker could either make or lose money.

Understanding this key point, we can now grasp the essence of bookmaking, which is the need to control the "betting balance sheet" and not allow players to bet at will. What needs to be controlled is precisely the "Projected Payout" column.

As mentioned earlier, the formula is:

**Projected Payout = Bet Amount × Odds**

In other words, as long as the bookmaker can control the bet amount or the odds, they can naturally control the payout. Additionally, it's worth mentioning that some bookmakers look directly at the bet amount, although this method is not accurate. Since the odds for each ticket are different, solely looking at the bet amount does not allow for an accurate grasp of profitability.

However, because bet amounts are easier to tally and can provide a rough idea of the profit range, some still use this method.

## Balance of Fate

In online sports betting platforms, the term "balance" is often used, with common phrases such as "the betting balance sheet needs to be balanced," "the betting lines need to be balanced," "bets need to be balanced," or "the scales need to be balanced," etc. All of these phrases refer to the same thing, which is the betting balance sheet we discussed earlier, and the "Projected Payout" column within it.

The concept of "balance" is crucial as it directly affects the profitability of the bookmaker. Whether the bookmaker can make money or has to pay out depends entirely on whether the betting lines are balanced.

Apart from using the "betting balance sheet" to monitor the betting situation, bookmakers have another powerful tool at their disposal, known as the "betting scales." Here's an example:

| Team A | Total Bets  (600) | Team B |
|---|---|---|
| Payout  (540) | | Payout  (540) |

The above representation is essentially a simplified version of the "betting balance sheet," reducing the entire betting details to just three numbers. First, the total income. Second, the projected payout for Team A. And third, the projected payout for Team B.

This simplified table looks much cleaner. With just three numbers, one can understand the profit situation of the entire betting line. In fact, this table is precisely what the so-called "risk control managers" or "line managers" look at on a daily basis.

There are three primary reasons for this simplification:

- The betting scales are usually generated in real-time by computers. With each incoming betting ticket, the numbers on the scale change instantly, allowing the bookmaker to grasp the current betting situation at any time.

- Bookmakers are often overwhelmed due to the multitude of betting lines they manage daily, sometimes numbering in the hundreds. They don't have the time to examine all the numbers individually, so they rely on simplified tables. While the betting balance sheet is useful, its plethora of numbers can be distracting.

- Most importantly, to control a betting line, these three numbers are actually sufficient.

Looking back at this table, it somewhat resembles a "scale," with Team A on one end and Team B on the other. The projected payouts represent the weights on the scale. As the payout number increases, it implies a heavier weight, causing the scale to tilt.

Since this table looks and behaves like a scale, and we operate it in a manner similar to a scale, it's referred to as a "betting scale." That's why you often hear bookmakers saying phrases like, "which way is the betting line tilting?" or "which side is it leaning towards?" These expressions are derived from the characteristics of this table.

Please note that this concept will be used continuously throughout our discussion.

Now, with this betting scales tool, bookmakers can instantly discern whether the tickets they've collected will make money or cause a loss. Through this table, they can ask two crucial questions:

Is the projected payout for Team A less than the total income?

Is the projected payout for Team B less than the total income?

If the answer to both questions is "yes," the bookmaker can rest easy knowing that no matter the outcome, they will make money. However, if the scales are imbalanced, and one of these questions returns a "no," then there's a problem, and actions must be taken to restore balance to the scales.

In fact, experienced bookmakers can manage with just two numbers—the projected payouts for both teams. As long as these two numbers are equal, the bookmaker is assured of making money, regardless of which team wins. Thus, the "total income" number on the scale can be considered somewhat redundant.

The key to balance lies in ensuring that the projected payouts on both sides are less than the total income. As long as this condition is met, a slight tilt in the scales doesn't matter. However, perfect balance is preferred as it ensures the most stable profits for the bookmaker.

Now that we understand what bookmakers aim for, it's time to delve into how they achieve it. What actions are taken post the release of a betting line to ensure the stability of the scales of fate?

## The Life Cycle of a Betting Line

In the previous chapter, we discussed that the key to being a bookmaker in sports gambling is maintaining the "balance" of the betting line. Only when the betting line is balanced can the bookmaker earn the "juice." This leads to a critical issue: once the betting line is released, the bookmaker cannot allow it to become imbalanced, or the chances of losing money are quite high.

Fortunately, betting lines are manipulable. We can liken an imbalanced betting line to a common ailment of the bookmaker, and like any other ailment, it can be both "prevented" and "treated."

So, in the following, we will discuss how bookmakers deal with imbalanced betting lines—how they prevent and how they treat such imbalances, and why "prevention" is better than "treatment."

Before we dive into how bookmakers balance betting lines, we must understand the concept of a betting line and the concept of a player.

The primary task of an online sportsbook every day is to release betting lines, which then allow players to go to betting sites, purchase betting tickets, and place bets. Every day, hundreds of betting lines are released, creating this lively gambling ecosystem.

However, the life cycle of a typical betting line rarely exceeds 24 hours. Usually, once the day's games are over, the sportsbook releases the betting lines for the next day's games based on the pre-announced schedule, starting to accept bets—a process known as "opening the line" or "releasing the line," allowing players to place bets.

Post opening, players can purchase betting tickets and place bets. This betting period lasts until five minutes before the actual game starts, known as the "betting period." However, there could be instances where betting is temporarily halted, perhaps due to sudden news like a player injury or other unforeseen events. But such halts are brief, often lasting only a few minutes, after which betting resumes.

As the game is about to commence, the sportsbook formally stops accepting bets, a process known as "closing the line" or "pulling the line," beyond which players can no longer place bets on that particular game. If they wish to bet, they'll have to wait for the next game.

Generally, the life cycle of a betting line is 24 hours. You might wonder why betting must end five minutes before the game starts, but that's a topic for later discussion when we talk about the sportsbook's "arbitrage."

Now let's look at the concept of "player." Since the beginning of this book, we've used this term countless times, and we know that "players" are the individuals who actually place bets. But do you know how many players a sportsbook has to deal with once a betting line is released? Is it one, two, or seventy-eight?

The exact number is hard to determine. Big sportsbooks and small sportsbooks have different levels of recognition and hence different volumes of business. As we've mentioned before, a sizable sportsbook having daily turnovers in the hundreds of millions is quite common. We can also reference the numbers from the Hong Kong Jockey Club. In Hong Kong, on average, each person buys $100 worth of betting tickets daily. This gives us a rough idea: government-sponsored sports gambling attracts about a hundred thousand purchasers daily, while private company sportsbooks, though having fewer customers, may have higher contributions per customer.

We also know that a sportsbook releases hundreds of betting lines daily. So, these hundred thousand players won't all cram into one game. On average, popular betting lines might attract around ten thousand bettors.

This is not an exact number, just an estimation to provide a concept of how many players a sportsbook might have to deal with daily. And when we discuss controlling betting lines later on, we are talking about manipulating these ten thousand players.

**The Essential Skill of Bookmaking: "Line Management"**

With the two concepts outlined above, we can envisage that once a sportsbook releases betting lines daily, around ten thousand players would gradually come to place their bets. They would randomly choose and bet on their favored teams. Observing the betting line balance at this point, we'd notice the balance continuously swaying left and right or gradually tilting towards one side.

In such a scenario of random betting by players, the balance of the betting line is certainly not going to remain stable. Ultimately, when the betting line closes and the balance becomes fixed, there will definitely be a disparity— one team would have attracted more bets while the other less. Let's examine an uncontrolled example to provide a clearer understanding.

| Team A | Total Bets (1M) | Team B |
|--------|-----------------|--------|
| Payout (0.93M) | | Payout (1.3M) |

This is indeed a terrible balance scenario. Without careful management, if Team B wins, the sportsbook would incur a loss of three million dollars. This essentially places the sportsbook in a gambling position akin to the actual bettors, a consequence of players betting randomly.

So, the essential skill for a sportsbook is how to prevent such a scenario from occurring, avoiding a gamble against the players. This skill is termed as "controlling the line" or simply "line management," also referred to as "manipulating the line" or "line manipulation." Hence, let's delve into how sportsbooks manage lines.

Broadly, line management embodies two concepts: "Prevention" and "Treatment."

- **Prevention** entails maintaining the balance of the betting line during the betting phase when the balance is constantly changing. This approach aims to prevent severe imbalance at the closure of the betting line, which would be troublesome to address at that late stage.

- **Treatment** is needed when, at the closure of the betting line, the balance is still off. Since the betting line is closed and the balance won't change any further, the sportsbook must adopt additional measures to perfectly balance the line.

These two concepts form the crux of line management by sportsbooks - prevention followed by treatment to balance the betting line, ensuring the sportsbook earns the "juice" or commission. The adage "Prevention is better than cure" aptly applies here. Let's discuss "Prevention" in this segment, and "Treatment" will be elaborated in the following section.

## Adjusting the Betting Line Balance

Discussing the prevention of line imbalance may seem peculiar, frankly, as the balance is actually in the hands of the players. When more bets are placed on one team, the balance tilts towards that side. The balance simply reflects the betting situation, and it can't just be shifted at will.

Moreover, player bets are unpredictable. As previously estimated, a popular betting line might attract ten thousand players. With so many players purchasing betting tickets, is it feasible to legislate something like "people with an odd last digit in their ID should bet on Team A, and those with an even digit should bet on Team B"? Obviously, this is unfeasible and if such rules existed, nobody would participate in sports betting.

There's also a misconception that needs addressing, illustrated by the following example:

|  | Bets |  | Payout |
|---|---|---|---|
| Team A | 1 million |  | 1.8 million |
| Team B | 2 million |  | 3.6 million |

Here we have a horizontal balance scale. From this, we can see that the anticipated payouts for the two teams are not equal, resulting in a severe imbalance. Given that the total bet is 3 million dollars, the outcome would either be a profit of 600,000 dollars or a loss of 1.2 million dollars.

So, some might suggest, since there's an imbalance, why not adjust it to create balance? Consequently, the table would be modified to look like this:

|  | Bets | Odds | Payout |
|---|---|---|---|
| Team A | 1 million | 1.80 | 1.8 million |
| Team B | 2 million | 0.90 | 1.8 million |

This involves adding the odds to the equation. According to their reasoning, since the sportsbook sets the odds, why not set it this way, right? Moreover, they would further deduce, based on this table, with a total bet collection of 3 million dollars, regardless of which team wins, only 1.8 million dollars need to be paid out. Hence, they argue, under any circumstances, we net a profit of 1.2 million dollars.

Please note, this understanding is entirely erroneous.

Firstly, this brings about a "which came first, the chicken or the egg?" dilemma. The sportsbook needs to publish the betting lines first, only then can the players choose the odds to place their bets. It's impossible to wait until the sportsbook collects the money and then inform the players of the odds. Therefore, the odds must be provided upfront.

Next, once the odds are released, they are printed on the betting tickets. When the time comes, players will be cashing in according to these tickets. So how is the sportsbook going to amend the odds on these ten thousand tickets? It's impractical to notify each player to inform them of altered odds after the lines are closed.

Lastly, we're not in elementary school doing multiplication tables, how could we arbitrarily alter the table? Adding the odds in this manner holds no meaning; the amount the sportsbook owes to the players cannot be shortchanged by a cent.

Therefore, while the balance needs adjusting, it's not about arbitrarily changing the table. The balance is merely a tool reflecting the betting situation; if we need to make adjustments, it should be on the actual betting circumstances.

## Manipulating Players

However, a problem arises. The sportsbook itself doesn't place bets, so why would anyone, after setting up the book, go and bet against themselves? Thus, when we talk about controlling the betting situation, we are actually referring to manipulating the players, making them place bets on both sides of the book, as per the sportsbook's wishes.

But manipulating players, while sounding simple, is incredibly difficult in practice. Firstly, the brains are the players'; they'll bet how they wish to, not as the sportsbook dictates. It's not like when the sportsbook suggests betting on one team, they will obediently follow.

So the first problem emerges, the sportsbook really has no way to command the players. Unless you hire a hypnotist to brainwash them. Alright, even if we could hire a hypnotist, but with so many players, would the hypnotist be able to handle it all?

Next is the second problem, the betting period is so long, stretching up to 24 hours, and during this time, players keep trickling in. This means, even if we manage to balance the scales this minute, it could tilt again the next minute.

Thus, manipulating players is not as straightforward as one might think. When we actually discuss controlling the book in practice, we are talking about a meticulous and complex operational process. When a sportsbook controls a book, it aims to influence all the players who come to bet, and this process is quite lengthy, covering the entire 24-hour betting period.

Returning to the topic of manipulating players, as just mentioned, controlling all players is a whimsical notion, an impossibility. But looking from another perspective, the sportsbook doesn't really need to do this, because the crux of controlling the book lies in seeking balance. Therefore, even in the worst-case scenario, assuming all ten thousand players bet on the same side, the sportsbook just needs to sway half of them, that is five thousand players, to the other side.

We also know that players place bets randomly, so it's impossible for all of them to bet on the same side. There will definitely be bets on both sides, just unevenly distributed, which is a better situation. This implies that the sportsbook only needs to influence a small portion of them, enticing them to switch sides, and the scales could balance.

Furthermore, luckily, if only a fraction of players need to be influenced, this task becomes much easier. The sportsbook just needs to provide some "incentives," which are never lacking in the realm of sports betting.

Now, let's discuss the issue of the prolonged betting period, which elevates the complexity of controlling the book. Due to the extended time, players will keep coming in to place bets, making the bets that the sportsbook sees come in one by one over 24 hours.

This means:

- The scales will keep swaying, making it hard for the sportsbook to discern the trend.

- The sportsbook won't know the final state of the scales until the very last moment.

However, this can also be looked at from a different angle. Firstly, the longer duration allows the sportsbook to observe gradually, not needing to control the book at every moment but only when a trend is discernible.

Moreover, the longer duration has a bigger advantage: the sportsbook doesn't have to act heavily all at once. It can provide just a slight incentive, slowly guiding some players to the other side, thereby restoring the balance bit by bit. This can stabilize the tilt of the scales, preventing drastic shifts.

Then there's the issue of the sportsbook not being able to predict the final state of the scales. This isn't a big deal, as we've discussed, the focus during the preventive phase is merely to prevent the scales from tilting too severely. Achieving perfect balance at this time is impossible. So, all the sportsbook needs to do during this period is to try its best not to let the book tilt to one side too much.

Therefore, to be precise, the term "controlling the book" in sports betting signifies the sportsbook's continual efforts to entice players to switch sides throughout the entire betting period.

**Standard Operating Procedure**

Combining all the above inferences, we can deduce the sportsbook's "Standard Operating Procedure":

Initially, once the book is open, the sportsbook starts observing the scales. Once a tilt is noticed, actions are considered to entice players to bet on the other side.

Then, the sportsbook continues to monitor the scales to see if players have taken the bait! If there's no effect, they up the ante, enhance the incentives, until the scales gradually come back to balance.

So, throughout the entire 24-hour betting period, the sportsbook keeps employing this cycle of observation, action, re-observation, and re-action.

What exactly are these "incentives"? We'll discuss that later. But in summary, during the sportsbook's control of the book, the scales keep wobbling until the book closes.

This operating procedure is crucial for the sportsbook. So, when players look at the book at the betting sites, there are people and even computer programs behind the scenes, continually monitoring and taking actions to balance the book.

We can imagine, with such rigorous control processes, by the time the book closes, the scales are already largely balanced. Of course, perfect balance won't be achieved, but getting close is already quite good.

Also, we have mentioned while discussing the betting balance table, a perfectly balanced book is great, as it means the sportsbook can earn the same amount of money regardless. However, a slight tilt is acceptable. Only at this point, depending on the game results, the sportsbook will know if they are making more or less.

Having discussed the entire operating process, we still missed out on a key point: What are the incentives? What exactly does the sportsbook offer to entice players to change their minds?

## Enticing Players To Switch Sides

In this section, we will discuss the incentives provided by the sportsbook. What do they use to entice some players to switch sides for their bets? But you probably have some idea already. Why do players engage in sports betting? Essentially, it's to win money. Hence, as long as the sportsbook provides conditions for players to win more money, players will willingly switch sides.

### Using "Odds" to Control Players

The simplest way to direct players to bet on a particular team is through manipulating the odds. Higher odds imply that with the same stake, players can receive more winnings. And everyone who plays with betting tickets wants to win more money; no one would want to be harsh on their own wallets.

So, when the book tilts, the sportsbook's first reaction is to increase the odds for one of the teams. As the odds increase, some of the subsequent players will be influenced and will bet on this team. This way, there's a chance for the book to gradually regain balance.

Moreover, we discussed the concept of "juice" earlier; the sportsbook's total odds must be fixed. If the odds for one team are increased, the odds for the other team must decrease. The total odds must always be less than 4.00; this mathematical formula must not be violated.

For instance, if initially, the odds for both teams were 1.80.

| Football league | |
| --- | --- |
| Team A | Odds 1.80 |
| Team B | Odds 1.80 |
| | |
| | Total Odds 3.60 |

now, with the scale tipped, the website needs to boost the incentives for Team A. As a result, they adjust the odds for Team A to 2.00.

| Football league | |
| --- | --- |
| Team A | Odds 2.00 |
| Team B | Odds 1.60 |
| | |
| | Total Odds 3.60 |

After adjustments, the odds for Team A rise to 2.00, but at the same time, the odds for Team B have to drop to 1.60. So, if you raise the odds on one side, the other side will definitely drop, which is a basic formula for the sportsbook to earn juice, creating an even stronger incentive.

Taking this example, a player would think, now my stake is $100, if I bet on the team with odds of 1.60, I can only get back $160 if I win. But if I place the bet on the "2.00" side, that's $200, so naturally, they would want to bet on Team B.

Therefore, the "odds" itself is an excellent incentive. As long as the sportsbook utilizes this well, influencing players is almost a sure bet, which makes "odds" a pervasive element in all the betting methods on the sportsbook, becoming a fundamental aspect of sports betting.

## Money Line

This method of managing odds is widely adopted in Europe, hence, a betting site that utilizes odds to control the betting from start to finish is referred to as the "Money Line." However, in this industry, many look down upon the Money Line method of managing the betting, arguing that sports betting is about predicting the outcomes of sports events, which are predictable to some extent. For instance, in a match between a strong team and a weak team, would anyone bet on the weak team winning?

This perspective is quite insightful. No matter how high the odds for the weaker team, it remains the weaker team. It's unlikely for bettors to be enticed by higher odds and take on higher risks. Therefore, it seems that the effectiveness of this method of managing the betting by the online sportsbooks is limited. Nonetheless, we can defend the Money Line with three points:

1. High odds are indeed a good incentive. We can look at traditional lottery games where numbers are drawn; this can be considered the pinnacle of odds control. In such games, the probability of hitting the jackpot is usually one in tens or hundreds of millions. Frankly, buying such lottery tickets is akin to a sure loss, yet there's no shortage of buyers. This is because the odds are high enough; with a few tens of dollars, one can win up to hundreds of millions, translating to odds as high as several millions. Hence, odds do serve a purpose; as long as the odds are high, there will be buyers.

2. The odds don't need to affect all bettors. From the online sportsbook's perspective, the effectiveness of the incentive is measured by whether it balances out, not by whether it affects all bettors or has a significant impact. Sometimes, it's enough if a small portion of bettors switch sides due to the odds.

3. On the betting balance, what matters is the "expected payout," and we know that

**Expected Payout = Amount Bet x Odds**

This implies that the amount bet by players is not important to the online sportsbooks; what's important is how much they have to pay out. So when the odds are adjusted, and the strong team is set at lower odds, even if many more people bet on the strong team, the expected payout for the strong team will not be too high, preventing the balance from tilting too severely.

Therefore, the widespread popularity of the Money Line is not without reason. It covers all bases in terms of mathematical logic and understanding human nature. Consequently, many online sportsbooks still primarily use this method for managing the betting.

## Using "Point Spread" to Control Players

The concept of the Money Line is solid, and it indeed works well in European and American countries. By influencing players with odds, slowly but surely, the balance of the betting can be achieved. However, this method doesn't resonate much with Asian players, who are known for their "stubbornness".

When online sportsbooks open betting in Asia, no matter how much they increase the odds, it doesn't seem to affect the players. As the saying goes, "you have a thousand plans, I have my way," Asian players won't budge if they decide not to.

And there's logic to it:

1. Through detailed analysis, players indeed have ways to predict the general outcomes of matches. It doesn't make sense for them to bet on the losing side just for the sake of higher odds. After all, players are not here to lose money deliberately; they don't have money to burn.

2. The odds in sports betting have their limits. There's only so much online sportsbooks can do to increase the odds. As mentioned before, from the perspective of income and expenditure, the total odds shouldn't exceed 4.00; otherwise, the payout from the online sportsbooks would surpass the income, leading to a guaranteed loss situation.

No matter how the online sportsbooks set the odds, they can't go beyond a payout of four times the bet, which is incomparable to lottery games. Given the limited height to which odds can rise, the attraction they hold for players is naturally limited.

Looking back, players in Europe and America perhaps are not as shrewd, thus being led by the Money Line. Based on relevant statistics, it's evident that most of them engage in sports betting for entertainment purposes, not particularly aiming for strategic betting.

In Asia, however, everyone bets shrewdly, and merely adjusting the odds doesn't make a big difference. Therefore, besides the odds, online sportsbooks need to employ the second tool, the "Point Spread."

What is the Point Spread? In simple terms, when online sportsbooks open betting, they set a strong team to give a few points to the weaker team as a head start. Let's look at an example directly.

|  | Point Spread |
| --- | --- |
| Team A | -2 |
| Team B |  |

This is a point spread betting line. When the online sportsbook opens the betting, it decides that Team A has to give 2 points to Team B, so on the betting line, it shows a -2 points.

What's the use of this?

It indicates that now Team A has to win by more than two points to be considered a win. Otherwise, it's a loss. Let's illustrate this with two examples.

| Match Result | Outcome |
| --- | --- |
| Team A scores 9 points, Team B scores 8 points | Team A wins, but since it's not by more than two points, Team A is considered to have lost. |
| Team A scores 9 points, Team B scores 6 points | Team A wins by more than two points, so Team A is considered to have won. |

Now we can see, by employing the point spread, the predictability of the match outcome becomes less straightforward. The relationship between the strength of the teams and the winning or losing of the betting ticket is also diminished. Hence, some people argue that the point spread used by online sportsbooks is to obscure the match, making it hard for players to predict the outcome, thus leading them to randomly place bets on which team will win. This is seen as a method to promote fairness in the game.

This kind of argument might give many people a wrong impression, assuming that it's natural for the stronger team to give a few points to the weaker team, or even without bothering to judge which team is strong or weak, just by looking at the point spread one could recognize who the strong team is. Even many news media adopt this approach, informing the public about the stronger team based on the point spread odds.

However, this is not the case. The point spread used by online sportsbooks is merely a tool; it's not meant to make it difficult to guess the winner, its primary function is to balance the betting line. There's no rule stating that the stronger team must give points to the weaker team, and in reality, there are instances where the weaker team gives points to the stronger team. Whenever the betting line is unbalanced, the online sportsbook will adjust the point spread accordingly, irrespective of which team is strong or weak.

Online sportsbooks only care about one thing, which is the balance of the scale. Hence, both the point spread and the odds are tools for the online sportsbooks, and once the betting line is open, both will be adjusted continually. But the impact of the point spread is much more significant than that of the odds. Especially in low-scoring games like baseball and soccer, usually a one-point movement could result in a large number of players changing sides.

In summary, seeing a side with lower odds or a higher point spread doesn't necessarily mean that team is stronger. From our online sportsbook's perspective, the real reason is that too many people are betting on that team, and we don't wish to accept more bets on them. Conversely, a team with higher odds or receiving points is not necessarily weaker; it just means the online sportsbook wants to attract more bets on that side.

The strength or weakness of the teams is irrelevant to the interests of the online sportsbooks, and thus, some savvy players can take advantage of the point spread or odds, making a big score when everyone else gets it wrong. This is a characteristic of this game. So if you have done in-depth research on the competing teams and have confidence, you don't have to follow the crowd. You don't need to be swayed by the point spread or the odds; just place your bets on the team you have confidence in. The host of the game only cares about the balance of the betting line, not who will win.

## Asian Handicap

In Asia, online sportsbooks often use the point spread and odds in conjunction, and the formal academic term for this kind of betting line is "Asian Handicap," also known as "Asian Handicap Betting," with its English name being "Asian Handicap." As the name suggests, this is a betting method prevalent in Asia.

As for European and American countries, they didn't have this type of betting line before. However, under the trend of globalization, they are gradually adopting this betting line, primarily to attract Asian players.

Now, let's take a look at an Asian Handicap betting line.

|  | Point Spread | Odds |
|---|---|---|
| Team A | -2 | 1.80 |
| Team B |  | 1.80 |

In this type of betting line, both the point spread and odds are set by the online sportsbook, and can be adjusted at any time. Due to the significant impact of the point spread, once it's altered, the balance of the betting line on the sportsbook can drastically sway. Therefore, once the point spread is set, it's seldom changed, making the "odds" a tool for fine-tuning at this point. As long as the online sportsbook can appropriately adjust the point spread and odds, balancing the betting line won't be too challenging.

However, someone might spot a problem here - what if the match ends in a draw? Taking an example, suppose Team A and Team B score 98 to 96 respectively, so Team A wins. But after deducting the point spread, the score becomes 96 to 96, resulting in a draw.

A draw is troublesome because it raises the question for the players who placed bets: is it a win or a loss? So, to avoid such awkward situations, many online sportsbooks simply add a 0.5 point to the point spread to eliminate the possibility of a draw. Referring to the example above, initially, the line was set at Team A giving two points, which could easily result in a draw. So, instead of setting it this way, we now change it to…

|  | Point Spread | Odds |
|---|---|---|
| Team A | -2.5 | 1.8 |
| Team B |  | 1.8 |

Now Team A gives 2.5 points, meaning that no matter how the two teams play, there won't be a situation of a draw. Let's look at an example.

| Team A 8 points, Team B 6 points | Win margin is not over 2.5 points, Team A loses. |
|---|---|
| Team A 9 points, Team B 6 points | Win margin is over 2.5 points, Team A wins |

This is why in the spread betting method, a spread is often followed by 0.5 points to avoid the awkwardness of a tie, eliminating any confusion on how to calculate wins or losses. However, not every online sportsbook adopts this type of spread with an additional 0.5 points. The reason is simple; firstly, a spread with 0.5 points can confuse newcomers.

How could there be a score of 0.5 in a sports game?

Moreover, experiencing a tie in a game has its own charm. As long as there is a pre-established method to handle ties, everyone will know how to calculate the outcome, and that's fine; it's not a bad thing.

Thus, a specific term emerged, called "Draw Game." This is a method predefined by the online sportsbook before the game starts to handle ties, but each sportsbook has its own method.

- Since the score is tied, declare it a draw. All players take back their money, treating it as if the bet was never placed. This is the fairest method for players. However, it's rarely adopted because if everyone takes back their money, the online sportsbook gains nothing, which is unfair to the sportsbook.

- Win half, lose half. This one is also simple; in the event of a tie, everyone's bet is treated as if they had bet half the money. Since Team A gave two points, those who bet on Team A win, known as winning half. Those who bet on Team B lose, known as losing half.

This method benefits the sportsbook since betting half still constitutes betting, meaning the sportsbook can earn half the commission. Hence, this "win half, lose half" method is widely adopted by various sportsbooks, using this method to handle ties.

But the Draw Game isn't always a clear-cut win half, lose half. Some sportsbooks complicate it further, for instance, in a tie, those supposed to win half, win 40%, and those supposed to lose half, lose 40%. This can even be represented by the spread, for example, Team A gives -2.4 points, representing this scenario. But this rule is too complex, so let's not delve into it.

In the Asian Handicap, there are three basic elements: the spread, the odds, and the Draw Game. To manage the betting pool effectively, an online sportsbook must understand the timing and impact of these three elements, which also make this betting method complex and difficult to understand.

The lack of popularity of the Asian Handicap in Europe and America is understandable. A good sports betting game should be entertaining, but now with the spread, odds, and even the Draw Game, it's tormenting for players. Frankly, even buying stocks, with its highs and lows, isn't as complex.

But in Asia, it's inevitable. Players here are too shrewd. If only relying on the European style, the sportsbook might never achieve a balanced betting pool. And it must be said, in Asia, sports betting is hardly seen as entertainment, partly due to the complexity of the Asian Handicap.

However, the Asian Handicap isn't the most complex betting method. In Taiwan, there are even more challenging ones.

## The Handicap Within a Handicap.

For online sportsbooks, it's well-known how meticulous Asian bettors are, and among them, domestic bettors are particularly famed. What makes them special? In a word, they are exceptionally sharp.

From the beginning of this book, we've reiterated a concept that the interests of online sportsbooks and players do not directly clash. What sportsbooks desire is simple: a small portion of players obediently betting on specific teams. This isn't without a cost; they either offer better odds or more favorable spreads. This exchange is quite fair.

However, domestic players are not easily swayed by this tactic. Starting with the spread, whether betting on baseball, soccer, or basketball, if the spread is not adequate, players won't place bets. Yet, as soon as the spread changes, a large group of players follows suit, embodying the phrase "fence-sitters who sway with the wind."

Thus, the balance of the betting pool in sportsbooks is never stable; it tilts one way or the other, making it impossible to maintain a steady equilibrium. Imagine a seesaw; sportsbooks use the spread to press down on one side, but the other side immediately bounces up, resulting in no balance after much effort.

Next is the matter of odds. If adjusting the spread proved too impactful, then minor adjustments to the odds should work, right? Unfortunately, this method is ineffective too because it doesn't change anything. Domestic players act as if the odds don't exist. The common sentiment is, as long as they win, even winning a dollar is still winning, which is better than losing. Due to this mindset, no matter how much sportsbooks lower the odds, players will still bet on strong teams. Moreover, there's a rule that the odds must be greater than one, ensuring players win some money.

These scenarios occur because domestic players are exceptionally astute in betting. They have a near-certain grasp on the outcomes of games, and they understand the appropriate spreads better than the sportsbooks. Therefore, a change in spread sends them scurrying faster than rabbits.

But a disbalanced betting pool is unsustainable as it impedes sportsbooks from making profits, threatening the continuation of this game. Over time, a unique type of betting pool emerged in this region, known as the "Taiwan Handicap."

## Taiwan Handicap

What is a Taiwan Handicap ? At first glance, it's a peculiar looking betting pool.

|  | Taiwan Handicap | Odds |
|---|---|---|
| Team A | 1 + 30 | 1.80 |
| Team B |  | 1.80 |

It bears some resemblance to the Asian Handicap, featuring both a spread and odds, but there's a distinct difference in the spread, illustrated here by "1 + 30". Understanding such a spread might be a tall order for many, so let's delve into its principles. In domestic circles, since everyone has a good grasp on the probable outcomes of games and a better sense of the suitable spreads than sportsbooks, the latter compromise. Whatever spread the players propose, the sportsbook implements.

In this instance, the "-1" represents the standard spread, functioning the same as in Asian Handicaps, with the odds in the pool also resembling those in Asian Handicaps. Some generous sportsbooks might even declare a fixed odd, given players rarely pay attention to odds, setting it at 1.80 on both sides from start to finish.

So in Taiwan Handicaps, the "odds" remain static, and the "spread" is collectively agreed upon by players. Under such circumstances, as soon as the betting pool opens, it almost always presents a balanced scenario (while this might not reflect objective reality, it certainly aligns with domestic players' perception).

One could imagine, in such betting pools, the distribution of bets among players would be fairly even, preventing drastic fluctuations in the sportsbook's balance. Yet, the story doesn't end here, as this setup doesn't guarantee a balanced book, so sportsbooks need a tactic to entice bets.

This tactic is the aforementioned "Draw Handicap". Since the spreads in Taiwan Handicaps are player-approved, as soon as the betting pool opens, it's destined for a draw outcome (of course, this doesn't mean the teams will definitely end in a draw, but it speaks to the players' mindset).

Since Taiwan Handicaps often lead to a draw scenario, the handling of Draw Handicaps naturally piques every player's interest, providing a leverage point for sportsbooks.

Initially, sportsbooks refine the Draw Handicap further, departing from the simple win-half, lose-half system. Instead, they introduce dynamic adjustments, such as, in the event of a draw, "those who bet on + win thirty percent, while those who bet on - lose thirty percent," which is what the "+30" in the spread signifies. Note that this rule only applies when, after accounting for the spread, the teams end in a draw.

Here's an example for better understanding:

|  | Meaning |
|---|---|
| +90 | People who bet on + win 90%, others lose 90% |
| +80 | People who bet on + win 80%, others lose 80% |
| +50 | People who bet on + win 50%, others lose 50% |
| +30 | People who bet on + win 30%, others lose 30% |
| +10 | People who bet on + win 10%, others lose 10% |

In the realm of handicaps, both "plus" and "minus" signs naturally exist. Where a "plus" sign indicates an advantage, a "minus" sign represents a disadvantage.

|  | Meaning |
|-----|---------|
| −90 | Those who buy − lose 90%, while others win 90% |
| −80 | Those who buy − lose 80%, while others win 80% |
| −50 | Those who buy − lose 50%, while others win 50% |
| −30 | Those who buy − lose 30%, while others win 30% |
| −10 | Those who buy − lose 10%, while others win 10% |

What's the utility of this, you may wonder? For instance, if Team A is set at "+ 30," it signifies that in the event of a draw, betting on Team A yields a thirty percent win. Now, if the sportsbook raises the spread to "+ 40," it implies a forty percent win for bets on Team A in a draw scenario, serving as an incentive.

Moreover, when a sportsbook desires to lure more players, it can flip the "plus" to a "minus." For instance, if the current spread is "+ 30," betting on Team A reaps a thirty percent win. Yet, if too many are betting on Team A, the sportsbook could alter the spread to "-30," turning the tide and causing bets on Team A to lose thirty percent. Now, players might ponder whether betting on Team B is more beneficial.

Through such incentives, sportsbooks regain control over the betting pools. In Taiwan Handicaps, the power of Draw Handicaps falls somewhere between true spreads and odds. Given the inherently balanced nature of Taiwan Handicaps and the shrewdness of domestic players, they pay extra attention to these minor spreads, affording sportsbooks the means to entice players to bet as desired.

This overview merely scratches the surface of Taiwan Handicaps; the finer nuances are omitted as it's a complex evolution of the spread betting, far surpassing mere entertainment. There's no need to delve into it as not many sportsbooks offer Taiwan Handicaps. The reluctance roots in the complexity of Asian Handicaps, making the promotion of Taiwan Handicaps an uphill battle, almost necessitating an educational course before play. The gaming experience becomes too strenuous when such extensive learning is required.

From the discussed incentives, it's evident that both theoretically and practically, they serve to effectively lure players. This is the result of decades of refinement in sports betting, transitioning from spreads, to odds, and then to Draw Handicaps. Implementing these incentives as needed, sportsbooks can successfully dictate betting trends, restoring balance to tilted betting pools.

However, these tactics can't achieve a perfect balance as last-minute bets can tip the scales, and sportsbooks, lacking clairvoyance, can't predict the final balance. Hence, a lack of balance is inevitable, occasionally landing sportsbooks in a betting duel with players.

In the following, we will delve into the prevention and remediation of imbalanced betting pools, particularly exploring how to rectify an imbalanced pool post-closure, sans any further bets.

## Perfect Balance of Betting Pools

Starting from the section on online sportsbooks, we have been introducing a series of methods to control the betting lines, as well as the operational processes. Now we have come to the end, where the sportsbook stops accepting bets, and the scales are set. However, this scale is far from balanced, and the "juice" the sportsbook can earn is not yet determined. So, in this chapter, we will see how the sportsbook can perfectly balance the scales without any bets being placed.

We all know that when a sportsbook operates the betting lines, it relies on creating an incentive to form a betting trend, to gradually restore balance to the scales. Although this method cannot achieve precise balance, under ideal conditions, when the betting lines are closed, the scales should only tilt slightly, not becoming too unbalanced. Let's look at the balanced state of the scales after ceasing to accept bets.

| Team A | Bets ( 0.95 million) | Team B |
|---|---|---|
| Payout (1.1 million ) | | Payout (0.7 million ) |

Through meticulous operations, the scale hasn't achieved complete balance, and there's still a possibility for the online sportsbook to lose money. However, this level of tilt is acceptable, and we have ways to amend it.

First, let's look at the scale, the total bets accepted currently stand at $950,000. If Team A wins in the end, $1,100,000 will need to be paid out, causing a loss of $150,000 to the sportsbook. If Team B wins, only $700,000 needs to be paid out, netting a profit of $250,000 for the sportsbook. From this, it's evident that the sportsbook stands to either gain or lose a large sum, and this risk is too high, which is why insurance needs to be purchased at this point.

Buying insurance in this context has a specific term, generally referred to as "laying off". Assuming we are the sportsbook, let's look back at this betting scale; for it to be perfectly balanced, the anticipated payouts on both sides should be $700,000 each. It's precisely because on Team A's side, there's an excess of $400,000, that we have this current imbalance.

Therefore, the first step in "laying off" is to take out this $400,000, to restore balance to the scale initially.

| Team A | Bets ( 0.95 million) | Team B |
|---|---|---|
| Payout (0.7 million ) | | Payout ( 0.7 million ) |
| | | |
| 0.4 million | | |

After taking it out, it signifies that we don't wish to payout these winnings because doing so carries a risk for us. Hence, after taking it out, we aim to transfer this risk onto someone else. The practical method is to search the market for other online sportsbooks willing to cover this $400,000 payout.

It's worth mentioning here that there's a network of relationships among different online sportsbooks. Not only do domestic sportsbooks know each other, but some large-scale sportsbooks also connect with even larger foreign sportsbooks. No sportsbook operates in isolation, so it's quite easy for a sportsbook to seek out others.

Now, let's go to the market to see which sportsbooks are still accepting bets. Suppose after some search, we find a sportsbook still offering a line for "Team A with odds at 2.00", this becomes our target. Since we need them to cover this $400,000, reverse calculating based on the odds of 2.00, we can bet $200,000 with them, and they will cover the $400,000 payout for us. This solves the problem, and this betting action is referred to as the sportsbook's "laying off".

Let's look at the scales post "laying off".

| Team A | Bets ( 0.75 million) | Team B |
|---|---|---|
| Payout (0.7 million ) | | Payout ( 0.7 million ) |
| | | |
| | Laying off (0.2 million ) | |
| Payout (0.4 million ) | | |

Now the scale is divided into two halves, but we'll first look at the payout. The anticipated payout for Team A remains at $700,000 + $400,000 = $1,100,000, and for Team B it remains at $700,000. This indicates that, even after laying off, the amount to be paid out to the players hasn't reduced by a single cent. Please note, this is the focal point of laying off. The money to be paid out to the players is absolutely indispensable.

In the lower half of the scale, as mentioned earlier, this represents the money bet with other online sportsbooks. We have to place a bet of $200,000 on Team A, and if Team A indeed wins, we can collect $400,000 in winnings from them.

Now, let's look back at the upper half of the scale, which represents our own scale. Since we took out $200,000 to place a bet, the total income of $950,000 now reduces to $750,000. However, the scale is now perfectly balanced. At this point, we can calculate the profit, as the total bets are $750,000, and regardless of which team wins in the end, only $700,000 needs to be paid out, resulting in a net profit of $50,000.

**"Juice" Is Only an Ideal**

Once the sportsbook completes the laying off, the day's work can be considered done, and what remains is probably heading home to count the money. Mind you, the game hasn't even started yet. This key point is the trick to the trade for the sportsbook. Whether the sportsbook can make money is entirely unrelated to the game's outcome, and profits can be calculated even before the game begins.

Here, it's also visible that the actual "juice" received by the sportsbook is only $50,000. From the total income of $950,000, only $50,000 is earned, translating to an actual profit rate of 5.2%. This figure, compared to the previously set "juice" ideal value, whether it's 7% or 10%, falls short.

However, this is inevitable as players place bets of their own free will, and until the last second, no one knows which way the scale will tip. Therefore, a perfectly balanced scale is impossible in the end. Under such circumstances, part of the principal must be taken out to purchase insurance from other sportsbooks.

This results in sharing the profits that were initially supposed to be ours, with others, which manifests the difference between the ideal and reality. But risk and profit are two sides of the same coin, desiring larger profits necessitates bearing larger risks, and once the risk exceeds the threshold the bookmaker can endure, risk diversification is imperative, and hence, profits are also dispersed.

The term "laying off" is used because, during the acceptance of bets, it's also termed "accepting goods", hence taking the "goods" out to other sportsbooks is called "laying off". Laying off is also referred to as "throwing lines", implying the act of throwing out the betting lines.

**Replenishing from Other Sportsbooks**

What was discussed above is "laying off", pushing out excess money to achieve balance, but actually, the reverse can also be done. The so-called "replenishing" is about accepting bets from other sportsbooks. For example, in the previous scenario, we cut down the anticipated payout for Team A to $700,000, but we could actually choose not to cut it. Instead, we could elevate Team B's $700,000 to $1,100,000.

| Team A | Bets  (1.2 million) | Team B |
|---|---|---|
| Payout<br>( 1.1 million ) | | Payout<br>(1.1 million ) |

This method entails exploring the market to see if there's any online sportsbook wanting to place bets with us, specifically on Team B. If we indeed find such a sportsbook, the scale could be balanced. As everyone can see, now someone comes to bet on Team B, elevating the total income to $1,200,000, balancing the scale. In the end, regardless of which team wins, a profit of $100,000 can be made.

Compared to "laying off", actually "replenishing" is more beneficial for the sportsbook. Everyone can see, under the same balanced situation, the previous method could only earn $50,000, but now this method can earn

$100,000. It's imaginable that everyone would prefer to do this kind of "replenishing".

Regrettably, there's no such thing as a free lunch, other sportsbooks can do the math too, and it's not easy for them to hand over hard cash to us. Likely, they would prefer to wait for us to come to them. At the very least, both parties need to have a good discussion regarding the odds.

So, "replenishing" has some element of luck involved, whether or not goods can be replenished in time is hard to say. But "laying off" is no problem, as this is giving away the "juice", other sportsbooks are mostly very welcoming, and this is a reason why "laying off" is more common than "replenishing".

## In-Play Arbitrage

The laying off introduced above is a method conducted by the sportsbook after the betting lines are closed. Therefore, once laying off begins, it's impossible for the sportsbook to accept further bets. However, there's another form of laying off, occurring during the betting process, and the sportsbook can do this at any time without closing the betting lines. This variation of laying off is termed as "in-play arbitrage".

We all know that, after the betting lines are opened, the sportsbook will continuously adjust the odds to attract players to place bets. During this time, the sportsbook will also continuously observe the betting tickets coming in. If, after observation, it's found that some tickets have a large bet amount and the odds are not high, this is when "in-play arbitrage" comes into play.

For instance, a betting ticket of $100 is received with odds at 1.80, the sportsbook would immediately check the market to see if other sportsbooks offer better odds. If better odds are found, say a sportsbook offers 2.00, then an arbitrage opportunity has been identified by the sportsbook.

Below is the arbitrage calculation table used by the bookmaker:

|  | Bets | Odds | Payout |
|---|---|---|---|
| Income | 100.00 | 1.80 | 180.00 |
| Other Online Sportsbook | 90.00 | 2.00 | 180.00 |
|  |  |  |  |
| Profit | 10.00 |  |  |

Upon receiving a betting ticket of $100, the expected payout is $180. The basic concept of arbitrage, similar to laying off, is to have another sportsbook cover this $180 payout. However, since they offer higher odds of 2.00, the amount we need to bet is only $90.

So, after receiving this $100 betting ticket, the sportsbook just needs to quickly use $90 to place a bet with another sportsbook, netting a profit of $10. This is a type of risk-free arbitrage transaction. Moreover, during in-play arbitrage, the sportsbook selectively targets tickets with large bet amounts, hence avoiding excessively large bets that could impact its balance, achieving two goals with one move.

**In-play arbitrage** is very common among sportsbooks, and the method is the same as laying off, placing bets with other sportsbooks. However, it's crucial to understand here, "in-play arbitrage" refers to the sportsbook earning a price difference during the betting process, earning 'juice' from others. Whereas "laying off" is a method post stopping bets, where the sportsbook sacrifices its profit for insurance, giving the 'juice' to others. Both are distinct and shouldn't be confused.

An issue in sports betting is the lack of standardized terminology; every sportsbook has its own terms, creating a chaotic nomenclature. A group discussing could use "laying off", "throwing the line", or "risk dispersal", all referring to the same thing, sounding complicated but all pointing to the same action.

## Risks of Laying Off

We've discussed the essence of laying off by sportsbooks, which seems simple and safe, seemingly sacrificing some total revenue for safe profits. However, it's not so straightforward. In the simple example given, a significant issue arises when no other sportsbook accepts bets, or offers too low odds making it unprofitable for the sportsbook. What to do then?

Indeed, this highlights the key risk of laying off; it may not be possible to execute. If no sportsbooks are willing to accept your bets, you can't lay off. This is unavoidable, and there's no better solution, thus, being a bookmaker in sports betting does entail risks.

For sportsbooks, prevention is better than cure. Before closing the betting lines, various strategies must be employed to influence players to maintain balance; this is a primary task and an essential checkpoint. The better the balance, the lesser the amount needed to be laid off, minimizing the risks of laying off.

Ultimately, "laying off" is a last resort, discussing giving away 'juice' to others, where the sportsbook can only hope for lesser losses rather than gains. The safest approach is still to balance the scales, which is why we've discussed at length how to manipulate players earlier on. Manipulating players doesn't rely on luck, but laying off does. And it's due to this reliance on luck that sportsbooks charge a high 'juice' in this game.

## How to Reduce Risk?

Coming back to it, although there's no way to completely eliminate risk, there are some methods to slightly reduce it. Addressing the first concern from earlier, if other sportsbooks also stop accepting bets, leaving us with money but nowhere to place it, what can be done?

Prevention is indeed better than cure in this scenario. One approach is to close our betting earlier, for instance, ending it five to ten minutes before the event kicks off, instead of dragging it till the event starts. If that still feels uncertain, closing it even earlier, like an hour or two before is also an option.

This way, there's ample time to look for other sportsbooks, and the odds obtained may also be better. Hence, as discussed during the operational procedure discussion, general sportsbooks will cease accepting bets five minutes before the event starts, following this logic. Ending the acceptance of bets earlier allows for earlier lay off. But this can't guarantee an opportunity every time, hence, it's merely a risk reduction tactic.

Onto the second concern, other sportsbooks offering too low odds! Revisiting the earlier example, suppose we can no longer obtain odds of 2.00, and the maximum odds now are only 1.25, then the scale would tip this way:

In this scenario, to cover the $400,000 payout, more capital is needed. Calculating backwards with the odds of 1.25, the capital now needed is $320,000, leaving our total revenue at $630,000. This implies that no matter which team wins, we'll incur a loss of $70,000.

| Team A | Total Bets (0.63 million) | Team B |
| --- | --- | --- |
| Payout (0.7 million ) | | Payout (0.7 million ) |
| | | |
| | Laying off (0.32 million) | |
| Payout (0.4 million ) | | |

In order to meet the payout of $400,000, more capital needs to be invested. Using the odds of 1.25 to calculate backwards, the capital now needed is $320,000, leaving our total revenue at $630,000. This means that regardless of which team wins, we'll have to incur a loss of $70,000.

The situation looks pretty bad, as the sportsbook will lose money either way. However, this "lay off" is better than not doing it at all. Compared to not laying off at all where the sportsbook could lose up to $150,000, "laying off" only incurs a loss of $70,000, which is relatively better. Therefore, even if the odds are not favorable, it's still necessary to lay off to reduce some risk.

## House Always Wins

The adage "House always wins" holds true in sports betting as well, but running a sportsbook is not easy. In many other games like lottery tickets and jackpot pools, sportsbooks can earn steadily by simply following basic prize distribution principles and mathematical formulas. However, in sports betting, skills are essential, and merely having a formula to earn the "juice" isn't enough.

In this section, we introduced a crucial concept that every sportsbook must grasp, that is "Balance." Only when the betting lines reach a balanced state, will the formula of revenue and expenditure work, enabling the sportsbook to earn the "juice." We also introduced two major monitoring tools for sportsbooks, the "Betting Balance Sheet" and the "Betting Scale." With these two tables as references, sportsbooks can take action to ensure their profits.

Furthermore, we can notice that earning the "juice" isn't that easy, at least it's not something you can earn while lying down. Sportsbooks need to assign personnel to monitor the betting lines at all times, enticing players to bet on both sides of the line. In the end, money must be spent on insurance to ensure steady profits.

## Luck Can't Beat Math

However, we need to circle back to the point that "laying off" for a sportsbook isn't always a must-do. In fact, if a sportsbook aims to maximize its profits, the mathematical suggestion is not to lay off. Keep all the money and directly bet against the players, which in industry parlance, is called "sportsbook takes all."

Why is this suggested? Because there's a very safe mathematical formula at play here, the juice formula. The most crucial concept of the juice is that the sportsbook's expenditure will always be less than its revenue. Conversely, the players' expenditure will always be greater than their revenue.

Since players are destined to lose money, the sportsbook will make a steady profit, making laying off irrelevant. Besides, "laying off" means giving the juice to other sportsbooks, which isn't economically sensible from a business standpoint.

Yet, there's another perspective. Betting against players, no matter how advantageous, is still gambling. As long as there's gambling, there's an element of luck involved. So, there's a chance, albeit slim, that the sportsbook might keep losing money due to bad luck. There have been instances of extremely unlucky sportsbooks losing money continuously for a month.

Moreover, the total amount wagered by players is enormous. Assuming a daily betting volume of $100 million, a sportsbook might inadvertently end up betting $10 million against the players and lose. Losing $10 million a day translates to $300 million a month, a figure painful for anyone to cover, no matter how rich.

So, if a sportsbook decides to take all bets, its capital becomes extremely crucial. The capital must be robust enough to withstand long-term losses and sustain long-term operations. If all these conditions are met, then taking all bets makes sense since luck can't beat math over the long term. Sooner or later, players will lose all their money to the sportsbook.

However, this doesn't mean that laying off is an unnecessary tactic. This deduction is based on the premise that the sportsbook will operate long-term and that players will keep playing. It's easy for a sportsbook to stay in business as it's a profitable venture, but what about the players? Who would want to stay in a losing business? Therefore, adequate risk aversion is essential; otherwise, if someone wins big and leaves, the sportsbook can't always win.

Furthermore, sports betting revolves around competitions, and some competitions, like the FIFA World Cup or the Olympics, occur only once every four years. In such cases, luck plays a significant role. It's better to lay off some bets to reduce risk because if you want to win back the next time, you'd have to wait for another four years.

In conclusion, whether or not to lay off, the sportsbook's advantage in this game is pretty apparent due to various tactics they can employ. In contrast, players don't have as many options. However, this doesn't mean that players can only buy lottery tickets and are doomed to lose money. We'll introduce other options in the player section, as savvy players have quite a few choices too.

**Game Flaws**

While sportsbooks generally have the upper hand over players, this is a broad view. As we calculated before, a popular betting line could attract ten thousand bettors, and not all of them will lose. In reality, only the average players are set to lose, while savvy players, just like sportsbooks, can take advantage of opportunities.

From this chapter, we can deduce that sportsbooks do not concern themselves with the details of each betting ticket. They do not care whether a player's odds are high or low, or how much has been wagered. What sportsbooks care about is the total revenue versus the total payout.

This means that sportsbooks are indifferent to the odds on your ticket. Whether you get "1.10" or "2.75" odds, it's all the same to them. They are also indifferent to whether you win $11,000 or $27,500. Hence, the interests of sportsbooks and players do not conflict.

This is why there's a distinction between savvy and average players in sports betting. Savvy players can seize opportunities to secure higher odds for themselves, which sportsbooks allow. For instance, you and your friend both bet on Team A, but you get odds of 2.10 while your friend only gets 1.50. This scenario is entirely plausible.

The biggest flaw in this game is that knowledgeable individuals earn more than those who lack understanding. While everyone makes use of this knowledge to earn extra money, sportsbooks can't do much about it. Actually, they can't do anything about it since the rules and operating tactics of this game are fixed. If sportsbooks change the rules or the way they operate, they will either lose players or lose money.

We will discuss more tactics like these in the future, which you can also utilize to strive for higher odds and win more money. Now, some might be itching to rush to the nearest betting station saying, "Boss, give me a ticket with the highest odds."

Hold on! Don't do this. I am not advising this, and taking things out of context can be dangerous, especially in a guide discussing "betting". If you only listen halfway, you are jeopardizing your own money. You can strive for higher odds, but not like this. To understand the crux, you'll need to patiently read through to the "Player Section".

Returning to sportsbooks, since they lay off and let others earn the juice, "juice" becomes a theoretical value. But even without laying off, the "juice" remains theoretical. Typically, if a sportsbook sets a 5% "juice," achieving half of it, i.e., 2.5%, over a year would already be considered highly successful.

Why is that? Because in this game, the tactic of earning the juice is known not just to sportsbooks, but to many others, like savvy players, agents, and you who are reading this book. With the understanding of sportsbooks' principles, of course, there are ways to extend this tactic, reverse it, and earn the sportsbook's juice.

The higher juice set in sports betting is due to this reason; not only do sportsbooks take risks to make money, but many people are also making a cut from it. This makes running a sportsbook challenging. Next, we will delve into how others mimic sportsbook tactics to do business.

This introduces the concept of agents. In this game, besides sportsbooks, this group reaps the most profits. In fact, in many places, agents earn significantly more than sportsbooks.

# Agent

## Agents and Their Role

In Hong Kong movies, there's a common scene where the protagonist receives a call from a friend asking if they want to place a bet that day. The friend enthusiastically recommends which teams are playing that night and how enticing the odds are. If the protagonist finds it unappealing and declines, the friend keeps calling to provide the latest odds and predictions until the protagonist finally decides to ask the friend to buy a betting ticket on their behalf.

Ever wondered why this Hong Kong friend is so eager?

There's a reason for it. The friend wants to earn the sportsbook's "juice." We've discussed the concept of juice, which is the sportsbook's profit. As long as everyone places bets according to the sportsbook's odds, the sportsbook earns a percentage of the total wagers as "juice." However, this concept isn't exclusive to sportsbooks; others can also earn this juice, and we'll discuss the rationale behind this.

Let's assume today "Team A faces Team B," and we have five friends who want to buy betting tickets together. Two of them ask us to bet on Team A, while the other three bet on Team B. Do we really need to run to the betting station to buy these five tickets?

Certainly not; buying just one ticket for Team B will do. This demonstrates that we've assumed the role of a sportsbook, accepting our friends' bets and earning the juice that would have gone to the sportsbook.

How is this achieved? Firstly, we retain the money for four of the tickets—two for Team A and two for Team B. For simplicity, let's assume the projected payouts for both sides are equal, so no matter which side wins, we can use the money from the losing side to pay off the winners. Since the sportsbook has already set aside the juice when determining the odds, if they set a 10% juice, then after paying out, we're guaranteed a 10% profit. For instance, if the four tickets amounted to $10,000, the profit would be $1,000.

Simple and safe, this is the sportsbook's original juice, but now it's in our pockets. However, there's a crucial point to note. Now that we've accepted the bets, all the rules that apply to sportsbooks now apply to us.

Hence, we must adhere to the sportsbook's principle of balancing the betting lines between both sides. That's why we need to take the extra ticket for Team B to the betting station, a process known as "laying off." We can't retain all the money because when the balance is off, we're essentially betting ourselves— a big taboo in the world of sports betting.

Buying betting tickets for friends is actually a bit more complicated, so next, we'll walk through a practical operation to see how to buy tickets ensuring we get the "juice" without accidentally losing money.

Firstly, everyone needs a piece of paper and a pen. Then draw the following table on the paper.

| Team A | | | Team B | | |
|--------|------|--------|--------|------|--------|
| Bets | Odds | Payout | Bets | Odds | Payout |
| | | | | | |

Let's assume this is a match between "Team A vs Team B," and your friends now come to you to buy betting tickets. They are all buying simple point spread tickets, so they are either betting on Team A or Team B. When they come to buy, you need to fill in the betting information in this table. Please see the table below.

| Team A | | | Team B | | |
|--------|------|--------|--------|------|--------|
| Bets | Odds | Payout | Bets | Odds | Payout |
| 100 | 1.90 | $190 | 200 | 1.90 | $380 |
| 100 | 1.90 | $190 | | | |
| | | | | | |

In this example, we have collected three betting tickets. Two of them are for Team A, and one for $200 is for Team B. The amount in the "Bets Received" column is decided by your friends; whatever amount they want to bet, that's the amount you take. The odds are based on the lines given by the online sportsbook, which you can check online or at betting sites. In any case, you should fill in the odds at the time of purchase (please note, this is very important, it must be the odds at that time, it cannot be higher, a little lower is fine, but whether your friends will accept that is uncertain).

In this table, there is a column called "Projected Payout", which you need to calculate yourself. The formula is simple:

**Projected Payout = Bets Received X Odds**

Since we only have these three tickets, let's sum them up now.

| Team A | | | Team B | | |
|---|---|---|---|---|---|
| Bets | Odds | Payout | Bets | Odds | Payout |
| 100 | 1.90 | $190 | 200 | 1.90 | $380 |
| 100 | 1.90 | $190 | | | |
| | | | | | |
| Payout $380 | | | Payout $380 | | |
| | | | | | |
| Bets $400 | | | | | |

After tallying, we derive three figures, among which two are the total projected payouts for each side, which simply add up the projected payouts, and the remaining one is the total bets received, which is the sum of all the bets received.

Now, doesn't this table look familiar? Correct, this is the betting balance sheet that online sportsbooks normally use. Since the goal is to earn the juice, of course, we must utilize the tools of the online sportsbook. And this table allows us to easily see how much money can be made.

According to this balance sheet, we can see that not only is the total projected payout on either side less than the total bets received, but the total projected payouts on both sides are also equal. This can be described as a perfect balance. And a perfect balance means, first, we can make money; second, regardless of the outcome, whether Team A wins or Team B wins, we can earn the most juice.

So, when the betting balance sheet is perfectly balanced, everyone doesn't have to do anything, just sit at home after collecting the money, and wait for the game to end. As you can all see, no matter how the payouts go, the most that will be paid out is $380, and we can net a profit of $20.

**Profitable Betting Balance Sheet**

The above is the simplest betting balance sheet, mainly for understanding the concept. What we did is very simple, but in reality, it's hard to encounter such a perfect scenario, so we need to look at more complex situations, which are the more common betting balance sheets you'll encounter.

| Team A | | | Team B | | |
|---|---|---|---|---|---|
| Bets | Odds | Payout | Bets | Odds | Payout |
| 100 | 1.90 | $190 | 200 | 1.70 | $340 |
| 100 | 1.90 | $190 | 100 | 1.50 | $150 |
| | | | | | |
| Payout $380 | | | Payout $490 | | |
| | | | | | |
| Total Bets $500 | | | | | |

In this example, the scale is slightly tilted, and there isn't a perfect balance, but this is more reasonable, as it's indeed hard to encounter a situation where the bets received are just right. In this betting balance sheet, the bets for Team B have undergone a subtle change. You can see that one betting ticket of $200 has odds of 1.70, while another ticket of $100 only has odds of 1.50.

This is because we assume that these two friends made their purchases at different times, and the sportsbook had adjusted the odds in the meantime, resulting in different odds for these two friends. Please pay special attention to this point; the odds must strictly follow the ones provided by the sportsbook at the time of the bet, and any deviation could lead to significant losses. For the principles behind this, please refer to the discussion on juice in the "Online Sportsbook Section".

Now, looking back at the betting balance sheet, the scale is not balanced. As those who have read the previous sections would know, if this were an online sportsbook, it would need to "lay off" bets to achieve a perfect balance at this point. However, considering this situation, I would advise conserving some energy, as the situation isn't that dire.

You're not professional sportsbooks, so there's no need to be so meticulous. It's fine as long as you can get by. After all, the total payout on either side doesn't exceed the total bets received, meaning we can still make money regardless, it's just a matter of how much. So, after collecting the money, you can still sit at home and watch the game.

Only now, watching the game will have added excitement, because if Team A wins, we can earn $500 - $380 = $120. But if Team B wins, we can only win $500 - $490 = $10.

## Loss-Making Betting Balance Sheet

The above illustrates a more common betting balance sheet, but things won't always be this rosy, and not every day is a celebration. Sooner or later, you will encounter a misbalanced scale, so let's look at more complex, potentially loss-making betting balance sheets.

| Team A | | | Team B | | |
|------|------|--------|------|------|--------|
| Bets | Odds | Payout | Bets | Odds | Payout |
| 100 | 1.90 | $190 | 100 | 1.80 | $180 |
| | | | 100 | 1.80 | $180 |
| | | | | | |
| Payout $190 | | | Payout $360 | | |
| | | | | | |
| Total Bets $300 | | | | | |

In this scenario, if Team B wins, it would result in a loss, as the total bets received amount to $300, but the anticipated payout for Team B reaches $360, leading to a $60 loss should Team B win. Hence, it's essential to purchase some insurance by "laying off" bets, just like how online sportsbooks do.

The method for laying off is straightforward. First, subtract the payout amount of Team A from that of Team B:

**360 - 190 = 170**

This $170 is the amount we hope the sportsbook would payout. So now, we should hurry to the betting site to check the odds for Team B. Suppose we find that the current odds at the betting site are 1.70, we can work backwards to figure out that we'll need to put forth a principal of 170 / 1.70 = 100 dollars.

So now, we need to purchase a $100 betting ticket for Team B. After doing so, the betting balance sheet will be updated as shown in the table below:

| Team A | Team B |
|---|---|
| Payout 190 | Payout 190 |
| Bets 200 | |
| | |
| laying off 100 | |
| | Payout 170 |

Now everyone can see that $100 is missing from the total bets received, which is used to purchase the betting ticket for Team B. However, the entire scale has been restored to a perfect balance, and this could be considered a job well done. Regardless of which team wins in the end, we can steadily earn $10.

Points to Note

Above is the principle of pooling funds to buy betting tickets. This is why that Hong Kong friend is so enthusiastic about helping to buy betting tickets on behalf of others. By pooling funds to buy betting tickets according to the procedures mentioned above, he can steadily earn the "juice" that originally belongs to the online sportsbook.

However, it's more apt to say "pooling funds but not buying betting tickets," as the Hong Kong friend hopes to keep the betting balance sheet balanced, keeping all the money to himself, without actually going to the betting site to buy tickets. Going out to buy tickets, a process known as "laying off," means giving away his juice to the online sportsbook.

On the flip side, if the scale is indeed unbalanced, "laying off" is necessary. If he doesn't lay off, he's betting against his friends, and betting entails winning and losing. It doesn't guarantee he'll make money, whereas earning juice is the real insurance.

Having discussed the principles, let's talk about some considerations in practical operation. The principles of these laying off operations can be applied to three types of betting:

## 1. Money Line

The so-called Money Line is a method where there is no point spread between the two teams, and the sportsbook purely manipulates the scale using odds. Therefore, the odds will change from time to time. In this method, buying betting tickets on behalf of others directly applies the principles mentioned above. The key point is that the odds your friends get when they come to buy tickets must be the odds offered by the sportsbook at that time.

## 2. Point Spread

In this method, the sportsbook may use point spreads to balance the scale, for example, "Team A gives one point." In this scenario, since the point spread may change, multiple betting balance sheets need to be prepared. With the point spread varying at the time your friends buy tickets, corresponding sheets should be prepared, for example,

| Team A  (-1) | | | Team B | | |
|------|------|--------|------|------|--------|
| Bets | Odds | Payout | Bets | Odds | Payout |
|      |      |        |      |      |        |

| Team A  (-1.5) | | | Team B | | |
|------|------|--------|------|------|--------|
| Bets | Odds | Payout | Bets | Odds | Payout |
|      |      |        |      |      |        |

| Team A  (-2) | | | Team B | | |
|------|------|--------|------|------|--------|
| Bets | Odds | Payout | Bets | Odds | Payout |
|      |      |        |      |      |        |

In the example above, there are three tables because the website offers three different point spreads, so we need to create three tables, one for each point spread.

However, when acting as a proxy to purchase point spread tickets, although the odds are primarily based on what the website offers, the point spread doesn't necessarily have to be. At this point, you can look at the state of your tables and decide on your own how many points to give to your friends.

For instance, if we find that there's a need for more bets in the "Team A giving 1 point" scenario to balance the table, we could persuade our friends to place their bets there. After all, the game hasn't started yet, and it's really hard to say how many points should actually be given. The best scenario would be to unify the point spreads to avoid creating too many tables.

If multiple tables are created, it would require us to separately monitor the balance of each table, and when it comes to "laying off" to balance the bets, it needs to be done separately for each table. What does separate laying off mean? It means looking for betting sites offering the specific point spreads as per each table and buying tickets accordingly.

This, of course, can be challenging, so it's important to pay attention when receiving bets and try to unify the point spreads to avoid hassle later on. Alternatively, another approach would be to find friends who haven't bought lottery tickets yet when it's close to game time, and offer slightly higher odds to entice them to place bets, achieving the "laying off" purpose.

### 3. Over/Under Bets

This type of betting involves wagering on whether the total score of both teams will be over or under a certain number of points. This "certain number" is referred to as the base score, for instance, 199 points. So, the betting line might look like this:

"Team A vs Team B, will the total score be over or under 199?"

We have detailed this type of betting in the "Player Section," but the operational method is similar to the first and second points above. Firstly, we need to check whether the website only manipulates the odds.

If the base score remains static, the operational method is similar to the first type, the Money Line. However, if the website manipulates the base score, it's akin to the second type, the Point Spread.

The above covers all methods of collective ticket purchasing. Frankly, this is the standard operating principle for online sportsbooks. Hence, what our friend from Hong Kong is doing is essentially the job of an online sportsbook.

Since he's taken on this role, he's subject to all the risks that a sportsbook would encounter, and must adhere to all its rules; otherwise, he won't be able to earn the juice (commission). For detailed operating principles of online sportsbooks, you can refer to the "Online Sportsbook Section" in this book, which will not be repeated here.

Other Betting Types

You might wonder about other betting types offered by online sportsbooks, such as guessing the exact score or the total number of goals. These types will be discussed in detail in the "Player Section."

Basically, we do not recommend engaging in betting types where the probability of winning is less than ½ without thorough analysis. The reason is simple: they are designed for players to lose. So, if friends ask us to purchase these lottery tickets on their behalf, we, as friends, should advise them against it and suggest simpler bets like wagering on the game's outcome or the Over/Under.

There are many ways to "do charity", and one doesn't have to go against one's own money by engaging in high-risk, low-reward games. However, if they still insist, then of course it can be done, and we will look into how to operate it better.

Primarily, online sportsbooks, for these low probability betting types, usually adopt a take-it-or-leave-it approach without laying off. With mathematical probability as a backing, there's only a gain in the long term. Nevertheless, a betting balance sheet is still necessary, mainly to ensure that the total income always exceeds the total payout. For instance, in exact score betting, players can guess whether the total goals will be 1, 2, or 3, 4, 5, 6, 7... etc. Here, the payout for each goal count should be less than the total income.

Yet, as there's still a factor of luck involved, if the payout for a single goal count exceeds the total income, a well-resourced sportsbook might still accept the bets and gamble with the players, given the substantial probability advantage it holds. Over the long term, it's a winning proposition. However, lesser-resourced sportsbooks or individuals looking to collectively purchase lottery tickets might encounter bad luck and end up losing a lot on these bets, which has happened before. Therefore, extra caution is needed when acting as a proxy for these types of tickets.

If you decide to accept all bets and collect the money, be prepared to pay out the winnings if they win in the end. However, to operate in such a manner, there are two conditions that must be met.

- Regular Purchases: It is essential that the ticket purchases for friends are done on a regular basis—daily and for every game. It's not advisable to buy a ticket sporadically now and then.

- Financial Strength and Steadiness: The odds for these types of games are quite high, so if you're not careful and a friend guesses correctly once, the loss can be substantial. Therefore, having substantial financial strength is imperative.

For such proxy purchasing, our suggestion is to genuinely act on their behalf —whatever they want, we go to the betting site and purchase exactly that. However, there's still room for discussion with friends. You can charge a small service fee; for example, if they buy a ticket with odds of 3.00, you could take a 0.30 odds share. This way, if they win in the end, you also get a share of the prize money, ensuring that your efforts were not in vain.

It's a reminder for all, if you're interested in doing this, ensure to go through relevant materials, understand the relationship between odds and probability of guessing correctly in each type of game. Once you grasp the principles, the actual operation isn't complicated. All you need is a piece of paper and a pen, or if you're diligent, you can create an Excel spreadsheet on a computer which would be much more convenient.

Lastly, there's one point to note; we don't know whether the friend from Hong Kong, mentioned at the beginning of this article, gave the protagonist the official odds. As seen from the earlier discussion, official odds are constantly changing, there's no fixed number.

What if this friend reported an official odd of 1.90 as 1.80? That's quite shrewd. In this way, besides earning the official 10% odds, he also made an extra 10% from the protagonist. Since the protagonist doesn't check the betting lines, even if he did, it's hard to notice this due to the constantly changing odds.

## Is "Collective Ticket Purchasing" Legal?

After going through the Hong Kong example of collective ticket purchasing, the major concern is, "Is collective ticket purchasing legal?". Indeed, this is a great question. Collective lottery ticket purchasing isn't a new thing; people domestically and internationally have a habit of pooling money to buy lottery tickets, and stories of hitting jackpots through collective purchasing are often reported in the news. So, the initial impression might be that it seems legal.

But is it really legal? Let's discuss. Firstly, we need to break down the phrase "collective ticket purchasing" into its components: two actions and one objective.

- Collective Funding - This refers to the act of pooling money with others.

- Proxy Purchasing - This refers to the act of purchasing lottery tickets.

- Lottery Ticket - This is the objective of the purchase.

Starting with the third item, the lottery ticket, domestically, only government-approved legal sports betting is allowed. So, if we are to purchase, it has to be this type. Underground lottery tickets remain illegal, so regardless of whether it's a collective purchase or an individual one, it's not permissible.

Moving on to the second aspect, "Proxy Purchasing" behavior, there is no need to delve deep into this. It's absolutely legal as long as the item being purchased is a legal commodity. There have been no instances where purchasing items on behalf of someone is considered illegal, and government-approved sports lottery tickets are undoubtedly legal commodities.

Lastly, we come to the first aspect, the act of "Collective Funding." Frankly, this is where the question gets substantial. Why? Because the major difference between sports betting and lottery is that during collective ticket purchasing, the person collecting the funds could potentially profit from it.

The example of the individual from Hong Kong illustrated this point well. Hence, a particular law comes into play here, which is the crime of public gambling under the criminal law.

"Intending to profit, providing gambling places or public gambling, is punishable by up to three years imprisonment, and may also incur a fine of up to three thousand dollars."

So, whether or not there is an intention to profit during collective funding for sports betting, at least it appears suspicious to others. Hence, the act of

"Collective Funding" is almost seen as "Intending to Profit." However, intending to profit is not a crime. Everyone works to earn money, which is also intending to profit.

For this gambling crime to be established, there are two more elements, first, providing a place for gambling, and second, public gambling. If either of these two elements is established, it would be considered as committing a gambling crime.

Firstly, providing a place for gambling. This implies that if collective funding is done publicly or in public places, it's not allowed. For example, doing so in schools, companies, or setting up a stall on the street would be considered as providing a place for gambling, and would certainly be a violation of gambling crime.

Secondly, public gambling. This gets a bit more complex. Let's look at what public gambling means in legal terms?

"It refers to gathering an unspecified number of people to participate in gambling. This crime is established based on whether the individual gathers people to gamble together or entices others to gamble, regardless of whether they themselves participate in gambling, or entices others to gamble, this crime can be established."

This is the crux of the matter. From this, it seems that "collective funding" is not permissible by law, because collecting funds to purchase lottery tickets definitely gathers a majority of people to participate in gambling. Regardless of whether you're merely helping others buy or buying for yourself and helping others along, it establishes a gambling crime.

Moreover, even without helping everyone collect funds to buy lottery tickets, if you are instigating others in the office to go to the betting stations and buy lottery tickets, that's also not permissible as it's considered as "enticing others to gamble."

Therefore, my conclusion is, domestically, the act of "Collective Proxy Purchasing of Lottery Tickets" is not permissible by law, but if it's merely "Proxy Purchasing of Lottery Tickets," there should be no problem. The distinction lies in whether you are actively "gathering" people or "enticing" others. If you are active, then it's not allowed.

However, if you are passive, and friends actively come to you for help privately, then the law probably wouldn't apply. Because there's neither "providing a place for gambling" nor "public gambling" in such scenarios. So, in the example of the friend from Hong Kong, if this scenario were to be portrayed in a domestic movie, the narrative would need to be reversed. The protagonist would need to actively call the friend for help in purchasing the lottery tickets.

The above is purely personal opinion, and for an accurate legal interpretation, consulting a lawyer or relevant expert is necessary. However, I am quite curious about one thing— in the future, when government-approved sports lottery tickets are advertised, would that be considered as "enticing others to gamble?"

**Tripartite Standoff in Sports Betting**

In this extensive section, we are going to discuss a fascinating character in the realm of sports betting—the "Agent". You might wonder why we kickstarted this discussion with the anecdote of "a Hong Kong individual collecting funds to buy lottery tickets".

There's a reason for this. Many might assume that an "Agent" is nothing but a betting station on a website, and government-approved betting stations are dime a dozen, available for players to buy lottery tickets. Moreover, franchising a betting station merely requires having a storefront, possessing sports knowledge, and teaching players how to play. So, what's the big deal about it?

If you think along these lines, you are mistaken. The importance of this "Agent" is far from ordinary. Moreover, the concept of "Agent" is vastly different from what many might imagine. Indeed, a betting station is a type of "Agent", but an "Agent" is not limited to a betting station. Our Hong Kong friend from the earlier narrative is also an "Agent".

In our definition, anyone can become an agent, not necessarily needing official recognition.

Furthermore, the concept of a betting station in sports betting and the one you visit to buy numerical lottery tickets are entirely different. Their monetizing methods are poles apart and incomparable. If you have been paying attention to the news, you'd notice that individuals keen on setting up sports betting stations are significantly more compared to traditional betting stations. Have you ever wondered why?

That's why we have devoted this section to discuss the agents in sports betting.

Their definition is vague, and anyone can become one.

They reap the most benefits but almost have no obligations.

They can transition their roles freely; they can become a website or a player whenever they wish.

## What Is an Agent?

What is an agent? An agent can be easily identified as someone who accepts bets from players but does not set the betting lines themselves. Betting Sites are included in this definition because they allow people to purchase betting tickets. Our friend from Hong Kong is also an example, as he helped others buy betting tickets. Agents do not require licenses, examinations, or government registration. The only requirement is that players trust you enough to place bets or purchase tickets through you.

So, anyone can become an agent. However, people usually become agents because there's significant financial gain involved. For example, our friend from Hong Kong took advantage of helping friends buy betting tickets but kept the money himself. He essentially "skimmed the juice" from the online sportsbook by balancing the bets. This technique is the basic skill set for every agent, known as "balancing bets."

Why do agents do this? The focus is on the financial benefit. Agents aim to take the "juice" from online sportsbooks, which we've estimated to be around 10% to 12%. This is much higher than transaction fees. We haven't even started talking about other profitable methods in sports betting. If you include those, the potential profits could reach up to 25%.

What does 25% signify? Let's take a small betting site for example. Suppose it has a daily turnover of $100,000. If the site only charges a transaction fee, then the daily profit would be 6% of $100,000, or $6,000. In a month, that's only $180,000, not accounting for rent and personnel costs. But what if instead of charging a transaction fee, the site earns money from the "juice"? In that scenario, the maximum profit could be 25% of $100,000, which is $25,000 per day, or $750,000 per month. Of course, the actual profit may vary, but even at a 50% discount, it's higher than the standard transaction fees.

So, based on the profits, we can clearly differentiate between agents and betting sites. Moreover, regular betting sites have a fixed profit margin of 6%, but if you are good at controlling the betting lines, then the money you can make can approach the amount of "juice" available.

## Role Transition

The allure of becoming an agent is greatly due to the substantial benefits it offers along with the ease of operation, which is why many veteran players transition into this role, making the earlier mentioned case of the friend from Hong Kong a common scenario in reality. Becoming an agent doesn't require any official permission or registration with the online sportsbook, making it a nearly inevitable journey for astute players in this game to privately accept bets and transition into agents.

The foremost advantage of being an agent is the ability to earn all the juice from the online sportsbook without incurring any costs. It's known that online sportsbooks have to set lines, hire traders to control the lines, and invest in expensive computer hardware and software, which incurs high costs. However, agents, functioning under the online sportsbooks, can directly leverage these resources. They merely need to use the lines set by the online sportsbook to earn money, making it almost a zero-cost business.

Nevertheless, solely relying on the online sportsbook's lines has a downside: the betting balance sheet won't balance out, and achieving balance is crucial for earning the juice. Therefore, seasoned agents, over time, will set their own lines to entice their players to balance their bets, and truly rake in substantial earnings. Hence, transitioning from an agent to an online sportsbook is a natural progression.

The thrill of this game lies herein. An individual starts as a minor player, gradually climbing up the ladder, first becoming an agent, then advancing to an online sportsbook. If an error occurs along the way, resulting in business failure, they'd revert to being minor players and start afresh.

On a global scale, wherever sports betting exists, there will be online sportsbooks, players, and agents - three roles that are bound to interchange. There's no permanent sportsbook or player, and agents act as a bridge between the two, playing a pivotal role in this game.

Moreover, in numerous places, agents hold stronger positions than the online sportsbooks. However, agents are rarely mentioned in the news, and their significance is severely underestimated, often causing people to overlook this role. Hence, in this section, we will delve into the role of agents, exploring their functions and tactics.

**Revisiting Betting Sites**

Since many general players are willing to become agents, how could the owners of official betting sites resist? Indeed, according to normal regulations, sports betting sites, representing online sportsbooks, must transfer betting tickets to the online sportsbook, and they also collect the deserved handling fees. Therefore, logically, they shouldn't act as agents.

Looking at traditional lottery tickets already issued, we can see that everyone abides by the law. When we go to buy number-drawing lottery tickets, we have never heard of betting site owners proposing private transactions or offering better odds. However, when put plainly, this is not a big deal.

In the case of lottery tickets, if one hits the jackpot, the prize money is $100 million. No betting site owner could afford to cover such an amount. Even if they could, probably no one would trust them, hence when buying lottery tickets, private transactions are non-existent. Moreover, there's nothing to say about the odds; the odds for lottery tickets are already sky-high. We've calculated that it's already at 2 million. So, even if the owners raise it to 3 million, what's the point? The odds of 2 million are already very appealing.

However, it's a different story with sports betting. Theoretically, there's a high possibility of private transactions at sports betting sites. No matter how we look at it, owners might absorb the betting tickets themselves, without transferring them to the online sportsbook behind.

The logic is simple. When players engage in sports betting, they definitely check the odds first. For example, at an odds of 1.80, betting $100 could yield a maximum of $180. With such an amount, a betting site owner can absolutely afford to cover it. More importantly, players would also believe they can cover it. Thus, a trust relationship can be established in sports betting, something that can't be achieved with lottery tickets.

Next is the issue of odds. The odds in sports betting are low, like the aforementioned 1.80, which is extremely low compared to lottery tickets. And what players aim to win is just a small amount of money. With these odds, betting $100 would win just $80. From this perspective, betting site owners have the opportunity to use slightly higher odds, like 1.90, to attract players for private transactions. For players, this is a good deal! Initially, they could only win $80, but now they can win $90. Calculating the return on investment, it's an increase of 10%, so what's not to like?

Taking a holistic view, official betting sites can gain players' trust, and have the means to attract players for private transactions, plus, the allure of "juice" is so enticing. So if these betting sites claim they have never accepted bets privately, it's hard to believe. Looking back, in the news related to sports betting, everyone is eager to join betting sites, and this is indeed thought-provoking.

## Who Is the Culprit?

Given that the role of "agent" is so lucrative and the operation is so simple, it's safe to say, from the inception of sports betting, this entity has been an inherent part of the game. So, one might ask, does the online sportsbook know about this?

Of course, they do. If we know, how could the online sportsbooks not know? Moreover, when we discuss the money agents make, the most direct victim is the online sportsbook itself. To be more explicit, in this scenario, both agents and players benefit, while the real victim is the online sportsbook.

And the culprit here is the agent. Think about it, if someone has been victimized for a long time, wouldn't they know who the culprit is? Moreover, most online sportsbooks start from the grassroots, climbing up step by step, and of course, have operated as agents at some point, so they are well versed in the various tricks of the trade.

You must be thinking, there's a problem, so solve it. If the online sportsbooks realize their money is being made by others, how could they not think of a solution? Would they just sit idly and await doom? Moreover, sports betting, having developed over decades, should have some countermeasures by now. Otherwise, who would want to run an online sportsbook? Everyone would rather be an agent.

Exactly, in our discussion, every problem requires a solution. But there's a prerequisite, the problem itself must be solvable. Unfortunately, regarding the "agent dilemma" for online sportsbooks, there basically isn't a way to eradicate it. It's a situation where everyone is at a loss.

The logic is simple, whether it's the private acceptance of bets by betting sites or savvy players privately pooling funds. The crux of such private transactions lies in the word "private." Since it's not public, it's hard to catch.

Think about it, if you and your friend bet privately, can the online sportsbook control it? How could they?

Another regrettable point is that this game never lacks online sportsbooks. If one online sportsbook finds it hard to make money and quits, naturally, someone else will take its place. This won't disrupt the game's balance or development. So, despite decades of development in sports betting, this problem has never been resolved.

The reason there's never a shortage of online sportsbooks is simple, agents will eventually have to operate online sportsbooks. As we discussed in the "Online Sportsbook Chapter," to make "juice" money, balance is essential, and to achieve balance, one must control the betting lines. So, if an agent is both controlling betting lines and accepting bets, naturally, they become an online sportsbook. As mentioned earlier, it's inevitable.

The law of natural evolution applies here too. If an agent has no natural predators in this game, they won't be eliminated. So even if online sportsbooks know the culprit is the agent, there's nothing they can do. And we can anticipate, as long as sports betting exists, there will be people making a living by being agents.

**The Only Victim?**

In fact, after being victimized for a long time, online sportsbooks have developed a "123 Rule." It stipulates that when a savvy player emerges, they will bring along two friends, resulting in the online sportsbook losing three betting tickets. The logic is simple: as a person engages in sports betting for a while, they gradually understand what "juice" is and how to profit from it. Hence, they will voluntarily buy betting tickets for their friends, becoming an agent. We all know that to achieve balance and earn juice money, at least two people are needed, so they will bring along at least two friends. Eventually, since this person knows how to act as a bookmaker, they naturally won't buy betting tickets themselves, so the online sportsbook will lose three betting tickets in total.

Following this rule further, a terrifying result emerges. Suppose in a group of ten players, only one knows how to act as an agent, then according to the rule, the online sportsbook would lose nearly one-third of its revenue. If we calculate based on a daily turnover of one hundred million dollars, that's a loss of thirty million dollars, translating to a net loss of three million dollars a day, amounting to a loss of one billion dollars annually.

This is only when one in ten players knows how to be an agent. If sports betting has a longer history, or if the online sportsbook is situated in a less favorable region where players are too savvy, and this number rises to one in five players being savvy, then running the book becomes unappealing. This is because the turnover would halve, and the loss in profits would double.

We could even argue that the "123 Rule" is just a baseline, the savvy players in reality will bring along more than two friends. According to the operational principles in the betting balance sheet, the more people placing bets, the better, as this maximizes the juice money, and the balance is better maintained. So, savvy players, if intending to snatch customers, won't bring just two people; they will bring along a large group of friends. Therefore, the loss to the online sportsbook is absolutely incalculable.

However, upon careful differentiation, there is also the issue of agents stealing juice money from each other. Let's take a betting site with private acceptance of bets as an example; the boss of this betting site, who continuously engages in private transactions with customers, will eventually train these customers to become savvy.

Thus, we have another savvy player, and this player, following the 123 Rule, might also snatch business from the betting site boss, so beneath an agent, another agent could easily emerge.

But in this scenario, we still cannot consider the betting site boss a victim. Because if an agent doesn't run a betting book, it's a no-cost business. Only the true online sportsbook, which opens betting lines, controls the lines, and spends heavily on computer hardware and software, is the real victim. No matter how small an agent's business becomes, they can never lose their capital.

Moreover, in this tripartite situation, besides affirming the online sportsbook as the ultimate victim, we can also infer that the ultimate beneficiaries are the savvy players. We are not saying that savvy players must act as agents, but rather, a good player can choose the best odds for themselves.

Since the game has online sportsbooks and so many agents, who compete to offer better odds to entice players to place bets, it's easy to imagine that with a little inquiry, it's easy to find higher odds. And as we will introduce in the "Player Chapter," high odds are crucial for players as they relate to whether a player can profit in the long term. If players can choose the odds, then in our inference, their chances of making money are greater.

So, the more agents there are, the more profits players make, yet the heavier the loss online sportsbooks suffer, but for the agents themselves, it's neither here nor there, as this is a no-cost business after all. Moreover, they can offer higher odds to attract players from the online sportsbooks.

On the victimized online sportsbook side, another disadvantage is that they have to invest capital to run the business. Since there's capital involved, they need to earn more profits to offset the costs, so generally, online sportsbooks can't offer too high odds, or else who would want to run a loss-making business. But agents don't have this problem, even if the juice money collected is only half of that by the online sportsbook, and the odds offered are much higher than the online sportsbooks', they won't suffer a loss.

**Fair Game**

So, we have always believed that sports betting is a fair game, although its "fairness" is exceedingly peculiar, it is fair nonetheless. Upon examination, it appears that the online sportsbook is destined to be the unlucky one, yet paradoxically, everyone still wants to be in the online sportsbook's position. As previously inferred, players starting from the grassroots level buying betting tickets will gradually rise to the position of the online sportsbook, driven by human nature, making the unfortunate online sportsbook a position everyone has a chance to rotate into.

We may not know whether the inventor of this game considered the agent issue, but it's certain that the unyielding agent has become a pain point for the online sportsbook, something they wouldn't want to see. We also can't ascertain whether they've proposed a solution, but logically deducing, it seems the agent is destined to never vanish.

Yet, the indomitable nature of the agent doesn't mean the online sportsbook has nothing to do. In fact, it must take action. Similar to the necessity of controlling the lines to defend the juice money, the online sportsbook must exert effort in dealing with agents. It has to continuously employ various means to diminish the influence of agents, striving to maintain its juice money unscathed and players unpoached, it cannot just sit and wait for doom.

For the online sportsbook, this is an endless battle because agents can never be eradicated. Yet, this battle is indispensable, as only by constantly finding ways to deal with agents can the online sportsbook's profit approach the figure set by the juice money. This classic offensive strategy to defend its domain is a way to preserve its territory.

So, next, let's see how the online sportsbook handles the challenging "agent" issue.

## Direct Customer Contact

In plain terms, a "Direct Customer" is a direct client of the online sportsbook. As long as a player places bets directly with the online sportsbook, we can consider them a "Direct Customer." This entity exists only with the online sportsbook; agents don't have direct customers.

A hundred percent "Direct Customer" is the dream of every online sportsbook because it signifies that all players are buying betting tickets directly from the online sportsbook, with no one engaging in private transactions. There are no agents, no betting sites, and certainly, no interference from our Hong Kong friend.

If everyone is a "Direct Customer," the online sportsbook no longer worries about a decrease in turnover, juice money being stolen, or having to pay commission to others. Moreover, they can charge the juice money as they please, and profits can be as high as desired. Not only can the initial investment be recovered, but the well-being of family members can also be secured in the future. What a wonderful situation that would be!

Regrettably, this is unrealistic. There is no such thing as a hundred percent "Direct Customer" in this world. Moreover, fast-forwarding a decade or so, even dreaming of "Direct Customer" might have been far-fetched. In the past, due to the lack of information, people had a vague understanding of sports betting; to place bets or buy betting tickets, they had to rely on others, seek guidance. Given the limitations in manpower and resources, it was impossible for the online sportsbook to cater to all players, thus developing a Direct Customer system was out of the question.

However, in recent years, this situation has undergone a drastic change. Hence, the emergence of this article, the path of the online sportsbook to Direct Customer engagement.

**The Rise of the Internet**

The Internet has thoroughly changed everyone's lives, whether it's online gaming, e-commerce, researching online, or simply making friends on the web, all have become integral parts of our lives. Concurrently, the Internet has also transformed the game of sports betting, providing the online sportsbook with an opportunity to fully develop a Direct Customer base.

Even those who have never participated in sports betting might have heard of "online betting." It's where the online sportsbook sets up a website, posts the betting lines, and accepts wagers from players. This is nothing new, and we won't delve into it much. In short, the Internet is an excellent channel for placing bets, and for players, it is incredibly convenient. In practical experience, winning money by placing bets on a website is easier than shopping online.

The betting transaction systems used by online sportsbooks have already perfectly integrated with online betting, so this is essentially my old line of work, and we will discuss more about such systems in the "Other Roles" section. Additionally, online betting holds special significance for players, a point we will elaborate on in the "Player Section."

Returning to the topic of Direct Customers, why do we emphasize online betting particularly? Many people think that online betting is merely a marketing strategy adopted by online sportsbooks to expand their market, especially in this digital age, attracting these new players is a challenge for the online sportsbook.

However, we want to highlight that for online sportsbooks, there is a more crucial thinking behind developing online betting, which is the development of Direct Customers. It's clear to see that players who place bets on the online sportsbook's website are essentially Direct Customers, with absolutely no room for anyone else to intervene in between.

This implies that if the online sportsbook successfully directs all players to online betting, even inadvertently, then the dream of a hundred percent Direct Customer base becomes a reality, achieving the beautiful scenario we depicted earlier. Hence, we say that developing online betting is synonymous with developing Direct Customers, a matter of life and death for the online sportsbook, far beyond a mere marketing tactic.

Nevertheless, agents are not fools, and they certainly can see through this crucial factor.

## The Agent's Counterattack

Direct Customers are a boon for online sportsbooks, but a bane for agents. Should the sportsbooks successfully absorb all the players, agents would be left with no avenue to earn their juice. The luckier ones might still retain their positions as betting shop owners, earning a 6% commission. But the less fortunate ones, like our friend from Hong Kong, would likely be out of a job.

Hence, certain government-sanctioned sports betting operators, who have traditionally operated through physical betting shops, suddenly sought the government's permission to open "virtual channels" one day. These virtual channels refer to online and mobile betting, as opposed to the physical nature of betting shops, hence deemed virtual.

This move was met with unanimous opposition from the physical channels, where not only did betting shop owners resist the virtual channels, but they also took to the streets in protest, demanding the cessation of online and telephone betting. The reason was simple - this move threatened their livelihoods. With online betting in place, the business at physical betting shops would undoubtedly suffer. Moreover, the physical channels have a unique characteristic of serving the public welfare, thus virtual channels were seen as an indirect exploitation of the vulnerable.

Following the strong counterattack from the physical channels, sports betting operators typically propose profit-sharing rules, meaning a portion of the profits earned from virtual channels would be shared with the physical channels. However, this suggestion was not accepted, and various protests and resistance continued to emerge.

The above narrative is a common phenomenon we observe, with two intriguing key points. First, why would sports betting operators risk facing the condemnation of the masses to insist on launching virtual channels? Second, why were betting shop owners in various regions unmoved by subsidy policies, continuing to believe their interests were significantly harmed?

We hadn't mentioned one basic rule of agents in previous articles, that is, the more players an agent deals with privately, the better. And how is this achieved? The more friends an agent has, the better. The more private transactions with players, the easier it is for agents to balance their books. The more people agents know, the higher the likelihood of converting these individuals into players for private transactions.

Connecting the "Agent Dilemma" in sports betting with this phenomenon is quite intriguing. The global sports betting industry is striving towards the path of Direct Customers. Meanwhile, our agents are sparing no effort to prevent this from happening.

Of course, we might be assuming the worst, and the situation might not be as depicted. However, here we can tell everyone that globally, whenever a sportsbook wholeheartedly develops Direct Customers, it will undoubtedly face resistance from agents. We've deduced this logically. Moreover, we've also deduced that sportsbooks have no choice but to develop Direct Customers.

The costs for a sportsbook are substantial, so without diligently developing Direct Customers, would they just allow themselves to be slaughtered? We've calculated that agents earning juice is no small matter. If not curtailed, the sportsbook would soon be unable to continue operations, making the development of Direct Customers a matter of life and death for sportsbooks.

But the reaction of agents is understandable. If sportsbooks are to make money, shouldn't agents as well? It's not too much for sportsbooks to enjoy the meat while agents sip the soup. Moreover, agents do earn their keep. They initially introduce new players to the sportsbook, acquainting them with sports betting, which eventually opens opportunities for private transactions. From a market expansion perspective, they do contribute to the sportsbook.

So, we won't judge the parties involved in this news piece. Everyone is fighting for their interests, and their actions are somewhat justified. But we must point out that the most pitiable group here is the players themselves.

Think about it, sportsbooks and agents are clashing heads, but what they are fighting for is the money in the players' pockets. We've discussed their operating principles before, and aside from a little capital from the sportsbooks, the funds they use to run their operations mainly come from the players. Yet, in this whole affair, the most aggrieved party, the players, aren't even mentioned in the news. But not to worry, in the "Player Section" of this book, we'll look at things from the player's perspective, discussing how players can protect themselves amidst such scenarios.

## A Series of Compromises

The development of Direct Customers by online sportsbooks is not news in the industry. The resistance of agents against Direct Customers has a long history. Hence, in the evolution of sports betting, aside from continually refining the game itself or integrating internet technology, managing the relationship between online sportsbooks and agents is a crucial aspect of this game.

There's an intriguing aspect here; sportsbooks can't eliminate agents, and agents can't eliminate Direct Customers. We've inferred before that agents are inherent to this game and will persist until the very last day of its existence. But what about Direct Customers? Can they be eliminated?

Indeed, to some extent, Direct Customers can be seen as natural adversaries to agents, yet they are irremovable. One significant reason is the strong support from sportsbooks, along with various incentives, making players willing to be Direct Customers. Moreover, being a Direct Customer holds special importance for players. We will discuss more on this in the "Player Section," but for now, let's just say to be a good player, one must take advantage of various benefits offered by this game.

Therefore, agents can't stop a sportsbook from developing Direct Customers, and similarly, sportsbooks can't prevent agents from accepting bets privately. The opening of virtual channels is an inevitable matter, something we dare to assert, as it's "very important" for players. As for betting shop owners conducting private transactions, it's just something no one openly admits.

Nevertheless, in its evolutionary process, sports betting has found a way to address this issue, and the solution boils down to one word: "Transparency." Sportsbooks openly declare their intent to develop Direct Customers, and agents voice out their desire to keep collecting money from players privately. Since neither party can stop the other, why not sit down and discuss, finding a compromise that could work for both?

Initially, both sportsbooks and agents have their challenges in making money from sports betting. If everyone lays their cards on the table, there might be a mutually acceptable solution where they complement each other's strengths and weaknesses. Moreover, the money they discuss isn't from their pockets but from the players. So, why fight each other, providing a spectacle for players, when they could unite and collectively reclaim the money from players? Hence, they may reach a series of agreements and compromise on a method.

Before delving into the specifics of these agreements, shall we first explore what challenges they face?

## The Challenges Faced by Agents

Firstly, agents need to manage their own betting balance sheets if they are to accept bets privately, a method we've already elaborated upon in the article about our friends in Hong Kong. Besides managing the balance sheet, they also need to handle the intricate accounting for betting tickets. It is imperative that they get the collections and payouts to players right; the amount of prize money to be given can't be miscalculated either. Furthermore, agents must be cautious to mitigate risks. If they are not attentive to the guidelines previously discussed for operating as an online sportsbook, they may incur substantial losses.

So, for agents, there are mainly three significant challenges in conducting private transactions.

- Online sportsbooks offer hundreds of lines every day, which means agents have to create hundreds of betting balance sheets. The more bets they accept privately, the more tedious the task becomes. The laborious nature of the task isn't the only issue; accuracy is crucial. A single mistake can potentially lead to significant financial losses. This balance sheet needs to be updated continuously, just like the online sportsbook operates. It's not something that can be done once in a while. Over time, managing these complex balance sheets becomes a challenge in itself.

- Since the task involves creating betting balance sheets, achieving balance in betting is fundamental. You can't just assign this task to a temporary intern. At the very least, time must be invested in educating and training them to understand the operational principles. You also have to monitor the quality of work from these employees. If they make errors and throw the balance sheet into disarray, the agent is in trouble. Employing skilled staff implies higher wages, making this a problematic issue as well.

- There's risk involved. After completing the balance sheet, agents need to "arbitrage," similar to what online sportsbooks do, a concept we discussed in the "Online Sportsbook" section. Arbitrage comes with its own set of risks. Agents can still incur losses despite their best efforts.

Therefore, this matter is even more troublesome. You might privately collect numerous bets and still end up losing a significant amount of money. As for the sportsbook? They have their own set of problems:

- Because agents are accepting bets privately, the sportsbook's revenue decreases, subsequently affecting profits. With high operational costs involving expert consultations for setting up betting lines and designing computer systems, reduced revenue makes the business unsustainable. A decrease in the 'juice' would result in a substantial shortfall, not just a dollar or two but possibly billions.

- The odds could become uncompetitive. As we've mentioned in the "Online Sportsbook Section," there are standard numbers for the odds, which can't be arbitrarily set since they directly affect the sportsbook's daily earnings from the 'juice.' Agents, however, don't have to invest their own capital, so they might offer any odds to attract customers. If an uninformed agent sets the odds, it would be even more disastrous. If the sportsbook's odds differ too much from the agent's, players will become skeptical and might accuse the sportsbook of ripping them off.

- Agents could evolve into sportsbooks. This is the most critical point. As we know, if agents operate correctly, the profit they can make from the 'juice' is as much as a sportsbook. In the long run, agents could also become wealthy. They could set up their own betting lines, build their own computer systems, and compete directly with existing sportsbooks.

Both sides have challenges and reservations, so compromise and cooperation are necessary. This is understandable, and it's why sports betting has evolved to include a comprehensive set of public rules that precisely define everyone's rights and responsibilities.

## Institutionalization

In the world of sports betting, one of the great things is that there are systems, standards, and game rules everywhere. This is true for both online sportsbooks and agents. After reaching a consensus and establishing a series of compromises, they become an open system that each online sportsbook can choose to adopt depending on the situation.

Why do we call it a series of practices? Let's discuss the traditional method of subsidizing in the sports betting industry, which involves using the profits from the virtual channels to subsidize the physical channels. Many online sportsbooks adopt this approach. However, it may seem ineffective, as betting sites still push back. This isn't a flaw in the system, though. What agents really want is for the online sportsbook to have no direct customers, which is, of course, unfeasible. If they can't grow their direct customer base, they might as well shut down. So, no system can fully satisfy the agents, and these systems are all products of compromise. Nobody is entirely happy, but everyone can accept it.

The reason the subsidy system may not be effective is likely that everyone is too savvy, and the system doesn't hit the real issue. But it's still a good approach. If the agents are conducting their business properly, and the virtual channel incurs some transaction fees, then the online sportsbook should subsidize some of those costs. Virtual channels don't require much effort from the owners of the betting sites, so this subsidy can be considered a windfall, making it acceptable. This subsidy system is the first mature system we want to introduce.

In this subsidy system, the relationship between the online sportsbooks and the agents is clearly regulated. Both parties have rights and responsibilities, and it is fairly balanced. Therefore, it's no surprise that this is the first system rolled out by sports betting operators. However, this system has a limitation: it only governs what happens above board. What about the unspoken issues that happen behind the scenes? What if agents plan to accept bets privately to earn juice? Regardless of how good the "subsidy" is, it's merely a drop in the bucket compared to the "juice."

So we say, this subsidy system is good, but it doesn't hit the nail on the head. However, it's also important to note that many times, what can be done is probably just this much. It's not that the sportsbook operators don't understand, but rather, many things can't be openly discussed.

Can you imagine a betting site owner coming out and saying, "You're preventing me from making juice?" Or can an online sportsbook openly complain, "You guys are just trying to earn my juice, that's why you're so dissatisfied?" Such talk about juice here and there sounds terrible. If someone who doesn't know better hears it, they might think it's a group of robbers divvying up an uneven loot.

So, they definitely are in a position where they can't speak freely. Institutionalizing the relationship between online sportsbooks and agents is likely difficult, not to mention researching which system would work best. But that's okay; we don't have that problem. We directly look at it from an academic perspective, examining how other places openly discuss the matter and eventually create a win-win situation for everyone.

For a system to be accepted by both the sportsbooks and agents, we must acknowledge the existence of private transactions. We can't turn a blind eye to it. Otherwise, a compromise will never be found. So the first step in designing a system is for sportsbooks to admit that they want to develop direct customers, while agents must also acknowledge that they are engaging in private transactions.

With this premise in place, we can then proceed with regulations. We make the agents' private bet-taking a public activity, while the sportsbooks would allocate a portion of the juice for the agents to make money, thereby also solving their issues with line management. Once this is done by the sportsbooks, agents should not obstruct them from acquiring direct customers. In the end, it all comes down to who has more customers to make more money.

This could create a positive competition in economic terms, where everyone contributes to enlarging the pie, attracting the most players, and ultimately, everyone makes money. This way, unnecessary losses or mutually destructive outcomes can be avoided.

But when it comes to sharing the juice, there's a problem. This money can't just be distributed randomly; it has to be allocated wisely. First, not all agents can simply register to get money; that won't work. Second, sportsbooks still want to make more money, so they can't just give it away without a strategy to get more in return.

Therefore, there are various systems to discuss. In this article, we'll take a look at how sports betting in other places is regulated, particularly in terms of the relationship between sportsbooks and agents.

## Agent Commission System

Let's get straight to the point, focusing on the most important aspect: the "Agent Revenue Sharing System." The first questions that come up are, what is an agent and what does revenue sharing mean? An agent is simply an agent, but one that is registered—not with the government, but with the online sportsbook. The logic here is simple. If an agent wants to participate in all reward programs, then they must first make the sportsbook aware of their existence. Otherwise, how would the online sportsbook distribute the funds? Using our earlier example of a friend from Hong Kong, he would simply need to register on the sportsbook's platform to become an agent.

Next, what is the revenue sharing system? This is where the sportsbook takes a realistic approach. Since private transactions can't be avoided, the sportsbook decides to legitimize them. The thought is, aren't agents already enticing players to engage in private transactions? Why not make it easier for everyone? So agents officially start accepting bets, and the sportsbook directly agrees on what percentage of those bets belong to the agent.

For agents, the advent of the revenue sharing system essentially legitimizes what used to be private bet acceptance, and the profit model remains the same. Whenever a player purchases a betting ticket from the agent, a certain percentage of that purchase amount belongs to the agent. If the player loses, the agent directly keeps that percentage from the betting ticket. However, if the player wins, the agent must also pay out the winnings according to their revenue share.

Let's look at an example. Suppose a player buys a $100 betting ticket from an agent, with odds of 1.50. In this revenue-sharing agreement, let's assume it's a 70-30 split. Therefore, $70 goes to the sportsbook and $30 goes to the agent. We can further examine the detailed breakdown.

|  | Bets | Payout |
|---|---|---|
| Sportsbook | 70 | 105 |
| Agent | 30 | 45 |

First, if the player loses, both the online sportsbook and the agent make money. The online sportsbook takes $70 of the wager, while the agent receives $30. This is a 70-30 split. However, if the player ends up winning, the online sportsbook has to pay out $105 in winnings, and the agent has to pay out $45. This is also a 70-30 split. In this arrangement, the agent essentially acts as a mini-online sportsbook, making it an attractive proposition for them. Some might argue that such a commission-based system is less profitable compared to handling bets privately. Isn't this a disadvantage?

True, at first glance, accepting a commission-based system means that the agent has to give a cut to the online sportsbook, which may seem less profitable. However, there are other benefits to consider. For one, the agent doesn't have to balance the books or handle finances themselves, which significantly reduces overhead. Moreover, in a commission-based system, all revenue, expenses, and financial balancing can be managed by the online sportsbook's computer system. The agent only needs to submit all the betting tickets, and their share is automatically calculated—saving both time and effort.

From the online sportsbook's perspective, a commission-based system might seem disadvantageous because it cuts into their all-important juice or commission. If an agent takes even 10% of the commission, it means the online sportsbook's revenue will be reduced by 10%. If the agent takes 50%, the revenue is halved. Therefore, online sportsbooks are generally reluctant to agree to such terms unless absolutely necessary. Only large agents can negotiate such commissions with the online sportsbook, and even then, the terms are up for discussion.

However, as bad as a commission-based system may be for the online sportsbook, it's better than an agent operating privately and the online sportsbook getting nothing. After adopting a commission-based system, agents are required to submit all betting tickets, which allows the online sportsbook to see the agent's actual turnover. This makes it possible to negotiate and vie for a larger share of the juice.

In any case, for online sportsbooks in the sports betting industry, the juice doesn't just fall from the sky. They have to continually strive to maximize it. Therefore, this commission-based system is the most mutually acceptable arrangement between online sportsbooks and agents in this game.

## Three-Tier Agent System

After the development of the revenue-sharing model matures, the industry introduces a well-known three-tier agent system. Once an agent registers on the online sportsbook, we categorize them according to their capabilities, in ascending order, as:

- Agent

- General Agent

- Shareholder

What do we mean by capability? Simply put, it refers to the daily amount of betting tickets an agent can collect. Generally speaking, the more they collect, the stronger they are, and the higher their level on the online sportsbook. The highest level one can achieve is that of a shareholder.

Why categorize agents like this? The primary difference lies in the benefits available to the agents. In the aforementioned revenue-sharing model, the more significant the share an agent can claim, the more juice they will earn. This is subject to detailed scrutiny; for instance, securing an additional 10% could lead to millions more in juice earnings over a month. The share an agent can claim depends on their capability. If they become a shareholder, they are entitled to claim a share, and a powerful shareholder can even claim a larger portion.

However, this is not necessarily the case for smaller agents. If they can claim a share, it will undoubtedly be a small one. Some online sportsbooks might not even allow them to claim a share, given that they don't bring in many clients or significant betting amounts. However, a lack of revenue sharing does not mean that there are no other benefits. We will discuss later that there are still many advantages to being an agent, even without revenue sharing.

In addition to revenue sharing, the three-tier agents also have different benefits. In the various reward measures we'll discuss later, what the three levels of agents can earn will differ. Of course, there are numerous online sportsbooks worldwide, and not all of them use a three-tier system; some have seven or eight levels of agents, which we have heard of. Regardless, the three-tier agent system is the most basic.

Since revenue sharing most directly affects profits, agents start at the grassroots level and climb their way up to becoming shareholders. What they compete for is mainly this "share." However, another crucial factor is the ability to "control the line."

**agents controlling the odd**

In the past, hardly anyone knew about the concept of "agents controlling the line," and the reason is simple. An agent who wants to register as a representative for an online sportsbook primarily wants to avoid the hassle of line management. As we've mentioned before, if agents want to earn a profit through juice, they have to balance the bets themselves, which can be very tedious over the long run. Therefore, agents join sportsbooks to let the professionals handle it. In doing so, agents can go back to being the owners of betting sites, casually earning money by collecting betting tickets from players, without the headache of managing betting balance sheets.

So, agents don't really need to control the line themselves; otherwise, what's the point of becoming an agent? If they still have to manage the line, they might as well accept bets privately to avoid giving the sportsbook a cut. This is why no one talks about "agents controlling the line." However, there is a problem here. Sooner or later, agents will realize that becoming an agent for a sportsbook is not as lucrative as it seems. The profit can drop significantly.

Take a 50/50 profit-sharing arrangement as an example. Suppose an agent gets 50%, and the sportsbook also takes 50%. After handing over all betting tickets, the agent should ideally earn as much as the sportsbook, right? Well, if you think so, you're wrong! Usually, agents don't make much, but sportsbooks do. The problem lies in "line control."

Let's revisit what "line control" means. It involves manipulating players to place bets evenly on both sides of the line. This way, the scale is balanced, and the bookmaker makes money. Maintaining this balance is crucial for earning the "juice." Now, sportsbooks have multiple agents, and they also have direct customers. Their balance sheets are definitely different from individual agents. When sportsbooks manage the line, they do it based on their own balance, not considering the agents' cut.

In monetary matters, everyone is pragmatic. The sportsbook will only focus on its own balance sheet showing its share of the bets. Why would they care about how much money agents have collected? So, in the end, the sportsbook ensures that its balance sheet is perfect, but what about individual agents? Unfortunately, each agent's situation is unique, and their balance sheet may not match that of the sportsbook.

Therefore, it all comes down to luck for agents. If they're fortunate and their balance sheet happens to even out, they can make money. But in most cases, luck isn't so generous.

## Fine-Tuning the Odds

Of course, for online sportsbooks, not making money because of controlling the betting lines can be inevitable. However, for the agents, this is absolutely unacceptable. There's no way they'd tolerate a situation where the online sportsbook is consistently profitable while they're not. If that were the case, agents would be better off accepting bets privately, where at least they can control the betting lines and prevent losses.

Therefore, a compromise must be reached between the online sportsbook and agents. They must sit down and negotiate, which gives rise to another strange system known as "Agent-Controlled Fine-Tuning of Odds."

First of all, we must emphasize that an agent can never have full control over the betting lines. If they did, they would essentially become an online sportsbook. That's the basic rule of the game. However, to solve the issue at hand, agents can't simply let the online sportsbook have complete control either. Thus, this compromise allows the online sportsbook to maintain control while letting agents "fine-tune" the odds.

Here's how it works: The online sportsbook must control the lines in order to make money; there's no issue with that. However, agents also want some control because they have their own lines to balance. The solution is to allow agents to fine-tune the odds, making it acceptable for both parties.

For example, if the online sportsbook sets the odds for "Team A at 2.20," it may be because they haven't received enough bets on Team A. By offering higher odds, they hope to attract more players to bet on Team A. But let's look at an individual agent; they may have already accepted too many bets on Team A and don't wish to take any more. So, they exercise their authority to adjust the odds to "Team A at 1.90."

What players ultimately see is "Team A at 1.90," which is a compromised line. Team A is still attractive due to the high odds but isn't overwhelmingly appealing. This way, the needs of both the online sportsbook and the agent are considered.

However, there will be critics questioning this method, as it could result in dissatisfaction from both ends. The online sportsbook may fail to attract a large number of players through high odds, throwing off its balance. On the agent's side, despite not wanting to take more bets, the high odds still remain, making it difficult for them to balance their books as well.

Indeed, your concerns are valid; this method could lead to a lose-lose situation. Therefore, it's an odd system where everyone struggles with line control and profitability.

But there's no better solution. Each agent under the online sportsbook has their own state of accepting bets, essentially their own balance scale. The online sportsbook itself also has one. Hence, deciding whose balance to use for controlling the line is unreasonable. The only approach is for the sportsbook to control the main line, while each agent makes minor adjustments. In the end, whose balance remains stable comes down to luck.

So, let's circle back to what a third-level agent aims for. Besides claiming a percentage of the winnings, another crucial factor is how much they can adjust the odds. In typical market conditions, the range is usually between 0.10 and 0.50. Any more than that is difficult, and the sportsbook isn't willing to permit it since too much adjustment by agents complicates the sportsbook's line control.

Someone may wonder why these agents don't simply engage in private trades. If they still have to control the line and give a cut to the online sportsbook without guaranteed profits, it doesn't seem advantageous. To address this question, it's important to clarify that the computer systems for sports betting are costly. Setting up a sportsbook requires extensive expertise. So, if an agent wants to become a bookmaker, they need to meet these criteria, which is not easy. Moreover, not all sportsbooks dominate their markets. In many areas, the landscape comprises large agents and smaller sportsbooks. These major agents might account for up to 90%, leaving just a little for the sportsbook as management fees.

However, it's generally correct to assume that once an agent becomes a significant shareholder in a sportsbook, controlling both percentage and line, it wouldn't be long before they consider becoming a bookmaker themselves. In our logical reasoning, it's just a matter of time. After all, both expertise and system infrastructure can be acquired at a cost, which is trivial compared to the profits.

While you, the readers, might deduce this outcome, most people wouldn't think this far. Let's focus on the most critical character in this large narrative: our friend from Hong Kong. Would he ever consider becoming a bookmaker while he's still making a bit of "juice" by helping friends place bets?

To become a bookmaker and operate a sportsbook, there's a process involved—a slow and gradual one. It's incremental and organized. Once you reach a certain level, you encounter new problems. Solutions are found incrementally, giving birth to these compromised systems. Therefore, the existence of these systems, whether it's the percentage of winnings or controlling the line, is necessary.

It's also these systems that allow smaller agents to rise through the ranks, eventually reaching the level of running their own sportsbook. This has led to a runaway growth in the game, something we will discuss more in future sections on "Concepts."

## The Tiered Line System

The tiered line system is the most important incentive structure for agents and line controllers on the online sportsbook, but as we've said before, this system can be highly detrimental to the online sportsbook. So, it should only be used as a last resort. With that in mind, let's talk about a less impactful approach: the "Tiered Line System." Generally speaking, it's unrealistic for small agents to expect a share of the profits, especially if they don't know how to control the lines. However, the Tiered Line System is practical because it allows you to make money without needing to control the lines, and it's a stable source of income.

The way the Tiered Line System works is that the lines on the online sportsbook must be categorized into different tiers before they can be distributed. For example, when Team A is facing Team B and the online sportsbook sets the line, a tier chart must first be created.

| Odds | Juice | Tier |
|---|---|---|
| Team A odds 1.80, Team B odds 1.80 | 10 % | A Line |
| Team A odds 1.85, Team B odds 1.85 | 7.5 % | B Line |
| Team A odds 1.90, Team B odds 1.90 | 5 % | C Line |
| Team A odds 1.95, Team B odds 1.95 | 2.5 % | D Line |

The renowned "ABCD Line" in the industry is described above. The essence of this grading is based on how much "juice" the online sportsbook takes. As you move from the top tier down, the juice taken by the online sportsbook decreases, and consequently, the odds in the betting line increase.

What's the purpose of this table? It's quite simple. If a player directly comes to the online sportsbook to place a bet, then they're given the A line, which means the sportsbook aims to make a 10% profit from the player. But what if an agent comes to the sportsbook to get a betting line? It varies; they might get the D line or the C line.

Regardless, when the agent turns around to sell this to a player, they might offer them the B line. This way, the agent can pocket the difference. For instance, if an agent gets the D line, the online sportsbook is content with a 2.5% profit. However, when the agent sells this to a player, they offer the B line, which has 7.5% juice. Thus, the agent makes a 5% difference in profit.

This is similar to practices in the travel industry when selling airline tickets or hotel rooms. If you book a room directly with a hotel, the price might be higher compared to booking through a travel agency. The same logic applies to sports betting. The odds provided by the online sportsbook might not be as favorable as those given by an agent.

Thus, we can view the betting line as a product. If the profit margin for the online sportsbook is lower, then the profit for the agent is higher. Consequently, online sportsbooks can reward agents who place larger bets by offering them better lines, like the D line. On the other hand, agents with lower betting volumes might get a worse line, like the C line.

Using the bet amount to differentiate between agents has its reasons. If an agent conducts private transactions, their betting amount on the online sportsbook would not be high. On the other hand, an agent who hasn't engaged in private deals would submit all the betting tickets bought by players to the online sportsbook, leading to naturally high betting amounts.

The advantage of this "graded line system" is its simplicity. It's worth mentioning that not every online sportsbook divides into four levels. Distinguishing into seventeen or eighteen levels is also feasible. Under this system, being an agent is all about profiting from the spread. There's no need to control the line or manage the betting balance sheet. This profit is steady, and there's nothing wrong with it. The only thing agents aim to obtain from the online sportsbook is a better line.

Moreover, this graded system benefits the online sportsbook as well. How much can an agent earn from the spread? At most 5% to 10%. Earning beyond that is challenging. In comparison to private deals where the online sportsbook might lose 25%, this is much better. Furthermore, since agents profit from the spread, they don't rush to control the line. This allows the online sportsbook to freely control the line and easily earn the juice.

However, it must be pointed out that although the graded system is simple for an agent, the profits are much smaller compared to the revenue-sharing model. Therefore, in the long run, agents won't be satisfied and will eventually negotiate for the revenue-sharing model.

Another point to note is that online sportsbooks, in their quest to develop direct customers, have seen the shine of the graded line system fade. The reason is simple: in the tourism industry, agents cannot conduct private betting, so online sportsbooks cannot merely replicate strategies from the tourism sector, which often offers agents substantial benefits.

So, the online sportsbooks have gradually started to do the opposite. They now offer the best odds to players directly and give worse odds to agents, forcing these agents to cater to less informed players. However, this approach is somewhat understandable. For online sportsbooks, direct customers are the most important. As long as there are agents, the sportsbooks cannot keep all the profits for themselves. How can one sleep soundly beside a potential competitor?

## Subsidy System

Lastly, we have the subsidy system. Even though we use this term, it isn't as formal as the previous two systems we discussed. In the earlier systems, there were specific rules and methods, but the subsidy system doesn't have a fixed structure. It encompasses various practices, which we broadly refer to as the subsidy system.

We can't precisely detail every single method within the subsidy system, as sportsbooks could introduce new methods at any time. But one consistent aspect is that all incentive measures within the subsidy system are fixed amounts. Whatever amount the sportsbook promises, that's exactly what they give. Unlike the previous two systems where agents earn based on their efforts.

In previous sections, we observed many traditional sports betting companies decide to subsidize their physical outlets in order to develop their online sportsbooks or virtual channels. We term this as the subsidy system. Because no matter how many bets a betting site accepts, the profit remains consistent. Unlike the previous systems where the more they accept, the more they earn.

One can imagine that sportsbooks are very keen on developing this subsidy system. The money they distribute is fixed, and it's undoubtedly not a large amount. So, it's cost-effective for them. But what about the agents? Why would they abandon the advantageous commission system and tiered system to embrace this subsidy?

This comes down to the strength of the agent. Let's take our friend from Hong Kong as an example again. He usually just buys betting tickets for his friends, and the number of friends he has is surely limited. From this, we can easily infer that the number of betting tickets he collects daily wouldn't be many. Under these circumstances, if he registers on the online sportsbook as an agent, can he reap any benefits? Forget about the commission system; he wouldn't even qualify for a tiered system.

This is where the subsidy system comes into play. Since he has registered on the online sportsbook and can potentially bring in customers, the online sportsbook would provide some incentives. They can't let the agent put in the effort for nothing. While the amount of these incentives may not be substantial, they're quite interesting. Let's delve into them:

1. **Account Opening Bonus**: This is a reward the online sportsbook offers when an agent convinces a player to open an online betting account. One thing to note here is that once a player opens an account, they belong to the online sportsbook. All their subsequent transactions are directly with the online sportsbook. Only under the commission system would the player be attributed to the agent. Most of the time, this bonus is quite generous because it's essentially helping the online sportsbook develop direct customers, which they are keen on. Conversely, agents might not be too keen on receiving this type of bonus.

2. **Loss Bonus**: This might be a lesser-known practice, but every online sportsbook adopts it, so let's start from the beginning. Essentially, the online sportsbook would analyze and see whether the players brought in by each agent are winning or losing. The win-loss figures of these players are then aggregated under each agent's account.

So, every once in a while, the online sportsbook needs to check the reports to see if this agent is always losing money (which actually means his players are losing). If they are frequently losing, then the online sportsbook must reward this agent. The reward method is very similar to the bonus points of credit cards. Basically, the more you lose, the more rewards you get.

You might be wondering, why is there such a reward? We've mentioned that the wins and losses of each player have nothing to do with the online sportsbook. If you're losing, the online sportsbook isn't making money either.

That's right. Everyone's wins and losses have indeed nothing to do with the online sportsbook. But if you're always losing, it means someone is always winning (because of the constant payout theorem). At the very least, it can be said that other players are more likely to win, and these winners will definitely go out and promote it extensively, becoming a live advertisement for the online sportsbook.

So, in the final analysis, these agents who are always losing money are indeed contributing a lot. Therefore, the online sportsbook must reward them. Additionally, with the reward money, these agents might also appropriately compensate the real losing players to prevent them from constantly losing and eventually quitting.

3. **Advertising bonuses**. Here, all the agent needs to do is convince the player to visit the online sportsbook. Whether the player ultimately opens an account and places a bet is not a concern. This approach resembles typical online advertising. With the increasing advancement of the internet, this type of incentive is becoming more prevalent. After all, what online sportsbooks want most is to continuously seek new players from various channels. So, if you search for "sports betting" online, you'll undoubtedly come across numerous advertisements from these websites.

There are countless types of incentives, too many to discuss in detail here. So, we'll just touch upon these three unique examples. If you come across any interesting ones in the future, don't forget to let me know.

With this, we've covered all the rules regarding agents: how they survive and how they coexist peacefully with online sportsbooks. However, it's worth noting that not all agents operate legitimately. Sometimes, after an agent receives money, they might gamble with it themselves. If they lose, they simply vanish, which happens quite often.

So, when defining the role of an agent, it can be said they act as the proverbial "middleman". They can become an online sportsbook or a gambler at their whim, without any set guidelines. Moreover, the operating principle of agents is straightforward. Once someone understands it, they can venture into it themselves, which explains the proliferation of agents in sports betting.

Therefore, managing the relationship with agents effectively has become a crucial issue for online sportsbooks. To run a successful online sportsbook, it's essential to skillfully employ these three systems:

- The agent commission system

- The line grading system

- The subsidy system

In fact, these systems have undergone a long period of development and can be regarded as the ultimate solutions. If an agent can't be managed even with the use of these three systems, then there's no point in further negotiations. It might be best to just let them run their own bookmaker operations.

## Risk Issues

Another interesting phenomenon we've observed from the beginning of this book is that in this industry, high risk doesn't necessarily equate to high returns. On the contrary, online sportsbooks have higher returns than agents, but with lower risk. This is due to the factor of line management, as we've mentioned before.

While it's tough for agents to make money, they're still better off than players. We could say that agents have higher returns compared to players but with less risk. So, in terms of return on investment:

**Online Sportsbooks > Agents > Players**

And in terms of risk:

**Players > Agents > Online Sportsbooks**

Being an ordinary player in this game is unfortunate; not only is there high risk, but the returns are also low. Many savvy people, after being players for a while, decisively embark on the path of becoming agents. However, being an agent is no easy feat. In this context, we've seen that agents face numerous challenges, including being suppressed by online sportsbooks and the possibility of incurring losses. Therefore, many smart people ultimately choose to remain as **players**.

But they don't stay as ordinary players; they aim to be shrewd players. Sports betting is a game designed specifically for clever individuals. Being a shrewd player here may not necessarily make you a lot of money, but losing money isn't easy either.

So, we're about to delve into what everyone is truly interested in: the **Player Chapter**.

# Player

## The Juice Strategy

In previous articles, we've covered how online sportsbooks and agents make money. Now let's turn our attention to players. First off, how do players make money? The answer seems straightforward; many would say by placing bets on online sportsbooks. If you win, you make money.

Indeed, in our definition, a player has to bet on an online sportsbook; there are no other ways for players to make money since they don't have as many options as online sportsbooks or agents. However, we haven't said that you must "win" to make money. Note that savvy players don't necessarily care about accurately predicting the outcome of a game when they place a bet.

So, in this extensive section, we'll delve step-by-step into how to be a savvy player in this game. But before discussing techniques, we need to understand how many types of plays online sportsbooks offer and how should we, as players, engage with them?

Apart from this book, probably no one else would use a title like "The Juice Strategy." We dare to use this term because this book starts with how online sportsbooks make money. So, everyone is familiar with "juice." If you look in other books or ask at betting sites, you're unlikely to come across this term.

"The Juice Strategy" refers to Asian handicap and over-under bets, both of which are essentially blind guesses with a 50% chance of being correct; that's why online sportsbooks refer to them as such. So why call it this way? Since everyone's just guessing and has a 50% chance of being right, the online sportsbook can only profit from the juice. We'll also introduce "Non-Juice Strategies" later on, where the sportsbooks do not solely rely on juice for profit.

We've already discussed the operational specifics of these juice strategies from the sportsbook's perspective in the "Online Sportsbook Section." Basically, it involves manipulating the point spread and odds to entice bets on both sides of the line so that it balances out, ensuring profits for the online sportsbook.

So, in these types of plays, the interests of the online sportsbooks and players don't conflict; broadly speaking, it's a very fair way to play. Now, let's look at these juice strategies from the player's perspective: How should we engage with them?

**Betting Line**

Firstly, players need to look at the betting line when buying a betting ticket. Here's an example of a basketball betting line

|  | Time | point spread line | Odds | over/under | Odds |
|---|---|---|---|---|---|
| Team A (Home Team) | 18:30 | -2.5 | 1.80 | 198.5 | 1.80 |
| Team B |  |  | 1.80 |  | 1.80 |

The above are the betting lines most people commonly see. For ease of display, websites often display multiple types of bets side by side. In this example, it does just that. It offers two types of betting: the **point spread line** and the **over/under**.

The betting line will always indicate the teams playing and the start time of the match. It often indicates "home", indicating whether the team is playing at their home ground or not. This is because there's a so-called "home advantage", meaning the chances of the home team winning are usually higher. However, some websites will directly label the strengths and weaknesses of the teams, which is even more straightforward.

Once you've looked at the betting line, you can freely place a bet. But please pay attention to the start time listed on the betting line. You must **place a bet** a few minutes before the match starts. If the time is close, the website might close the betting line anytime, which is called "closing the line". Once closed, players cannot place bets anymore. As this is a betting line for a single match, the player's bet is also known as a "single game bet". And since we have to bet before the match starts, it's also called "pre-game betting".

After a player reviews this betting line, they can freely choose a game to play, whether it's the **point spread line** or **over/under**.

Firstly, let's talk about the point spread line. This type of betting is about guessing which team will win the match tonight. You can guess Team A or Team B. If the team you guessed wins, you will win money. However, there are four factors you need to consider first.

**Point Spread**

Firstly, it's about the point spread. In this example, Team A gave Team B a handicap of 2.5 points. In reality, it's 2 points, and we'll discuss the 0.5 later on. This means that Team A must win by more than two points to be considered as having won. Otherwise, they would still be considered as having lost. For example:

| Final Score | Result |
|---|---|
| Team A 99 points vs Team B 98 points | Won by less than two points, Team A is considered to have lost |
| Team A 101 points vs Team B 98 points | Won by more than two points, Team A won |

Please note, if you place a bet on Team A, then if they lose, you lose; if they win, you win.

**Draw Line**

The "Draw Line" in the point spread betting refers to a peculiar situation where there's a 0.5 spread. Of course, everyone knows there's no such thing as a 0.5 score. This 0.5 doesn't signify a score but represents a type of odds. For instance, in this betting line with a 2.5 point spread, if the final score is Team A 100 points and Team B 98 points, then after deducting the given spread of two points, it's a tie at 98:98. This is where the 0.5 comes into play.

In this scenario, those who bet on the team with the point spread will be considered to have won half of the bet, in this example, those who bet on Team A. Suppose you placed a bet of $100 with odds of 1.90, then it's as if you only staked half the principal, which is betting $50. So, you can win $50 x 1.90 = $95, plus the original principal of $50, which means you get a total payout of $145.

On the other hand, if you bet on the other team, in this example, those who bet on Team B, you'd be considered to have lost half. If your betting ticket was also $100, then you'd have lost $50, and you'd get back $50.

We have discussed the Draw Line extensively in the "Online Sportsbook" section, so we won't delve much into it here. Although the payout calculation might seem complex, players don't need to worry. How much a player wins or loses is calculated by the computer, and all one has to do is check the results and collect the money.

However, this Draw Line is a factor everyone needs to consider before placing a bet, as it determines whether a player wins half or loses half of their bet. Hence, our second consideration is the "Draw Line".

## Odds

The third factor to consider is the odds. Odds are determined by the online sportsbook. When the line is released with specific odds, you can only place a bet at those odds. You cannot set the odds yourself, nor can you negotiate with the owner of the online sportsbook. In short, what's set is set.

However, odds fluctuate over time, so you can wait for the right moment to place your bet, much like the "buy low" strategy in the stock market. But in sports betting, what we need to do is "buy high", as higher odds are better.

## Bet Amount

The fourth factor is how much you want to bet. This is your bet amount. The bet amount varies depending on the rules of each online sportsbook, your personal credit situation, or national regulations. There's no exact figure. Everyone should bet within their means, but please note, how much you can win depends on how much you initially bet. The formula is:

**Potential payout = Your bet amount x The odds at the time**

Once you've decided on all the above factors, you can go to the online sportsbook to place your bet, or go to betting sites to purchase your betting ticket. After placing your bet, wait for the game to conclude. At the end, did you lose? Or did you win? If you won, you can collect your winnings. If you lost, just throw away the betting ticket.

## Over/Under

Having discussed the point spread betting, and the factors to consider before placing a bet, let's move on to the second type of betting: Over/ Under. This involves guessing whether the total score tonight will exceed the benchmark score or not. The benchmark score is set by the online sportsbook, just like the point spread, and it can also change.

When betting on Over/Under, we have four choices:

First, we have the benchmark score. In this example, it is 198 points (we will ignore the 0.5 for now). So, we have to guess if the total score will be more than 198 or less than 198.

Secondly, this 0.5 is also a tie. So, if the final total score is precisely 198, those who bet on the over win half, and those who bet under lose half. The calculations are the same as point spread betting.

Lastly, we need to consider the odds and the betting amount, but this is the same as point spread betting, so we won't go into it further.

The two betting types introduced above are the most popular in sports betting, with an estimated 80% of players focusing on these two types. And there's a reason for this. Firstly, the probability of guessing right is high; you have a 50% chance even with your eyes closed. Secondly, they are predictable. Whether it's point spread or Over/Under, predictions can be made based on the strength of the two teams.

Predictability is crucial; otherwise, no one would play. For instance, there's a type of betting with a 50% probability of guessing right, but very few people play it: "Guess Odd/Even". It's about guessing if the final total score will be odd or even. Such a bet is entirely unpredictable, purely based on luck. Hence, no one wants to play it, and we won't discuss it further.

So, strictly speaking, within the "juice" betting strategy, there are actually only two methods. This number is quite limited. On the other hand, online sportsbooks have another type of strategy where they don't make money from the "juice", and there are numerous methods under that, at least dozens. Even though the number of methods in the "juice" strategy is few, they account for a significant portion of the total business volume. Therefore, it's extremely crucial for both the online sportsbooks and the players.

In just these few pages, we've covered how to play sports betting. Thus, becoming a player and engaging in sports betting is very straightforward. However, while placing a bet is simple, consistently making a profit over the long term is challenging. It's candid to say that most players are destined to lose.

In the methods we've introduced above, the online sportsbooks never directly bet against the players. And the highest probability of a player guessing right can approach 60%. So this is already the fairest method in this game. However, according to our deduction, if you play over the long term and bet frequently, you will inevitably lose money.

In the next chapter, we'll explore why that is.

## Even Immortals Lose in Long-Term Gambling

Why do we say that most players in sports betting are destined to lose? First, there's a common saying, "Even immortals lose in long-term gambling." However, just stating this would make many people discontented. After all, we can't blindly believe in common sayings. Furthermore, in the game of sports betting, our chances of guessing correctly can be as high as 60-70%. Merely stating "Even immortals lose in long-term gambling" and expecting that to suffice isn't acceptable.

So, let's look at the evidence, which lies in "economic observation." From the beginning of this book, we've discussed the operation mode of online sportsbooks. To become a bookmaker, you need powerful computer software and hardware, along with professionals, to operate this game, and all of this costs money. Besides the online sportsbook, many others also need to profit, such as agents, betting sites, and even regional governments that collect taxes.

Where does all this money come from? Everyone knows it's from the players. So, if you want to play this game, you're essentially supporting hundreds of thousands of industry professionals worldwide and paying taxes to the government. Based on the principle that money doesn't just fall from the sky, the money spent comes out of the players' pockets. Therefore, there's no logic to players not losing money.

Everyone understands this principle. However, many still harbor a speculative mentality, believing that those who lose money are others, not them. Why? Because they understand the game, often watch matches, and believe they can make money. There's also a common understanding in sports betting: players who guess correctly earn much more than those who don't. So, why should we be afraid? After all, making correct predictions, like guessing six or seven out of ten matches while watching games, is a common occurrence.

**Return on Investment (ROI) Formula**

Return on Investment (ROI) Formula

If you all think this way, then we're on the same page because sports betting is indeed such a game. Here's the formula for a player's ROI:

**Player's ROI = (Odds * Probability of Getting It Right) - 1**

From this mathematical formula, it can prove that the general perception is correct. The higher the probability of guessing correctly, the higher the player's ROI. Additionally, we can see another variable influencing the ROI, which is the odds. If you can get higher odds, it can also increase the ROI.

However, we shouldn't blindly trust the formula. We need to actually calculate to determine if this formula is accurate. Let's take a player who blindly places bets as an example to see if randomly buying betting tickets really means losing money.

Now, let's take a look at the line set by the online sportsbook.

| Team A | Odds 1.90 |
|--------|-----------|
| Team B | Odds 1.90 |

As mentioned before, in order for the online sportsbook to earn the juice, the total odds must always be less than 4.00. Therefore, this line only offers 3.80, implying that the online sportsbook aims to earn 5% of the juice. This line is also referred to as a 5-point juice line. We'll assume that this line was just opened, and both teams are evenly matched, so each team has odds of 1.90.

Now, let's go back to the player who makes bets blindly. Since he's betting randomly, theoretically, he has a 50% chance of winning. To further our assumption, let's say he places bets on ten such games, each with a wager of $100.

Let's deduce the results from there.

1. A bet was placed on ten games for $100 each, so the player's total bet is $1000.

2. The probability of guessing correctly is 50%, so out of the ten games, only five games can win money.

3. With odds at 1.90, the prize money one can retrieve from these five games is:

**Winning 5 games * $100 bet amount per game * odds of 1.90 = $950 in prize money.**

Having spent $1000 on ten games and only retrieving $950 in the end means the player has lost money. Specifically, they are down by $100. When translated into a return on investment, it's a "negative" 5%, specifically emphasized as -5%.

So, everyone's assumption is correct. When speaking of others who don't understand the game and make random bets, it's now calculated that they lose money, and for every $100 they spend, they lose $5. If one were to bet up to $100,000, they would lose $10,000. The more one spends, the more they lose.

Let's verify the previous formula again. Player's Return = (Odds * Guess Probability) - 1, to see if it's accurate. In this example:

**( Odds of 1.90 * Guess Probability of 0.5) - 1 = -5%**

Our ROI formula works, as it also calculates the return on investment as a "negative" 5%.

## Players Who Understand the Game

It has already been proven that players who don't understand the game and don't watch matches are destined to lose. Therefore, in general perception, people will tell you to start getting to know the matches better and pay attention to pre-match predictions by experts. Once we understand the game, we can escape the aforementioned situation and start making money. And at this point, all major online sportsbooks, betting sites, and agents will come to the same conclusion: it's time to watch matches, quickly absorb sports knowledge, and start making money fast.

But, is it really the case? Before they change the subject, let's look back at the return on investment. By continuing to examine the mathematical formulas, we can determine whether what they're saying is true or false.

Now, let's assume that we all understand the game. Let's assume that we all watch pre-match predictions and have ample sports knowledge. Not only are we fans, but we're also professional fans. Being frank, let's raise our prediction accuracy to 60%. Out of ten matches, we can definitely guess six correctly, which is not something those who bet randomly can compare to.

Let's apply the formula now:

**( Odds 1.90 \* Prediction Accuracy 0.6 ) − 1 = 14%**

According to the formula, we can now make a profit. What was originally a negative return rate has turned positive, and it's a 14% return. This means that if we bet $100, we can earn $14. If we bet $1 million, we can earn $140,000.

Hold on for a moment. Before we continue, someone is definitely going to have something to say. Is this return rate a mistake? We are professional sports fans who make very accurate predictions, and we are "betting" with high risk. Since this is betting, we expect high returns. Is 14% acceptable? To put it bluntly, you might get this rate even if you go to the bank and invest in financial products, or even higher. What, has the definition of gambling changed now? High risk implies high return; we expect even higher, especially since we are risking our hard-earned money.

Regarding this concern, our response is as follows. First of all, there's nothing wrong with the formula; we just verified it. Also, while guessing six out of ten games correctly is decent, you still lose in four games, which results in a less than satisfactory return on investment.

Moreover, don't be discouraged. Predicting six out of ten games is quite conservative. We've seen many professional players whose accuracy rates often reach 70-80% when they bet on games they are confident in. If you don't believe it, you can check out professional sports analysts in newspapers or online. Their accuracy rates can be astonishingly high. According to our data analysis, some players can even achieve a rate of guessing correctly in 9 out of 10 games, especially in soccer matches where there's a significant disparity in team strengths.

So, based on the above mathematical formula, because your probability of guessing correctly can be improved, we can reasonably adjust the return rate upwards, making you feel that this game is indeed like gambling, where high risks bring high returns. Your rate of return can be:

( Odds 1.90 ✳ Probability of guessing correctly 0.6 ) − 1 = 14 %

( Odds 率 1.90 ✳ Probability of guessing correctly 0.7 ) − 1 = 33 %

( Odds 率 1.90 ✳ Probability of guessing correctly 0.8 ) − 1 = 52 %

( Odds 率 1.90 ✳ Probability of guessing correctly 0.9 ) − 1 = 71 %

Investing $100 in a game can bring a return of $71, sounds great, doesn't it? By using this money-making method, not only can you make a living, but getting rich is entirely feasible. This is why many people are so engrossed in this game that they can't pull themselves out of it. The math is simple enough for everyone to understand, and this formula can give everyone a beautiful ideal: as long as we continuously improve our knowledge of the game, we can make big money.

But is this really the case?

While the mathematical formula itself is not wrong, regretfully, this is not a book about mathematical formulas. Look back at the cover, and you'll see we are discussing game theory economics. This mathematical formula is merely a component within the entire scope of game theory economics. There are countless other factors that influence your returns. In other words, the rate of return presented in the formula looks promising, but it's almost unattainable in reality.

The investment return rate discussed here purely refers to the "juice strategy." In this particular strategy, everyone already has an advantage, and the rate of return is already high. However, there are other strategies offered by the online sportsbook that you can play with. If you want to include these other strategies into your overall return calculation, you'll be shocked at how drastically the rate of return decreases, possibly approaching -100%.

Do note that a negative one hundred percent is the absolute limit; you can't lose any more than that. This can be considered a silver lining as it means you can only lose your initial investment and not any more than that.

## The Paradoxical Return on Investment

Looking around at friends who are involved in sports betting, and then turning to television news, we all know that those who frequently participate in sports betting hardly ever make a profit. What we keep hearing is the unchanging truth: "Long-term betting, even gods lose." The return on investment for most is not only below 14%, but even achieving a rate higher than -5% is tough.

Mathematical formulas, of course, don't lie.

**Return on Investment (ROI) = (Odds * Probability of Correct Guess) - 1**

In this formula, there are only three variables: 1. ROI 2. Odds 3. Probability of Correct Guess. We've mentioned before that the probability of a correct guess can be high. But common sense tells us that the ROI is very low. Thus, the problem must lie with the odds, which is indeed the most significant factor.

In the previous example, we used odds of 1.90 to apply to this formula. However, in reality, obtaining such high odds is almost impossible. Especially for those of you well-acquainted with sports matches, the more you understand the game, the more you watch the matches, sadly, the less likely you are to get such high odds.

The issue arises with the term "everyone." In the sports betting economy we discuss, those who truly have no understanding of the game are a minority. Those who buy betting tickets or place bets online have, to varying degrees, some knowledge and often make pre-match predictions. Moreover, many of them are avid fans who watch games daily. So, when we refer to knowledgeable players, we are actually referring to the majority. When we say "everyone" makes accurate predictions, we genuinely mean that most players guess correctly.

Furthermore, even those who completely lack knowledge and are somewhat lazy can refer to newspaper sports commentary columns. The predictions there are quite accurate and absolutely free.

Here's the crux of the matter: since everyone understands the game and since everyone makes accurate predictions, it's likely that most people are betting on the same team. We've previously discussed the operating principle of online sportsbooks: for the sake of maintaining a balanced betting line, they must adjust the odds downward. And the more people bet on a particular team, the lower its odds will be.

So, when everyone can accurately predict game outcomes, high odds are no longer available to them. It's easy to see that the odds for teams believed by the majority to win will be low, and those for the losing teams will be high. Otherwise, who would bet on a losing team? The betting line would be imbalanced.

What we're discussing is the economics of betting. It reflects the consequences of the majority behaving in the same manner. When the majority have high chances of predicting correctly and all bet on the same team, this naturally reflects in the betting line, leading to a drop in odds. This is an economic inevitability. Moreover, we can argue that the more accurate a person's predictions, the more likely they are to place bets alongside the majority. Since the majority are also accurate, the odds they get are lower, and ultimately, so is their return on investment.

So, what's the actual return on investment? The answer is **-5%**.

Because our initial line was set with a juice of 5%, this means the online sportsbook would take only 5%, with the rest returning to the player. Therefore, on average, each player would be losing 5%. The more events a player bets on, the closer they get to this number. Of course, not every online sportsbook charges 5%; some might charge 10%, which would mean the rate of return for everyone would be -10%.

Lastly, let's touch upon point spread again. As we've discussed, the point spread is a tool used by the bookmaker to balance bets. It doesn't represent the actual strength of the teams in a match. Whenever there's a rush to bet on a particular team, that's when the point spread comes into play. And this can be problematic.

If you're favoring a certain team, and so is the general public, then naturally, this team will have a point spread. They would have to give a few points to the other team. So now, your chances of winning reduce by those few points. If you initially had a chance of guessing 6 out of 10 matches correctly, now it might just be slightly more than 5. And this reduced probability of correct prediction also impacts your rate of return.

Therefore, while the odds for the point spread line remain unchanged, it can decrease the probability of correct guesses, subsequently lowering the rate of return. Ultimately, the actual rate of return, in the end, tends to gravitate towards -5%.

**Understanding the game**

Understanding the game doesn't make much of a difference. In real-world situations, with the interference of juice, odds, and probability of guessing correctly, your return on investment will definitely not reach 14%. We can even say that everyone's return rate is surely negative. The reason is simple: if everyone makes money, who will pay for it?

This means that online sportsbooks, betting sites, and agents continuously encouraging everyone to watch games and learn about sports is pointless. Because in the end, everyone still loses money. It's just a matter of how much you lose, and the difference isn't that significant. However, their perspective is understandable. Think about it: if a betting website told you that without understanding the game, you'd lose 8%, but with understanding, you'd only lose 5%, and therefore you should watch more games and learn more. If you still wanted to place bets after hearing this, that would be absurd.

However, there must be someone who would argue against this. There's a huge flaw in our previous deduction. As a savvy player, we don't necessarily have to bet on the same team as everyone else. We can do the opposite and specifically choose teams that most people don't like. Moreover, there's a benefit: these teams usually have higher odds. We know that the total odds are fixed. When the odds for one side decrease, the other side must increase. And this is the exploitable loophole!

## Going for the Underdogs?

Betting specifically on underdog teams is indeed a strategy. The odds for underdog teams are high, and this is an undisputed fact. Otherwise, how would the online sportsbook maintain a balanced line if no one bet on them? So, let's calculate the return on investment (ROI) for this "smart" tactic:

**( Odds 2.75 * Probability of guessing correctly 0.4 ) − 1 = 10%**

The above odds and probability are assumptions. We hope that in this ideal scenario, we can achieve a 10% ROI. In this scenario, we hope for odds of 2.75, meaning we're betting on high odds underdog teams. We also hope for surprising outcomes in the matches. We don't expect an upset in every game; if 4 out of 10 matches result in unexpected underdog victories that most people guessed wrong, then our strategy of exclusively betting on underdogs can be profitable.

This is why sometimes you might hear rumors of savvy gamblers specifically choosing underdog teams and making money. And the values in the formula above seem achievable - just find teams with high odds that most people overlook.

However, we must point out that the formula actually has a significant flaw. Achieving a 10% ROI based on the conditions above is undoubtedly a short-term stroke of good luck. We haven't seen anyone win money in the long run by continuously betting on underdogs based on this criteria.

We previously discussed the law of constant total odds, and in this example, the total odds are 3.80. This means that the odds for the other favorite team are extremely low, at 1.05. What does this imply? It means that for players betting on the favorite team, for every $100 placed, they can only win back $5. Such a low return rate is almost unappealing, yet people still bet on it. This suggests that the favored team's chances of winning are almost certain, almost a guaranteed victory.

Given the formula above, a 40% chance of guessing correctly is simply not plausible. A more probable figure would be only 10%. So, we need to adjust the formula:

**(2.75 odds * 0.1 probability of guessing correctly) - 1 = -72.5%**

Indeed, if you assume you bet $100 on each game, for a total of 10 games, with a total investment of $1000, you might end up losing $725. Unfortunately, if you only pick the underdogs, there's a good chance you'll end up with this result. Because in sports betting, what's most appealing is the predictability of the matches. That's a major selling point. So, if everyone's guesses are mostly accurate, then sports betting wouldn't be appealing. If you choose to stand against the popular team, you must face reality. The reality is that if most people can guess correctly nine out of ten times, then you're left with just one.

However, I can take a step back. Everything discussed above is about playing without point spreads, purely balancing the betting line with odds. But what if we play with point spreads? Because of the point spreads, the odds of an underdog team winning would be much higher. Indeed, after a popular team gives up a few points, the chance of an underdog team winning will greatly increase. For those who bet against the grain, the chances of guessing right could be a bit higher, certainly not limited to just four games.

But, you'll never get the odds of 2.75 again. After adjusting with point spreads, the chances of winning for both the favorite and the underdog teams will be roughly equal. Consequently, the odds will tend to be the same. In this example, both teams would probably have odds of 1.90. Even if there's a difference, it won't be significant.

The reason is simple. After the underdog team is given points, if they still enjoy high odds, then who would bet on the favored team?

So, this method of always betting on the underdog won't make everyone money, regardless of whether there are point spreads or not. In fact, if you just blindly pick teams, you might lose even less.

## Not a Get-Rich-Quick Game

In this article, we've actually discussed the return on investment (ROI) of this game. By the time you've reached this point, you're probably feeling quite disheartened. After all the calculations, it seems like you're always losing money and not making any. Whether you understand the game or not doesn't make much of a difference. At best, you might lose a bit less. But the bottom line is still a "loss."

Furthermore, even under the most optimistic scenarios, the return on investment is just a small amount, ranging between 2% to 8%. The issue is, achieving even this is almost impossible.

If you're thinking along these lines, then we're on the same page. Making a fortune in this game is simply unrealistic. However, if you can let go of that grand dream and aim to lose a bit less or make a little profit, then we do have some advice for you. It can help maximize that minuscule ROI. But if you're hoping to make a lot of money, we can't really help with that.

Sports betting isn't necessarily a losing game. In fact, it does allow a small fraction of people to make money consistently. However, the key to making money isn't about whether you understand the sport. When online sportsbooks or betting sites advise you to watch games frequently, it's mainly because those who watch games regularly are more likely to place a bet.

So when we talk about how to be a savvy player, we are not talking about sports knowledge. And whether you guess the game correctly or not is not the point because everyone is pretty accurate, but we still lose money according to our assumptions. To make money in this game, one must understand the principle of return on investment and ensure that every factor is in your favor. This is what is traditionally referred to as "betting smartly."

We will provide a comprehensive discussion in subsequent articles. However, everyone must accept one fact: in this game, no matter how smartly we players play, we are only vying for a few percentage points in return rate. Nothing more.

This is another fair aspect of the game. Whether it's the **online sportsbook**, agents, or players, everyone is vying for percentages. No one can earn more, and of course, no one can get rich overnight. The biggest victims of this game are the majority of players who "don't bet smartly." But there's nothing that can be done about that.

So how can one break free from the long-term pattern of 'gamble long enough and you'll lose'? We'll offer advice later on, but for now, here's a hint: the key lies in the "odds." The higher the odds, the better!

Next, before we delve into specific pieces of advice, we must first look at the other betting methods offered by the **online sportsbook**. This is the famous "no juice" betting method. As we've said before, if you don't understand these methods and play blindly, the player's return on investment will have to be revised downward. It's even possible to lose everything.

**No Juice Betting Methods**

Earlier, the betting methods we discussed were very straightforward. Players simply had to guess which one of the two teams would win, right? Or they would guess if the total score would be over or under a certain amount. The characteristic of these types of bets is that even if we were to blindly guess, there's a 50% chance of getting it right. So, for online sportsbooks to make a profit from these methods, they rely on the previously mentioned "juice", steadily earning little by little from the total wagers placed.

However, within sports betting, there are not only these types of bets. Online sportsbooks actually offer a wide variety of betting options for players' "entertainment." In many of these other betting methods, the concept of "juice" isn't as evident. Generally, we call these "No Juice Betting Methods."

Yes, it means no juice. But there's a significant difference between "no juice" and "no money." Even though they differ by just one word in expression, their meanings are miles apart. When we say online sportsbooks don't earn juice, what we're really emphasizing is that they might earn even more, and more effortlessly!

It's precisely because they earn so aggressively that online sportsbooks no longer need to painstakingly control odds to make "juice." This is why we name these methods "No Juice Betting Methods." What it really means is "methods where you don't have to work hard to earn juice." And in this section, we'll introduce these types of bets.

**Correct Score**

This is a common bet in soccer matches called the "Correct Score," known in Macau slang as "Bo Dan." Players have to predict the exact final score of the match. Here's an example of such a betting line:

| Correct Score | | | | | |
|---|---|---|---|---|---|
| Team A Win | | Draw | | Team B Win | |
| Score | Odds | Score | Odds | Score | Odds |
| 1-0 | 6.50 | 0-0 | 10.00 | 1-0 | 10.00 |
| 2-0 | 7.00 | 1-1 | 7.00 | 2-0 | 23.00 |
| 2-1 | 8.00 | 2-2 | 13.00 | 2-1 | 15.00 |
| 3-0 | 15.00 | 3-3 | 77.00 | 3-0 | 67.00 |
| 3-1 | 15.00 | | | 3-1 | 41.00 |
| 3-2 | 26.00 | | | 3-2 | 51.00 |
| 4-0 | 34.00 | | | | |
| 4-1 | 34.00 | | | | |
| 4-2 | 67.00 | | | | |

This game is very simple. We need to guess the final score. If you guess it right, you win and can claim money based on the odds. For example, if we bet $100 that Team B will win with a score of 3:2 and the odds are 51. If the final score is indeed as predicted, then we can claim a prize of $5100.

**Total Goals**

| Total Goal | | | | | |
|---|---|---|---|---|---|
| Team A vs Team B | | | | | |
| 0 Goal | 1 Goal | 2 Goal | 3 Goal | 4 Goal | 5+ Goal |
| 1.50 | 1.90 | 2.10 | 4.50 | 5.50 | 7.00 |

This is about guessing the total number of goals scored by both teams combined. For instance, if we bet that there will be a total of 3 goals scored and place $100 on it, and if it turns out to be true, we can claim back $450.

**Championship**

| Championship | | | | | |
|---|---|---|---|---|---|
| Team A | 2.50 | Team C | 7.50 | Team E | 12.50 |
| Team B | 3.50 | Team D | 9.50 | Team F | 11.00 |

This betting method takes a longer time. It's about predicting which team will become the champion at the end of the season. Players can start placing bets even before the season kicks off. Not just before the season, but throughout its course, you can continuously place additional bets. However, there's one thing to note: the online sportsbook will adjust the odds daily based on the betting trends for each team. From the start to the end of the season, it spans at least half a year. So, if you choose to play this way, you need to be patient and wait until the end of the season to claim your prize money. But the Championship Cup isn't just about league games. Events that occur every four years and last for a month, like the World Cup, also count. The time it takes to determine the champion in such tournaments is considerably shorter.

In this book, we categorize all betting types into two main categories:

- **Juice betting methods**: A typical example is the point spread line. For online sportsbooks to profit from juice, they need to carefully control the odds. Its characteristics are a 50% probability of guessing correctly and its predictability.

- **Non-juice betting methods**: Anything that doesn't fall into the first category is considered this type. The three methods mentioned earlier all belong to this second category, termed by online sportsbooks as "non-juice" methods. But we've only listed a fraction here. In reality, the number of "non-juice" methods is vast, with various names and styles. Furthermore, online sportsbooks continuously innovate, utilizing different topics to develop new methods.

However, these methods have a common trait. If we were to guess blindly, and the probability of guessing correctly is less than one-half, then this method is almost certainly a "non-juice" method. Additionally, we can infer from the odds; if you see odds greater than 3.00, then without a doubt, it's a non-juice method, and players should be extra cautious.

Why do we say this? Logically, how an online sportsbook profits shouldn't concern the player too much. Whether they earn from juice or other means, their goal is to profit. How does this relate to the player?

There are specific reasons for this, including:

- Not profiting from juice means one thing: the online sportsbook is directly betting against you, something you wouldn't want.

- When it's easy for the online sportsbook to profit, it means it's easy for the player to lose money.

- Online sportsbooks might discriminate against "non-juice" methods.

We'll discuss these one by one, starting with betting against the online sportsbook.

## Betting Against the Online Sportsbook

In the no-juice betting method, once the online sportsbook accepts bets, it keeps all of them, betting directly against the players. We've discussed before how online sportsbooks use "arbitrage" to avoid the risks of betting directly against players. But in this context, the sportsbook doesn't need to go through such troubles. When not profiting from the juice, whatever amount the sportsbook gets, it keeps and directly bets against everyone.

It's because of this direct betting that the interests of the online sportsbook directly clash with those of the players. This means that whenever players win money, the sportsbook loses. And for the sportsbook to make a significant profit, players must lose big. Therefore, in such scenarios, a player is bound to suffer a loss. Everyone understands this principle: no one engages in a loss-making business, and unless it's a sure win, the sportsbook won't bet against you.

How does the online sportsbook create a sure-win scenario? By controlling the relationship between the odds and the probability of guessing correctly. In an ideal situation, if your chances of guessing correctly are one percent, then the odds should ideally be 100.00 for it to be fair. This is what the sportsbook aims to control. If, through statistical analysis, it's found that everyone's probability of guessing correctly is one percent, then the sportsbook might consider adjusting the odds downwards, for example, reducing 100.00 to 70.00.

With these lowered odds as a safety net, the sportsbook can bet against you. In the long run, it's certain to profit without losses. Conversely, players are bound to continuously lose. This is a phenomenon we often notice when analyzing the profits of online sportsbooks. Even though these no-juice betting methods have a smaller turnover, their profits can often be quite significant.

The gameplay without the juice, at first glance, seems very fair. Because even after the online sportsbook adjusts, the odds still look very high, and this gives players a misconception. Taking the previous correct score as an example, the odds for Team B winning 3:2 are as high as 51.00. So many people might think that it doesn't matter if they lose ten or twenty times, because once they win, they can recover all their losses along with the profit.

But this is truly a misunderstanding. In this case, you're not just going to lose ten or twenty times. In my opinion, you have to lose at least a hundred times before you might win once. Of course, luck plays a big role, and not everyone has to lose that many times, but statistically speaking, most people do have to lose that many times.

So, the primary reason we don't recommend these types of games is that the online sportsbooks generally bet against the players. Whether the sportsbook is betting against you can make a big difference in the odds.

Firstly, in the gameplay without the juice, the only tool that online sportsbooks have to control the line is the odds. But to call it "controlling the line" might be a bit exaggerated because, generally, these types of games don't require much control. Once the betting lines are set with their respective odds, the computer takes over the control, without any human intervention. Later, we will discuss "oddsmakers" or "risk management traders", the experts inside the online sportsbook who specialize in adjusting the odds. However, their main focus is usually on point spreads and totals, and they usually don't interfere here.

Speaking of betting odds, as you all have just seen, using the correct score bet as an example, one game has nearly twenty odds. This number is not small. Twenty odds for one game, and two hundred odds for a hundred games. This is just for the correct score bet. If you include other betting methods, there would be at least a thousand, if not two thousand odds.

Why bring up the number of odds suddenly? It's because when we look at the quantity, we realize it's not something that can be manually set or controlled. Indeed, on the online sportsbook, methods that don't earn juice are mostly handled by computers, commonly known as the "betting transaction system". The odds are generated by computer programs.

There are generally two ways to generate them: first, copying; second, using formulas to calculate. Starting with copying, it's a common saying that all writings under the sun are copied, and it applies to betting odds too. There are actually very few online sportsbooks in the world capable of setting their own odds. Most of them copy. Whatever odds they offer, we offer the same, maybe with some added safety margin.

Then there's the formula calculation. Here, based on past betting records, an online sportsbook will create a reference table. This can generate correct score odds from point spread or money line odds. Such a reference table is the highest trade secret of the online sportsbook. It's not accessible to the average person. As long as the reference table is good, it's easy for the online sportsbook to make money. This kind of table is actually based on probability and statistics, plus some safety margin, and it's done.

After the odds are set, bets from players can be accepted. However, players can't just bet freely; these odds still need to be controlled. Let's take the example of Team B with odds of 3:2. If everyone is tempted by the 51:1 odds and starts betting like crazy, the online sportsbook might not be able to handle it. If by any chance the players guess correctly, the losses for the bookmaker would be immense.

Therefore, these odds still need to be controlled. But due to the numerous odds available, it has to be done by a computer. And when a computer controls the odds, it's not as flexible as when done manually. The main reason for this is that the odds only decrease and never increase. As we mentioned before, in the "juice" betting method, if the odds on one side decrease, the other side has to increase. But it's not the case here. With correct score betting, there are nearly twenty different odds. Does that mean if one set of odds decreases, the other nineteen have to increase? Of course not, the odds only decrease.

Some might feel this is unfair. For instance, if the odds change from 51:1 to 41:1 and the other odds don't increase, aren't the players at a significant disadvantage? Indeed, you're right, and this is why we don't recommend the "juice" betting method. In this method, the principles of controlling the odds by the online sportsbook are quite unfavorable for the player.

However, from a business perspective, it makes sense for the odds to be adjusted this way. The reason is simple: first, the odds in the "juice" method are already high, and whether they increase or not, they are already attractive. There's no reason for the online sportsbook to raise them further. Second, since the odds are already high, a slight decrease might not be easily noticed by players. For example, the drop from 51:1 to 41:1 is still offering quite high odds.

So, the approach that doesn't profit from the juice not only makes setting odds easier, controlling the line is also more straightforward, saving both time and effort. An added advantage for the online sportsbook is that there's almost no need for management. In the point spread line and over-under betting, we used a betting balance sheet and betting balance scale to introduce commonly used reports during online sportsbook line management. Monitoring these reports isn't a simple task. It requires constant attention, practically every moment of every day, to oversee the balance scale's situation.

However, the reports for the no-juice approach aren't like that. While it might not be as exaggerated as only checking monthly or quarterly reports, essentially, checking once a day to see how much money can be made is enough. If you find that the earnings are not up to mark, the management solution is simple too: adjust the computer program, tweaking the reference table or insurance values.

So, for an online sportsbook, making money in this area is quite effortless. But for a player, consistently profiting from these betting methods over the long term is undoubtedly a tall tale. There's another specific reason everyone should be cautious of these betting methods: the potential unique issuance rules and operational models that online sportsbook might have. Within these models, a peculiar restriction emerges, possibly making the no-juice betting method even more disadvantageous for players.

Firstly, it's not that the odds of winning these bets are low; the chances are the same worldwide. Whether you're guessing the correct score, the total number of goals, or predicting the league champion, there isn't much to discuss. Your likelihood of guessing correctly on one online sportsbook is the same as any other on the planet. What we want to talk about are the odds. Although these bets inherently have higher odds than juice bets, some online sportsbooks offer lower odds than others.

The reason lies in the operation of the sports betting business. Often, permissions or licenses are required to operate, and obtaining these permissions may come with a stipulation called the "total payout ratio." This ratio could be 75%, 80%, 90%, or any other figure. It means that of all the money taken in by the online sportsbook, they must pay out at least this percentage to the players.

For instance, if the total payout ratio is set at 80% and the online sportsbook takes in $100 billion in bets for the year, the bookmaker must ensure that at least $80 billion goes back to the players who placed bets. The remaining $20 billion is used by the website for taxes, operational expenses, and profit. (From this, you can see why we often say that regular players can only lose money at online sportsbooks; this total payout ratio ensures players will most likely lose money.)

Almost all government-licensed online sportsbooks worldwide accept these conditions, and some major websites will disclose their total payout ratios. As for underground online sportsbooks or smaller casinos, they might not disclose it, but they still internally maintain such a payout ratio.

Knowing the overall payout ratio is beneficial for players. Players can compare which online sportsbook offers a higher ratio, making it more favorable for them. Once the ratio is disclosed, it must be adhered to. Government agencies or institutions that grant licenses also scrutinize the financial statements of the sportsbook to ensure they are compliant.

The overall payout ratio has always been the tug-of-war outcome among the government, players, and online sportsbook. Hence, there's a vast difference in these numbers worldwide. For the government, the ratio shouldn't be too high because if more is paid out, there's less income for the government. Many governments permit sports betting because its revenue can supplement other areas, such as healthcare, education, and the care for the underprivileged. Naturally, higher revenue is preferred.

For players, on the contrary, a higher overall payout ratio is better. A high ratio means higher odds, meaning the prize money retrieved after a winning bet is more. Alternatively, if the winnings are too low, the game isn't worth playing.

For online sportsbook, the payout ratio should be well-balanced. On one hand, they need to ensure that the ratio is attractive enough to keep players engaged in the game. On the other hand, it can't be excessively high as they need to account for the government's income, taxes, and their own profit margins.

Once a payout ratio is mutually agreed upon by the government, players, and online sportsbook, it's up to the online sportsbook to execute. They achieve this by adjusting the odds for every match and every type of bet to ensure that, in the end, the annual overall payout ratio aligns with the agreed upon value.

## Discrimination by Online Sportsbooks

Once we have the overall payout ratio, we encounter a problem. That is the juice method. As we discussed earlier, the juice method also has a predetermined payout ratio, and it's usually very high. For a betting line set at 1.90:

| Team A | Odds 1.90 |
|--------|-----------|
| Team B | Odds 1.90 |

The translated payout ratio would be

**(1.90 + 1.90) / 4 * 100 = 95%**

This ratio is definitely higher than the previously agreed overall payout ratio, because if it's too low, you wouldn't play. But in this era of the internet combined with apps, checking the odds on major online sportsbooks is incredibly easy. And the juice method is the most straightforward betting method. You either bet on Team A winning or Team B winning. The only thing left to consider is the odds. Everyone is smart; if a website offers odds of 1.90, you won't go for 1.89 odds, after all, no one wants to lose money.

If online sportsbooks are rigid and insist on applying the overall payout ratio to the juice method, they will undoubtedly end up with unattractive odds. Taking the point spread line as an example, suppose the overall payout ratio is only 75%. This means the juice has to account for 25%. We all know that juice affects the overall odds. In other words, the overall odds can now only be set to 3.00. Going a step further, the betting line would now look like this:

|         | Odds |
|---------|------|
| Team A  | 1.50 |
| Team B  | 1.50 |

The payout ratio is unappealing, so of course, players win less. Look at this betting line; the odds are only 1.50, which is ridiculously low. Let's use the player return rate formula we discussed earlier:

**( Odds 1.50 × Hit Rate 0.6 ) – 1 = -10 %**

This means that even if you guess correctly six out of ten times, you'll still lose money. And for every $100 you wager, you'll lose $10. If you want to profit from such betting lines, you need to improve your hit rate. You'd need to correctly guess seven out of ten times, which, as we know, is hard to achieve after adjusting for the point spread.

In summary, when odds are this unattractive, players can't make money using the juice method, so no player would accept it. Naturally, no one would participate. Online sportsbooks are aware of this problem. This leads to the conclusion that online sportsbooks must keep the odds for point spread bets relatively high to make them attractive. Thus, the odds for juice bets (that is, point spread and over/under) are never low. This means that the overall payout ratio for juice bets doesn't vary much worldwide, staying between 85% to 95% to retain their appeal to players.

However, there's no such thing as a free lunch. If the odds for juice bets are increased, this means that the payout will be higher. But do you think the money for these payouts will come out of the online sportsbook's pocket? Moreover, the overall payout ratio is commonly agreed upon; even if an online sportsbook wanted to change it, they wouldn't have the authority to do so.

Therefore, there's only one solution: to lower the odds of the "no juice" bets as much as possible. This ensures that there's enough money to offset the juice bets. The reason is that the odds for these exact score and championship winner bets are originally high. Even if the online sportsbook adjusts them downwards, most people still won't feel that the odds are too low. For example, if Team B's odds were 51.00, we can cut them by half to 25.00. People would still find it acceptable since 25 is still higher than the odds in the point spread bets.

This is the discrimination of the online sportsbooks. On one hand (betting on which team wins or the over/under), the sportsbook tries to subsidize the players. However, this money is taken from the other side (exact score, total number of goals). As a result, players who bet on the juice games get a better deal, while others suffer a significant disadvantage.

Moreover, even if the odds are lowered in the "no juice" bets, sportsbooks can still capitalize on trending topics, continuously hyping the news to increase the betting allure. For example, they might use the participation of a famous soccer player as a topic. People can then bet on which match he will score a homerun. This is a classic "no juice" bet, but many would still place their bets because it's entertaining.

So, everyone should be especially cautious with these types of bets. No matter what guise the sportsbook uses or what topics they create, everyone needs to be extra vigilant. The way to judge is straightforward: if you realize that blindly guessing gives you a probability of less than ½ of getting it right, then you should tread carefully.

To be honest, the betting methods without juice are indeed attractive in terms of odds. To pretend not to see them is quite challenging for everyone. Moreover, everyone probably hopes for some insider tips to see if there's a way to break these limitations.

Regrettably, there isn't. In such betting methods, the best strategy is simply not to participate. If you really favor high odds, we have only one tip: directly buy those lottery tickets where you guess the numbers instead of engaging in sports betting. The odds in those lottery games can be as high as two million, which is sure to keep you enthralled.

Therefore, we must understand if a betting method involves juice. If it's too easy for the online sportsbook to make money, it's best to avoid it. In fact, all the techniques discussed in this book, whether applied to the online sportsbook, players, or agents, are all about the first type - the methods with juice. As for the second type, which doesn't involve juice, we entirely give up on it, and it's best for everyone to act as if they never saw it.

In the "juice" methods, the online sportsbook aims to earn from the juice, which is disadvantageous for the players. And in the "no-juice" method, the sportsbook is directly betting against you, which is even more unfavorable. This constant back and forth isn't good news; being a player seems tough. Isn't there a better way to bet?

Of course, there is. On the sportsbook side, not every betting method is against the player. In fact, there's one type of betting that's extremely favorable. The sportsbook is reluctant to offer it, but they have to, and this is the renowned "live betting" in sports gambling.

## The Thrilling Live Betting

"Live betting" is also known as "Live" or "Running Ball", and in places like Hong Kong and Macau, it's often referred to as "In-play". As the name suggests, live betting allows players to place bets while the game is in progress. This method is exactly as you'd imagine - you can watch the game, and when you feel that a particular team might win, you can place your bet. This gives bettors a significant advantage, arguably increasing their chances of winning.

Many are somewhat familiar with this type of betting, but there are also misconceptions about it. So, let's start from the beginning and take a closer look at how live betting works and how bettors can gain an edge. It's worth mentioning here that live betting is considered one of the toughest markets for online sportsbooks to profit from. As we've discussed before, it's not easy for them to make money, which means it's much easier for players to profit.

**Live**

|  | Point Spread Line | Odds | Score |
|---|---|---|---|
| Team A  (Home Team) |  | 1.80 | 8 |
| Team B |  | 1.80 | 6 |

The types of bets accepted during live games usually only include point spread and over/under. The focus is primarily on point spread. As we've mentioned before, these types of bets need to be placed before the game starts, which is known as "pre-game betting." On the other hand, if people place bets after watching the satellite broadcast of the live game, this is known as "live betting."

The online sportsbook sets up what's called a "live line" for these situations. Essentially, the live line is similar to the pre-game line, complete with point spreads and odds. The significant difference is an additional field called "live score." Since the game is ongoing, both teams will score points continuously, so this field displays their current scores. In this example, Team A has scored eight points, while Team B has scored six points.

Another distinction of the live line is that it will frequently be paused, a period known as "goal time."

| | Point Spread Line | Odds | Score |
|---|---|---|---|
| Team A (Home Team) | Goal | Pause | |
| Team B | | Pause | |

Once a team scores, the online sportsbook will immediately pause the betting line, preventing players from placing bets. Bets can only be placed again once the online sportsbook updates the "live score" field and reopens the line. This pause, known as "goal time," is very brief, lasting no more than a few seconds. If you're not paying close attention, you might not even notice it.

## Live Betting Misconceptions

After understanding how the line works, we can address some common misunderstandings about live betting. First, while players can indeed gain an advantage, it won't be in the form of scoring. In other words, if you're watching a TV broadcast and notice that Team A is leading Team B, and you decide to place a bet thinking that Team A has a better chance of winning, that's not how it works. If it were that simple, everyone would bet on the leading team during live betting, and who would bet on the other side?

This is where the "live score" field comes into play. When you bet on a live line, your betting ticket will definitely have a notation indicating the scores of both teams at the time of your bet. When the ticket is cashed, these scores will be deducted.

This means one thing: no matter when you decide to place your bet, whether the game has just started or is near its end, the score starts at 0:0 from your perspective. Using the previous example, let's say you bet on this live line, choosing Team A to win. In that case, your betting ticket would look something like this:

**"Team A wins, odds at 1.80, live score, Team A 8 points, Team B 6 points."**

Now, let's assume the game has ended and the final score is Team A with 8 points and Team B with 7 points. For the sake of simplicity, only Team B scored an additional point. In this scenario, you would lose the bet. Since the betting ticket deducts the live score at the time of your bet, the result for you would effectively be 0:1

|  | Final score | Live Score | Your Score |
|---|---|---|---|
| Team A | 8 | 8 | 0 |
| Team B | 7 | 6 | 1 |

Therefore, we say that you can't take advantage in terms of points. So, why do online sportsbooks often suspend the line? It's easy to understand now. Because live scoring affects all players, it's just too crucial. So, as soon as the bookmaker sees a team scoring, they must immediately suspend the line and adjust the score.

Having clarified this method of play, we know that players can't really get an advantage in terms of points. But why do we still insist that you have an advantage? This is because, compared to betting before the match where everything is unknown, you now at least know a bit more:

- You now know for sure who the players are for both teams in the match. We know that the starting line-up announced before the game isn't always accurate, and surprises can happen.

- You can sense the momentum; which team is dominant? Who is likely to win in the end? Or which team lacks momentum and is being dominated throughout the game.

- Online sportsbooks can make mistakes. And this point is crucial; once they make an error, your chances of winning money increase.

The first two points effectively increase the likelihood of making a correct prediction, thereby enhancing your return on investment. Those who often watch matches are aware of this, so we won't delve into that. Let's talk about the more exciting third point, which is actually the main reason many people play live.

## Goal Time

When betting live, both the online sportsbook and players might be watching the broadcast on TV together. So, when a team scores, guess who acts faster? Does the sportsbook suspend the line immediately? Or does the player act swiftly, buying their betting ticket before the suspension?

This is an intriguing question in live betting. If a player is quick enough and manages to buy a betting ticket before the online sportsbook adjusts for the live score, their chances of winning can increase significantly. Suppose we're talking about a soccer match, characterized by low scoring. In such a situation, if a player can gain a one-point advantage sneakily, it could be crucial for the outcome of the betting ticket.

Many would tell you that players can't get the better of the online sportsbook, insisting that the sportsbook would always suspend the line first, and players could never purchase their tickets in advance. However, I would say it's not always the case. Both in terms of mindset and in practice, sportsbooks do let a small percentage of players take this advantage.

After a team scores, if a player manages to bet before the online sportsbook suspends the line, there's a term for it — "post-score tickets." It's a big no-no for sportsbooks. Once identified, it's absolutely impermissible, and they would certainly cancel such betting tickets. But the challenge is that it's not easy to make this determination.

It's important to realize that during a match, players place bets continuously. A sportsbook can't simply decide that any bet made during a scoring moment is an attempt to take an advantage. Indiscriminately canceling such bets would upset players. Who would then want to play? Furthermore, just because a player gains an advantage doesn't mean they're guaranteed to win. The match isn't over yet, and no one knows the final outcome.

Lastly, and most importantly, in sports betting, there's no direct conflict of interest between the players and the online sportsbook. So, if the situation is just barely passable, why not allow players a sneak advantage? However, for a player, seeking an advantage in live betting isn't that easy. It depends on whether the online sportsbook makes a mistake or if the player has practiced for such opportunities.

During a match, the traders inside the online sportsbook, who control the betting lines, are definitely watching the game. As soon as a team scores, they will immediately suspend accepting bets and adjust the score. They are trained professionals and act quickly, so, generally, players don't have a chance to place bets first. But the act of suspending bets is human-driven, and wherever there's human involvement, errors can occur. For example, mistakenly pressing a wrong key on the computer, or having a momentary lapse in reaction. In such moments, there's a brief window of opportunity for players.

This is the gap players can exploit. If a player can seize this brief few seconds, they might be able to purchase a betting ticket after a team scores and before the online sportsbook suspends bets. Of course, this isn't easy. Consider this: after seeing a team score on TV, if you're not betting online, you'd have to sprint to the nearest betting site in your lane, take out cash, and ask the owner to get you a ticket. How much time would that take?

To complete a bet in such a short span, a player must, first, use online betting, and second, be logged into the site in advance, keeping a close eye on the betting line for that particular match. Only then, with a click of a button, can they place a bet in time. Those who rush to physical betting sites or place bets over the phone will undoubtedly miss this chance.

Here, it's also worth mentioning, why is there only a few seconds of window time? Sometimes, human errors are hard to determine; it might take several seconds to even a few minutes. However, when online sportsbooks face such situations, they often cancel all bets to avoid losses. Hence, if the human error is too severe, this window time doesn't exist.

Regardless, this golden goal time is a great joy for live betting. And it's not always about getting the score advantage. For example, in a baseball game with bases loaded and no outs, placing a bet at that moment can also be considered an advantageous position.

That said, live betting is arguably the most player-favorable mode in sports gambling. But, on the flip side, it's quite disadvantageous for the online sportsbook.

Looking from the perspective of the online sportsbook and considering live betting, it's, unfortunately, viewed more as a service rather than a revenue-generating product.

Why is this the case? Primarily because of high costs and low profits.

- Overall betting volume is low. Compared to pre-match betting, the scale of live betting is much smaller. And as we know, when the overall betting volume decreases, the juice, or commission, the online sportsbook makes is also reduced. Thus, even though both modes earn from the juice, pre-match betting is more profitable.

- High operational costs are a major concern when offering live betting lines. This not only requires more traders but also essential facilities such as satellite broadcasts and real-time news sources, all of which come with a price. Moreover, live betting only offers a short window, less than two hours, for line management, unlike pre-game betting which spans over 24 hours. Therefore, maintaining a balanced betting line in such a short time frame is considerably more challenging.

In the long run, online sportsbooks might struggle to make substantial profits from live betting. In fact, breaking even could be considered an achievement. From a business perspective, it might be more beneficial for online sportsbooks not to offer this type of betting. However, the catch is that live betting is immensely popular among bettors. If an online sportsbook does not provide this option, players might choose not to engage at all, causing the platform to miss out on potential pre-game betting profits as well.

As a result, online sportsbooks often treat live betting more as a "service" than a significant revenue stream. This isn't to say that all online sportsbooks can't make a profit from live betting. Many do, but this success is often tied to the volume of bets they handle and whether they employ skilled traders and sophisticated computer systems. Broadly speaking, the profit margins from live betting are typically lower than those from pre-game betting.

Why is live betting less profitable? The primary factor is "time." In pre-game betting, online sportsbooks have an entire day to gradually adjust the lines. They can also close betting earlier and engage in arbitrage to manage risks, as discussed in earlier chapters. However, during live events, there's only a limited window of one to two hours. This tight timeframe doesn't allow online sportsbooks ample opportunity to balance the lines or effectively use arbitrage. Consequently, they often have to take risks by betting against the players, making it challenging to ensure consistent profits.

So, some online sportsbooks might play around with the odds, charging more juice on live bets to cover their operational costs. For players, this means the odds become less attractive and not very advantageous.

Moreover, for players, live betting is not just relatively easier to win but also a way to hedge their risks.

Avoiding Betting Risks

Imagine this scenario: before the game, we've already placed a bet on one team, but when the game officially starts, something unexpected happens. The star player we were counting on faces an issue, like a twisted ankle or gets fouled harshly and is taken out. We all know accidents can happen in sports; it's inevitable.

However, such incidents can significantly influence the outcome of our bets. Now, without the star player, we might not be as confident in that team. So, what should we do in such situations? This is where live betting comes into play.

Suppose we initially bet $100 on Team A. During the game, all you need to do is place an additional $100 bet on Team B. Regardless of which team wins, you'll get back $190, which means you only lose $10. This is what we refer to as hedging because compared to losing the entire $100, you now only lose $10, which is considerably better.

This is the commonly mentioned "restocking" strategy in live betting, also known as "replenishing". However, it's essential to clarify that the "restocking" we're discussing here is purely from a risk-avoidance perspective, aiming to minimize losses. Online, you might find more aggressive strategies like "offense and defense" or "turning the tables after a defeat".

And the practices of these radicals, everyone should really pay more attention to, because these methods are problematic. If you want to "double down on your victory", you might end up losing two bets. Hoping to "turn defeat into victory" might result in even bigger losses. No one can predict the outcome of a game, so don't blindly trust these strategies. Using live betting as a hedge is an advanced technique and is not something that can be done carelessly.

Let's give an example to see how one might lose two bets consecutively.

| | Point Spread Line | Score |
|---|---|---|
| Team A  (Home Team) | -2 | 1.80 |
| Team B | | 1.80 |

First, this is the pre-match betting line, where Team A gives a two-point handicap to Team B. At this point, we favor Team A, so we place a bet of $100 on Team A to win.

However, once the game starts, a player from Team A gets injured, giving Team B the upper hand. As a result, the live betting line now shows

|  | Point Spread Line | Odds | Score |
|---|---|---|---|
| Team A  (Home Team) |  | 1.80 | 0 |
| Team B |  | 1.80 | 0 |

Please note that Team A is not giving any points now. So, if everyone blindly follows online rumors and bets recklessly, looking to hedge their risks, they might bet $100 on Team B to win. But here's the thing, this approach is not considered hedging, and there's a good chance you'll lose both bets. Some might not believe this, so let's do some math. Suppose the final match result is Team A with 2 points and Team B with 1 point, Team A wins. This means you will lose on both of your betting tickets.

On your first ticket, you bet on Team A giving two points, but in the end, Team A only wins by one point, so you lose this bet.

On your second ticket, you bet on Team B to win. Unfortunately, Team A still wins, so you lose again.

This is the most common scenario in restocking methods where one ends up losing both bets. Many think that the only way to lose both bets is by betting on the same team on both tickets. But we want to emphasize that beginners are more likely to make the mistake of betting separately on both teams.

Many forget the significance of the point spread and thus bet arbitrarily. They think that just placing a bet on both sides equals hedging. That's a huge mistake. If you want to hedge, you must pay attention to the point spread. Taking this example, if you want to hedge, you'd need to wait until Team A leads by two points before betting on Team B. Only then does it make sense, ensuring that no matter the outcome, you won't lose everything.

So, before planning your hedge, it's best to do the math first. If you want to hedge, ensure the point spread situation remains unchanged. If you're too lazy to calculate, then it's better to just bet on the money line. As we mentioned before, the money line has no point spread. Online sportsbooks purely manipulate players using the odds. Without the point spread, hedging on-site becomes much simpler.

## Our Recommendation

So, combining live betting with the money line becomes the best choice for players, and this is what we recommend to everyone. This is inferred from the profits of the online sportsbooks. Among all the betting types, their profits are the lowest in these two. It can even be said that they are running at a loss. Furthermore, controlling the odds in live betting and the money line is notoriously challenging. Therefore, if it's tough for them to make money, it provides a better opportunity for players to earn a bit more.

Moreover, when players engage in "live" betting, they can discreetly exploit the online sportsbooks. They can observe and see whose reaction is faster during the scoring. At most, the online sportsbook might just suspend accepting bets early. If you can't purchase a betting ticket, there's no loss. But, if you accidentally buy a ticket before the score gets updated, then it's an additional profit. All in all, it should be evident why savvy players opt for "live betting."

Additionally, it's worth noting that as long as the game's result isn't finalized, every online sportsbook has the right to cancel your bet in advance. In such cases, you can only retrieve your original stake as if you never placed the bet, without any disputes. So, even if you manage to exploit a loophole momentarily, it might not necessarily count. Until the end of the game, nothing is guaranteed, and all online sportsbooks follow this rule. However, on the flip side, you aren't at a loss. At most, your bet just didn't go through, and it's not a big deal.

The only thing to be cautious about in live betting is how much juice the online sportsbook charges. We have covered this part in our advice section, where we teach everyone how to identify the juice.

## Taking Advantage to the Extreme

Here I'd like to share with you about the most astute gambler I've ever heard of. His level of genius can be compared to the "Einstein" of the gambling world, and his "theory of relativity" has become a headache for many online sportsbooks!

What this gentleman aimed to challenge was the fundamental law of live betting: "The online sportsbook and the player watch the live broadcast together and are aware of the game situation at the same time." Does the player really have to watch with the sportsbook? What if they could know the results just a step ahead?

So he specifically chose international games, bought a plane ticket, and flew to the venue to watch the match live. We know that international matches are broadcasted via satellite, and with satellites, there's always a delay. This delay can be influenced by weather conditions. For the average person watching a satellite broadcast, a delay of a few seconds doesn't matter. But for this gentleman who was at the venue, it made a world of difference.

He also brought along a laptop and a mobile phone with internet access. We know that the internet is much more stable than satellite broadcasts. Everyone has accessed foreign websites and should know that no matter how distant the website server is, the response time doesn't differ much. You won't wait an extra ten seconds just because you're accessing a site in the U.S. So with these two theoretical advantages and the fact that this man was well-practiced in placing bets quickly and accurately online, you can probably imagine the outcome...

I won't continue the story, as the ending, whether he won or lost and by how much, isn't the point. After all, considering the money this gentleman spent (think round-trip plane tickets and accommodations) and the effort he put in, if I were the online sportsbook, I'd probably have to accept it. The main point of this chapter is to give everyone an understanding of the challenges of operating an online sportsbook and the endless ingenuity of players.

## Parlay

The betting method known as "Parlay" in English is also referred to as a "combined bet". What's unique about this approach is that players can bet on several matches at once, and if they predict all outcomes correctly, they can win a significant amount. Consider the following example:

| Parlay | | |
|---|---|---|
| Team A VS Team B | Buy Team A win | Odds 1.70 |
| Team C VS Team D | Buy Team C win | Odds 1.70 |
| Team E VS Team F | Buy Team E win | Odds 1.90 |

Think of this as a typical parlay ticket. Imagine it like a BBQ skewer, where players use their money to string multiple matches together, hence the nickname "combined bet". To win a parlay, you must guess all three matches correctly, known as clearing three stages. However, if you get even one match wrong, then, unfortunately, you lose.

It's evident that this method is considerably more challenging than the previous ones discussed. Still, many people buy these tickets, primarily because they hope to "win big with a small amount". Additionally, many believe that the odds in parlay betting are better, which is a misconception. The odds in parlay bets are the same as regular betting, but players can indeed win more money.

For instance, suppose you're very familiar with the six teams playing in these three matches. So, you decide to go to the Betting Sites to buy tickets for these three games. But once you arrive, you realize you only have $100 left. In this situation, you might consider using the "parlay" method to buy your tickets. If you predict all the matches correctly, you can win all three games at once.

**$100 x 1.70 (Team A odds) x 1.70 (Team C odds) x 1.90 (Team E odds) = $549.1**.

Placing a bet of $100 can yield a return of $549, which is much better than betting on a single game. However, you might be wondering, if we only brought $100 earlier, what if we had enough money? Would the outcome be the same? The answer is no! If you bet $100 separately on each game, the calculation would be like this:

**$100 x 1.70 + $100 x 1.70 + $100 x 1.90 = $530.**

In the "parlay" betting method, you use the money won from the first game to bet on the second game, and then use the money won from the second game to bet on the third. This way, you stand to win much more money compared to betting $100 on each game individually. However, the risk is that you either win it all or lose it all. In the first example, if you lose one game, you lose everything. In the second example, if you lose one game, you can still claim a prize of $340.

We used a three-game parlay as an example, but in reality, you can choose how many games you want to include in your parlay. The minimum is obviously two games, and you can go up to eight games. There's a term for this: if you are betting on two games in a parlay, we say you are "passing two stages," or "1 parlay 2." This means you are using one stake to bet on two games. If you bet on three games, it's "passing three stages," or "1 parlay 3," and so on up to "1 parlay 8." Some websites even allow you to go further, such as parlaying up to 16 games, but be aware of the odds. The chances of winning are actually quite slim. Let's assume you have a keen eye for games and are about 90% sure of the outcomes. In that case, your real chances of winning a three-game parlay would be **90/100 * 90/100 * 90/100 = 73%.**

Continuing this pattern, for an eight-game parlay, your odds of winning drop to 43%. What this means is that even when you are fairly confident in your judgments, after passing three stages, you only have a 73% chance of collecting the prize money. If you go up to eight stages, your odds of winning drop to less than half. And there's another issue: most online sportsbooks offer point spreads to make the games more balanced. So, your chances of winning are probably just slightly over 50%. Under these conditions, let's see what happens when you have a 50% certainty: For a three-game parlay, the odds of winning are 50/100 * 50/100 * 50/100 = 12.5%. For an eight-game parlay, the odds drop dramatically to 0.39%.

Yes, you read that right. If your chances of winning are only 50%, then the risk of doing parlays is extremely high. To actually pass eight stages and collect the prize money, your chances are less than one in a hundred. You can probably guess by now that for the sportsbook, this is a highly profitable product. In reality, that's exactly the case. Not only are the odds of paying out prizes low, but the sportsbook doesn't even need to allocate manpower for this, like risk management traders. It's low-cost and high-profit, which is why all online sportsbooks heavily promote this betting method.

## Unfair Parlays

Parlays, as a form of betting, essentially allow you to swap low probabilities for high odds. At first glance, this seems fair: betting on multiple games simultaneously means lower odds of winning, but the potential payout— referred to as "payout"—is much higher, making it a popular choice for many. However, as we've repeatedly emphasized, the website's definition of fairness isn't the same as yours, especially when it comes to parlays. The probabilities you're sacrificing are often a little higher than you might think.

To illustrate, let's consider the simplest example of a two-leg parlay. Assume you're betting on the point spread, only guessing which team will win or lose, and you're placing your bets blindly. In that case, the odds of getting each game right should be 50%, making the odds of hitting a two-leg parlay 25%. So if you buy four such parlay betting tickets, one should win.

Further assume that the odds you're given for each game are 1.80, and your bet for each parlay is $100. In that case, your profit comes only from the winning ticket.

**$100 * 1.80 * 1.80 = $324.**

Because you bought four tickets, your total stake is $400. Translated into a rate of return, it's a negative 19%. For every $100, you lose $19. And this is just a two-game parlay. You can calculate that the rate of return for a three-game parlay is even lower.

What if you don't play parlays? Let's calculate that. Suppose you don't buy four two-game parlays, but instead bet on eight individual games. All assumptions remain the same: your odds are 1.80, and the probability of guessing each game correctly is still 50%. For these eight games, your bet for each game is still $100.

Firstly, with a 50% chance of guessing correctly, out of eight tickets, four will win. Your profit will be:
4 * $100 * 1.80 = $720.
Now, because you bought eight tickets, your total stake is $800. But when we calculate the rate of return, it's now only a negative 10%. In other words, for every $100, you now only lose $10.

The key point is, many people think parlays are more profitable because it seems like the return is higher. This is wrong, because in reality, parlays are very easy to lose money on. Based on the mathematical argument above, if you're going to bet on the same number of games, it's better to split them and bet on individual games, because the rate of return is much higher.

## The Issue With "Draw" in Parlay Bets

Parlay bets have some odd quirks that can cause you to lose more than you anticipated. We've previously discussed something called the "draw line," which is a strange situation in point spread betting where there's a half-point (0.5) involved. Everyone knows that there's no such thing as a 0.5 point in a game; here, the 0.5 actually represents the odds. Let's say there is a line with a 0.5 point spread, and the match ends in a tie. If you bet on the team that was giving 0.5 points, you would win half your bet. For example, if you bet $100 at odds of 1.90, you'd win $95 back on a $50 bet, adding the original $50 to have a total of $145. On the other hand, if you bet on the other team, you'd lose half your bet, so with a $100 bet, you'd get back $50.

We won't go into the specifics or the reasons behind this system—those can be found in the "Online Sportsbook" chapter—but this is generally called a "draw line." Not every sportsbook has this, but it does happen in Taiwan Handicap betting, as we've noted before.

So, this issue applies to parlays too. Let's say you have a $100 parlay ticket, crossing two matches. In the first match, both teams draw. The calculation is the same as a single match; those who win half would get $145, and those who lose half are left with $50. Now let's assume you're unlucky and lost half; now, let's see what happens in the second match. If the second match is also a draw, and you win half, then everything is fine. Your earnings would be calculated from the remaining $50: $25 x 1.9 + $25 equals $72.5. But what if you lose half again? You might think that you would just lose half of the remaining $50 and end up with $25. You would be mistaken. If you lose half in both matches, you actually get nothing back. The logic from the sportsbook is that you've lost half of your original $100 in the first match, leaving you with $50. Then, you lose half of that $50 in the second match, making you a complete loser. This can be represented by the formula $1 - \frac{1}{2} - \frac{1}{2} = 0$.

By this point, you should be able to notice the differences between the two algorithms. Additionally, the monetary difference between the two is quite significant. In the player's algorithm, you could still get back $25, but with the website's algorithm, it's zero. However, there's no need to debate who is right or wrong, as the website's algorithm is already programmed into the computer system. **"Once you lose half of two matches, the calculation will definitely be a total loss, regardless of whether the losses are consecutive or not, and regardless of how many rounds this parlay ticket has passed."**

At this point, you might still have a question. If we must accept this rule, then by the website's logic, if we happen to win half of two matches during a parlay, the player should be considered to have won completely. Unfortunately, our website doesn't have such a rule. Once you win half of two matches, the outcome is still calculated according to individual matches. There's absolutely no possibility of winning a bit more. In short, the basic rule for bookmakers is to calculate in a way that minimizes the payout.

Also, when calculating the winnings for parlay tickets, the figures for each match often include decimals. For example, you might see winnings of $47.5. Whether the website uses "rounding up," "rounding down," or "rounding to the nearest whole number" is hard to say. Players may not pay much attention to these decimals, but on the website, they are not trivial at all. Accumulated over time, these can amount to significant sums. If you're interested, you can also calculate your own tickets to see how the website handles these decimal points.

Not all betting sites necessarily follow the judgment rules mentioned above, but they are a general trend. So, when looking at parlay calculations, please also pay extra attention to the winning probabilities you might be losing.

## Wise Guy: the Ultra-Smart Player

The English term "Wise Guy" is generally translated as "smart person," but those who watch movies may know that it's also used to represent "gang members." There's even a film focused on American gangs that uses this term as its title. In English, this term often has the connotation of "an arrogant and reckless person."

Why are we discussing this term now? That's because "Wise Guy" holds exceptional importance in the sports betting industry. It's just as critical as other terms like "placing bets," "odds," and "point spreads," all of which people need to mention every day.

What's so special about the term "Wise Guy" that everyone keeps uttering it? First of all, this term is not favorable on the sportsbook websites. When a website mentions a wise guy, it's usually bad news.

Let's take a closer look at what this term means in sports betting. It represents a small group of players who are experts in all the rules of the online sportsbook. They exploit the inherent loopholes in the game to place bets for profit.

To put it in layman's terms, these individuals are also players; they also place bets, but their purpose for betting differs from the majority. When most people place a bet, they hope that their team will win in the end so that they can make money. Wise guys are different; they don't need the team to win to make money.

Sounds mysterious, doesn't it? Therefore, in this article, we'll discuss in detail how these ultra-smart players, these wise guys, operate. We'll also explore why these techniques keep getting passed down and why the sportsbooks have not been able to completely block them.

## Utilizing the Fluctuations in Odds

Firstly, a common tactic used by wise guys is known as "Arbitrage," which shares the same name as the "Arbitrage" used by online sportsbooks, but the methods are entirely different. This is a technique for profiting from the difference in odds. Before diving into the principles behind this, let's take a look at how this technique is actually applied.

Today, the online sportsbook has opened a new line.

|  | Odds |
|---|---|
| Team A | 1.50 |
| Team B | 2.30 |

After the line is set, the Wise guy can start buying betting tickets. First, he purchases a ticket for "$100 on Team B winning, with odds of 2.30." But that's not the end. The Wise guy continues to wait. We all know that online sportsbooks need to adjust the odds regularly to attract players to place bets and balance the line. So, after a period of time, this line might change.

|  | Odds |
|---|---|
| Team A | 2.30 |
| Team B | 1.50 |

The line now has completely reversed from before, making Team A the one with the high odds. So, the Wise guy makes another move and buys another betting ticket, this time for "$100 on Team A winning, with odds of 2.30." At this point, the task is accomplished, and the "Arbitrage" technique has been successfully executed.

So, what do we have? Let's take a look at these two betting tickets in the Wise guy's possession.

|  | Bets | Odds | Payout |
|---|---|---|---|
| Team B | 100 | 2.30 | 230 |
| Team A | 100 | 2.30 | 230 |

He only bought two betting tickets, spending a total of $200, but no matter which team ultimately wins, he will receive $230 in winnings. Thus, what the Wise guy can earn is this $30. In other words, the return on investment for this method is 30/200, which is 15%.

We call this method "Arbitrage" because it's risk-free; you can earn money no matter which team wins. Therefore, it's considered more of an investment strategy rather than gambling, like how most players buy betting tickets.

The term "Arbitrage" is used for two reasons. First, the rate of return on this method is similar to the "juice" that the online sportsbook earns, both being a percentage of the total bet amount. Second, this method doesn't rely on a specific team winning; as long as there is a game happening, you can earn money, similar to how online sportsbooks operate. That's why the term "Arbitrage" comes into play.

Additionally, some people refer to this method as "earning the spread" because it takes advantage of the variations in odds to generate a profit.

However, the example given above is just a simple one. In reality, many people can see that such a complete reversal of strengths is unlikely to happen. But that's not a problem; the Wise guy doesn't need such an extreme example to make money. Let's now look at more common variations in the lines and advanced Arbitrage techniques

|  | original betting line | The line after a period of time |
|---|---|---|
|  |  |  |
| Team A | 1.65 | 1.89 |
| Team B | 2.15 | 1.91 |

In this change of odds, the fluctuations were quite subtle. The odds for Team A only rose slightly. Not to mention, there wasn't a complete switch in the perceived strength between the teams, and even the hierarchy of the odds didn't shift. After some time, the odds for Team B were still better than those of Team A.

However, this is a typical betting line. In the original line, Team A only had odds of 1.65, so fewer people placed bets on them. Thus, after a while, the online sportsbook increased the odds for Team A to 1.89 in an attempt to attract players. But sportsbooks usually prefer not to make drastic changes. If players shift too drastically, it's not favorable. A better approach is to slightly raise the odds and steadily control the line, hoping to gradually restore balance over time.

So, in such a scenario, is there an opportunity for a **wise guy** to make money? Of course, there is. But this time, the move needs to be smarter. Let's take a look at the two betting tickets that were placed.

|  | Bets | Odds | Payout |
|---|---|---|---|
| Team B | 100 | 2.15 | 215 |
| Team A | 114 | 1.89 | 215 |

This time, the Wise guy still purchased two betting tickets. At the original line, he bet on Team B, and after some time, he placed a bet on Team A. What's unique about his approach this time is that the bet amount for Team A increased. It was previously $100, but now it has become $114, and the odds remain the same as set by the online sportsbook. He purchased at the peak odds of 2.15 for Team B and 1.89 for Team A.

What was the outcome? Of course, he made a profit. The total bet was $100 + $114 = $214. No matter which team won, the expected payout was $215, yielding a profit of $1. The return on investment is 1/214, which is approximately 0.5%. Since the odds changed slightly, the Wise guy's profit decreased significantly. Compared to the previous line's 15%, it's a world apart. But even though the ROI is low, this is still a risk-free way to earn money. As long as the bet amount is large, there's still a good amount to be earned.

## The Principle of Arbitrage

After seeing the actual practice, we can discuss the principle that wise guys rely on. "Arbitrage" actually refers to buying two betting tickets, and it must be two, not just one, and not three. These two tickets should be for the teams that are competing against each other in the game. Relying on the ever-changing nature of sports betting odds, combined with basic mathematical principles, this method is achieved.

First, why do the odds keep changing? Those interested can refer back to the "online sportsbook" section; we won't discuss it here. So, what's the mathematical principle? It's simply that the expected payout from each of the two betting tickets must be greater than the total amount bet. Observing the examples above would illustrate this point. Moreover, we can identify some characteristics of wise guys when they use Arbitrage:

1. the combined odds of the two betting tickets must be greater than 4.00. This can be understood from a mathematical perspective. In mathematics, an odd of 2.00 represents our principal, and anything beyond that is the part of the winnings. If the additional amount doesn't exceed 2.00, it means that the winnings are less than the principal, and naturally, there's a loss. Therefore, the combined odds of the two tickets purchased must exceed 4.00, and the higher the better.

2. when purchasing the first ticket, the odds must be greater than 2.00. This consideration is due to risk factors. Since the combined odds of the two tickets must be over 4.00, a wise guy would prefer to secure odds greater than 2.00 with the first ticket. This is because there's uncertainty regarding how high the odds of the second ticket might be. So, when buying the first ticket, it's essential to look for odds significantly greater than 2.00, making the purchase of the second ticket easier.

3. the odds for the second ticket don't necessarily have to be greater than 2.00. As you've already seen in the previous example, it's ideal if it exceeds 2.00, but it's not mandatory. However, there are still many nuances to consider when purchasing this second ticket.

Firstly, the betting amount of the second ticket should not exceed the expected profit of the first ticket. Let's take a look at the previous example: If Team B is bet with $100, the expected prize money is $215, then the expected profit would be $215 - $100 = $115. This means that the betting amount for the second ticket should never exceed $115. The logic here is simple: if it exceeds this amount, the profit from the first ticket will not be enough to cover the loss from the second one, making the risk-free profit impossible.

Next, the expected profit from the second ticket should also exceed the betting amount of the first ticket. The logic is the same as the previous point. So, in the example, the profit for Team A is $215 - $100 = $115, which is greater than the $100 bet on the first ticket.

However, as long as you pay attention to the above two points when buying the second ticket, you can freely choose the odds and betting amount. Thus, we see that the wise guy was very smart when buying the second ticket. Although Team A's odds were not high, only 1.89, he was able to increase the bet amount, ensuring the profit was enough to cover the first ticket. Moreover, even though he increased the bet amount, it did not exceed the expected profit from the first ticket.

From the above, we can further deduce that if the expected prize money from both tickets is equal, then the profit from "arbitrage" will be maximized. This aligns perfectly with what online sportsbooks aim for when balancing their books. While sportsbooks strive to ensure that payouts are equal for both sides, a wise guy seeks to ensure that the payouts from his two tickets are the same.

Everyone can look back at the first two examples at this point. They both exhibit these three characteristics. By mastering these traits, you can harness the technique of "Arbitrage." However, we have to admit here that while Arbitrage seems straightforward, executing it is quite tedious. If you try it out yourself, you'll see that there are so many calculations involved. Not only is there a bunch of addition, subtraction, multiplication, and division, but for those who despised basic arithmetic in elementary school, this is undoubtedly a nightmare. Additionally, you must continuously monitor the odds to determine the right moment to place a bet on the second betting ticket. So, while the principle behind Arbitrage is simple, not everyone has the patience to do it. After all this explanation, I'm sure some readers are overwhelmed. Taking the time to slowly deduce the logic, especially with the rapidly changing odds, makes the calculations endless. And by the time you've finished, there's hardly an opportunity left to place a bet. The wise guys are of course aware of this, which led to the introduction of Arbitrage calculators.

| | Bet Amount | Odds | Expected Payout | Expected Profit |
|---|---|---|---|---|
| First Betting | (1) | (2) | (A) | (E) |
| Second Betting | (B) | (3) | (C) | (F) |
| | | | | |
| Total Bets | (D) | | | |
| Return Rate | (G) | | | |

This is a spreadsheet, and wise guys use Excel or other software to implement it. Once they have this sheet, wise guys just need to input three fields to derive all the numbers:

- This is the first betting ticket that has been purchased, where the purchase amount needs to be entered.

- This is the first betting ticket that has been purchased, where the odds bought need to be entered.

- This is the second betting ticket that they are preparing to buy, where the odds seen on the **line** need to be entered.

- With this information, the spreadsheet can automatically calculate potential profits. The answer can be found in column (G), allowing you to directly see what the return on investment is. So, the wise guy only needs to continuously update the odds in field (3) as seen on the current **line** to determine the best time to place a bet for the second ticket.

Why is this spreadsheet so magical? It's all about setting up all the formulas in advance for automatic calculations. This is where Excel comes in handy. Enter the following formulas in columns (A) to (F).

(A) = (1) * (2)

(B) = (A) / (3)

(C) = (B) * (3)

(D) = (1) + (B)

(E) = (A) − (D)

(F) = (C) − (D)

(G) = (E) / (D)

The above six sets of formulas are all based on the previously explained "Arbitrage" principle to calculate the maximum profit. We can use the previous example to determine the best betting strategy using this spreadsheet.

| | Bet Amount | Odds | Expected Payout | | Expected Profit |
|---|---|---|---|---|---|
| First Betting | **100.00** | **2.15** | 215.00 | | 0.03 |
| Second Betting | 114.97 | **1.87** | 215.00 | | 0.03 |
| | | | | | |
| Total Bets | 214.97 | | | | |
| Return Rate | 0.01% | | | | |

Using this spreadsheet, we can see that we could actually buy the second betting ticket when the odds were at 1.87. However, the profit is minimal, only 0.01%, which means you would only earn a dollar from a $10,000 bet. That's too little. Therefore, the wise guy chose to wait a bit longer and buy when the odds rose to 1.89. This decision was not without reason.

From the above, we can see the power of the Arbitrage calculation spreadsheet, and every wise guy has a similar tool to assist them. This is considered basic among basics, and we will introduce more auxiliary tools later on.

If you're interested in this spreadsheet but don't want to create it yourself, you can refer to the end of this book. There, you'll find a ready-to-use spreadsheet. Additionally, there are many other interesting tools that you can find there.

## Risks of Arbitrage

The above describes the principle of "Arbitrage." This approach can be applied to all matches within sports betting, whether it's soccer, basketball, baseball, or even beyond sports. As long as the odds fluctuate, this method can be used. However, executing "Arbitrage" is not risk-free. In fact, a wise guy, in addition to doing meticulous calculations and constantly monitoring the computer, risking dying of boredom, also runs the risk of losing money.

The first possibility is that the wise guy might never get the opportunity to purchase the second betting ticket. From the principle mentioned earlier, one can deduce that buying the second ticket is contingent on specific amounts and odds, not just any random purchase. If the chance never arises, the wise guy will only have the original betting ticket in hand. In this situation, he's just like any other player - gambling and relying on luck to win. This is the first risk of "Arbitrage," inadvertently finding oneself gambling.

The second possibility is that the online sportsbook may cancel the betting ticket. Even if a wise guy goes to great lengths and seizes the opportunity to successfully purchase two tickets and completes the "arbitrage" technique, this doesn't guarantee he will make a profit. This is because online sportsbooks despise this method. They will always have people monitoring to prevent individuals from employing this strategy. If the online sportsbook detects that the wise guy is engaging in arbitrage, then just before the end of the game, the sportsbook can directly cancel his second ticket, forcing him to bet against the online sportsbook. Alternatively, the sportsbook can also cancel both tickets, rendering his efforts fruitless.

And we know that such actions by the online sportsbooks are permissible because, before the end of a game, they have the absolute right to cancel any bets from anyone. Thus, this is the second risk of "arbitrage", being forced to bet against the online sportsbook.

It's precisely these risks that result in only a very few players becoming wise guys. Ordinary people don't have a strong enough heart, quick enough wit, or sufficient mathematical skills to become one, which is why the title of our article translates them as "ultra-smart players".

## Where There Is a Will, There Is a Way

However, wise guys don't just bluff. They have methods to mitigate these risks. The key lies in "increasing the number of online sportsbooks." Traditionally, sports betting was restricted to one region, and bettors could only purchase from one sportsbook. So, naturally, we had just one website, and thus, the associated risks. But what if we change our perspective and think about purchasing betting tickets from different websites separately?

We all know that there are at least thousands of online sportsbooks worldwide. None of these sites restrict player eligibility. Basically, anyone willing to place bets is welcomed. Under such circumstances, a wise guy placing bets online is even more convenient than the average person buying betting tickets at local betting sites. That's why they usually register as online members on several sportsbooks, diversifying their bets. This is what we mean when we say that wise guys can "increase the number of sportsbooks."

So, what are the advantages of increasing the number of sportsbooks? Let's examine from a few perspectives:

Firstly, each sportsbook offers odds for the same game, and with varying regions, the betting patterns of players differ. Consequently, the odds provided by each online sportsbook differ. This means that wise guys have more odds options to choose from. Whether buying the first or the second betting ticket, the process becomes much easier.

Secondly, a wise guy needs to purchase two betting tickets, and the total odds combined must exceed 4.00. In a situation with only one online sportsbook, he would first buy one ticket and then, after some time, purchase the second ticket when the odds change. This is because sportsbooks aim to profit from the juice, so they will never offer combined odds exceeding 4.00 for two teams at the same time. This introduces the risk associated with time.

However, in situations with multiple online sportsbooks, things change. Different sportsbooks might have varying odds for the same game, meaning that a wise guy could potentially purchase the first ticket from Sportsbook A and find the second ticket at Sportsbook B simultaneously.

Furthermore, the wise guy could adopt an inverse approach: continuously monitor the odds across various sportsbooks until both tickets reach a buying point. Only then does he make a move, simultaneously purchasing the two tickets from two different sportsbooks. If the opportunity never presents itself, he simply doesn't buy. This method eliminates the risk associated with time entirely, removing the gamble of purchasing the first ticket and then waiting for the second.

Thirdly, the betting tickets cannot be canceled. This is because the wise guy buys his two tickets from two different online sportsbooks. For either sportsbook, the wise guy has only purchased one ticket, just like any other player. Therefore, the sportsbook would have no reason to suspect he's engaged in arbitrage, or "water betting" as it's termed, and naturally, there would be no grounds to cancel the ticket.

What we've discussed above is the approach that a true wise guy would adopt. In essence, we can say that no wise guy bets on just one website. Conversely, players who are only familiar with a single site can't truly be considered wise guys. Of course, this isn't to say that "arbitraging" on a single site is unfeasible, just that it's "not savvy enough."

Our previously mentioned "arbitrage spreadsheet" can also be applied here, making it easier for wise guys to calculate arbitrage opportunities across multiple sites.

However, when we say "easier" here, it's only in relative terms. Using Excel for calculations might be a tad simpler than manually crunching numbers on a calculator. But in reality, just keeping an eye on the odds changes on one website can already be a hassle, let alone monitoring multiple sites simultaneously. Moreover, every website has its design and might display odds differently, so for a wise guy, this remains a grueling task.

## Arbitrage Bots

The saying "laziness is the mother of invention" couldn't be more accurate here. Wise guys, after engaging in arbitrage for a while, realize that mastering this skill takes a significant amount of time and mental energy, often involving tedious mathematical calculations. The whole process is arduous, to say the least. As a result, they came up with what is known as "arbitrage software," or simply "arbitrage bots." This is essentially a computer program that every wise guy will either develop themselves or commission a computer company to create. There are also pre-packaged software solutions available on the market.

So what can an arbitrage bot do? At its most basic, the program can simulate being a player. It scours the internet in real-time to capture the lines offered by online sportsbooks. This is because modern sportsbooks typically display their lines on individual web pages, which a computer engineer can parse to convert the odds into a format the bot can understand. Once the lines are obtained, combined with previously discussed arbitrage spreadsheets, the bot can continuously capture lines from various sportsbooks, cross-reference them, and identify the optimal moments for arbitrage.

The laborious work that humans find draining can be done by a computer with complete accuracy. Wise guys simply let the program run, allowing them to relax. When the bot issues an alert, indicating that it has found a favorable sportsbook and profitable odds, it's the wise guy's turn to take action. They then buy tickets from two different sportsbooks, guaranteeing a profit.

We can see that using computer programs to monitor betting lines eliminates the pain of watching odds, making arbitrage significantly more accessible. Over the years, as this method has matured and gained popularity, it has also rekindled interest in the basic theories of arbitrage. In the past, even if people knew this was a way to make money, the effort required deterred most. Now, there are even many programs advertised as "work-from-home" solutions, encouraging people to download software to make money from the comfort of their homes. These are actually applications of arbitrage bots.

That's the basic form of arbitrage bots, but there are more advanced versions as well. Wise guys find it tedious to manually place bets and buy tickets. Therefore, computer engineers, while developing these bots, not only have to parse the odds web pages but also need to understand the sportsbook's computer architecture in depth. They then design a program that can automatically fill out the necessary information and execute the actions to place bets and buy tickets.

Writing this kind of software is certainly not easy, but an experienced engineer can still accomplish it. After all, websites have an open architecture; if a person can place an order through a browser, a computer program can certainly simulate this action as well. So, if a wise guy uses this advanced arbitrage software, they basically don't have to worry about anything. In an ideal situation, the software would monitor the lines, make its own calculations, and even place bets by itself. What the wise guy really needs to do is probably just regularly check their account and withdraw their earnings.

But because the ideal is so tempting, people go online and Google "arbitrage software," only to find that a multitude of software companies are selling these kinds of packaged solutions, and new generations of arbitrage software are constantly emerging. However, people will inevitably be curious: Is this arbitrage software really that useful? Because intuition tells us that if it's so easy to make money with this software, the software companies wouldn't even need to sell it—they could just set up a few computers and arbitrate themselves.

Your suspicions are correct; the risks of using this kind of "arbitrage software" are indeed very high. But first, let's say that, both theoretically and practically, this kind of software is feasible. Many wise guys have developed such programs and actually kept them for their own use, rather than selling them. There are still quite a few people making a living off of arbitrage software. Next, let's address the concerns that many of you have—many of these software solutions on the market do indeed have a lot of issues. Let's take a look at what the problems are.

First, an arbitrage software is not something that can be used indefinitely after its initial development. As we've mentioned before, this type of software relies on scraping web pages from online sportsbooks to analyze them. However, web pages are frequently updated. If the odds suddenly shift or a new advertisement appears on the website, the arbitrage software may become unusable. Therefore, a good arbitrage software is constantly updated to synchronize with changes on the sportsbook websites, ensuring the program continues to function as intended. Unfortunately, many software companies don't inform customers about this issue, so the software often breaks a few days after purchase, without any warranty from the company.

Second, it's easy to get the odds wrong. Extracting odds from a website sounds simple but is actually complex. A software engineer needs to figure out the website's internal format and guess at the standards it might use to write the parsing program. This is unreliable because websites don't usually provide internal formatting documentation, leaving us to make educated guesses. Under such circumstances, the software might correctly capture 99% of the odds but mess up on the remaining 1%, either capturing the wrong number or the wrong team. Although the error rate is low, when a problem does occur, it can be substantial. The software will then use these incorrect odds or teams to determine profit, leading to the purchase of betting tickets, and potentially causing a wise guy to buy two tickets for the same team or just one ticket, thereby incurring massive losses.

Third, online sportsbooks are very opposed to the use of arbitrage software. Given the popularity of such software, these websites are well aware of their existence. When wise guys constantly make money using this method, it becomes unfair to other players on the platform. Hence, the engineers at these sportsbooks will set up various obstacles to render arbitrage software ineffective. They may also trace back to see which players are using these programs and then cancel their accounts or confiscate their winnings.

So these are the risks associated with using arbitrage software. This tool is by no means a guaranteed way to make money; its risks are not less than those of gambling. That's why software companies are reluctant to use it themselves and prefer to sell it instead—the profits from selling the software are more reliable.

In summary, using arbitrage software is essentially a battle against online sportsbooks using internet technology. Whichever side has better technology will make money, and vice versa.

## Online Sportsbook Countermeasures

After learning about how Wise Guys exploit the technique of Arbitrage, as well as the advancements in arbitrage software, it's crucial to also look at this practice from the perspective of online sportsbooks. First off, the technique of arbitrage takes advantage of inherent loopholes in the game, specifically the constantly changing odds. With thousands of websites globally, each offering different odds, it's impossible for any online sportsbook to outright ban arbitrage. We can anticipate that as long as sports betting exists, this technique will also continue to be around.

Although websites can't prohibit players from engaging in Arbitrage, they can still take steps to counteract arbitrage software. Proper prevention can minimize the damage caused by such practices, and there are usually several ways to handle this. One approach is to obfuscate the odds, making them visible to human players but difficult for computer programs to capture, thus increasing the challenges of designing arbitrage software. This would push Wise Guys towards other less secure platforms.

Another method involves routinely updating the website's layout, making small changes every week, for example. These subtle adjustments may not impact players, but they can disrupt the effectiveness of arbitrage software, causing Wise Guys to constantly update their programs.

Thirdly, tracking user behavior can be highly effective. A proficient arbitrage software will frequently access the website; therefore, by monitoring usage rates, one can identify whether a player is using such software. Once identified, countermeasures like IP blocking or account termination can be deployed.

There are other techniques, but discussing them would delve too deeply into the realm of computer technology, almost like a battle between computer viruses and antivirus companies, so we'll leave that aside for now. In summary, with human and financial resources, online sportsbooks are generally better equipped to combat arbitrage software.

The arbitrage techniques relied upon by Wise Guys are indeed effective in this field but also carry significant risks. There are rumors on the internet that someone made $2 million in a month using these techniques, and that's true. But it's also true that someone lost $2 million in a month doing the same.

As for individual players, it's best to use this technique as an insurance tool. After buying your first betting ticket, if you happen to notice a shift in the odds that offers an opportunity for arbitrage, you might as well take it. After all, there are no rules that say you can only buy one betting ticket on a sports betting website.

And from the perspective of the online sportsbook, there's not much more to say. Countering Wise Guys is something every site should be doing; otherwise, based on the principle of balance, if some people are consistently winning money, it becomes unfair to other players.

Finally, there are two types of "arbitrage" in this book. One is used by online sportsbooks, which serves as a form of insurance to generate steady income. The other form of arbitrage is utilized by players, specifically the "Wise guys" as previously mentioned. Unless otherwise specified, references to "arbitrage" pertain to the method employed by online sportsbooks. Only in this chapter does it refer to the players' use of "arbitrage."

## Advice for Players

From the section dedicated to players up to this point, we've already offered plenty of advice for those engaging in sports betting. Now it's time for a recap. However, we're somewhat reluctant to offer these pieces of advice. The reason is simple: there are two types of sports bettors.

- Those who are simply watching the games for enjoyment and want to add some excitement.

- Those who have some knowledge about the sports events but are primarily looking to make money.

If you belong to the first category, you can skip this advice. Spending money for entertainment is entirely justifiable. If everyone didn't lose some money, how could the game continue? So if this advice isn't necessary for you, writing it is moot for us.

In terms of spending money for entertainment, we could say more. These players primarily buy betting tickets to enhance their enjoyment of watching the game. They'll purchase tickets for their favorite teams before the game, and as both sides score points during the match, their emotions fluctuate accordingly. This is the essence of how buying betting tickets adds excitement to watching the game. After the game concludes and the winners are determined, you can show off your betting tickets to friends and family, proving your discerning taste. This sort of fun is much more engaging than just watching the game. If everyone belongs to this category, there's no need to worry about whether sports betting is fair or how much money online sportsbooks can make. Think of it as paying for a movie ticket; whether you win or lose doesn't matter, as you've already enjoyed the game. No one questions the fairness of watching a movie, right? This attitude is the healthiest way to approach sports betting, and it's the attitude that the government hopes everyone will adopt.

However, if you are not here solely for entertainment but instead belong to the second category, looking to make money, we must say that learning from these pieces of advice won't help you. This is because all the advice is meant for "everyone," not just the readers of this book. All advice, including discussions on the internet, is written for a general audience.

The issue lies precisely with this "everyone." In sports betting, there's an unwritten rule: "everyone" is bound to lose money; otherwise, the game cannot sustain itself. So, we can't teach "everyone" how to make money. This is not only beyond our ability, but also beyond anyone else's. If someone claims to have a foolproof strategy that can make everyone rich, they are either lying to you or you won't be able to execute the strategy they offer.

Worldwide, no sports betting community has disrupted this balance and allowed everyone to make money. So, no matter who gives this advice, it can't help the majority of players make money. After all the talk, the conclusion boils down to one point: if you want to make money, steer clear of sports betting. That's why we were initially hesitant to give this advice. When it comes to return on investment, sports betting falls short compared to stocks and funds. In terms of security, it's even worse than bank deposits. If you're considering making a living as a professional player, you might as well abandon that idea right now; there are no Warren Buffetts in sports betting.

But many argue that instead of investing in the stock market and potentially losing everything, or keeping money in a bank only to see it eaten away by inflation, it's better to invest in something familiar and interesting. After all, we watch sports all the time and it's far more engaging than combing through a company's financial reports. Besides, hasn't this book also mentioned that this game allows a small percentage of people to consistently make money?

So let's talk about some advice for players. Please note that this advice may not necessarily be sound. Even if it is, you may not be able to follow it, and even if you can, it doesn't guarantee that you'll make money.

Before diving into specific pieces of advice, let's first talk about some basics in the world of sports betting. In the long run, if you want to make money, securing high odds is crucial. That's why we emphasize the concept of "juice" so much. The lower the juice, the higher the odds you can get, which significantly impacts whether or not you can make money. If you're merely placing bets without considering the odds, you'll likely come up empty-handed in the long run. We'll talk more about juice later, especially its impact on players. For now, just remember that if the juice increases by one percent, your profits could potentially decrease by twenty percent.

Back to the topic of odds, patience is key, whether you aim to win or minimize losses. You shouldn't rush to place a bet as soon as you see the line. As a savvy player, you must wait for the odds to reach a point favorable to you. You don't have to bet on every game; if you don't see an opportunity, it's better to wait. As we've previously mentioned, online sportsbooks constantly adjust odds to balance the line. Sooner or later, a good opportunity will present itself. If it doesn't, keep waiting. If you can't win, it's better not to play at all. This, we believe, is the fundamental attitude every player should have.

## Advice One: Regional Specificity in Sports Betting

We've discussed before that sports betting sites may be subject to government regulations to obtain legal licenses, which may include payout ratios or, more colloquially, rules for distributing prize money. For instance, 10% could go to the government for charitable activities, 15% serves as the website's profit, and the remaining 75% is what is actually paid out to players.

This 75% is referred to as the website's payout ratio, and the remaining 25% is what we call the website's "juice." Those who have read the section on websites should know that this juice percentage is fundamental to the game. Every website needs to set a ratio to declare their profit and earn money from it. The number can be big or small, whether it's 5% or 25%.

For example, if a website sets a juice of 25%, this means if they accept bets amounting to $1 million in a day, their profit would be $250,000. If they collect $10 million, they earn $2.5 million. And if it's $100 million, it would be $25 million. Of course, this money isn't entirely theirs; they still have to pay taxes to the government. Furthermore, these profits are theoretical and are not guaranteed.

But the question arises: If the website sets a target of making a 25% profit, it's not just lip service. This figure will impact the entire game. Both internal staff and computer systems of the online sportsbook will adjust the odds and winning probabilities based on this target to ensure that it is met. In other words, no matter what type of gameplay the website introduces or what kinds of promotional activities it runs, one thing is certain: the money paid out every day will be only 75% of the revenue. To put it in simple terms, if everyone places a bet of $100, losing means you lose it all, but winning would bring you at most $75. The longer you play, the clearer this becomes.

You might wonder, is this fair? Our answer would be, it depends on who you are comparing it with. Frankly, the juice percentage is set by every sportsbook; they have to make money after all. So no sportsbook around the world is going to pay out 100% of their daily income to players; they will always retain a percentage for themselves. If you wish to engage in sports betting, you have to accept this reality; this is the so-called "fairness" in this game.

However, if we compare one sportsbook with another, we can still see a relative fairness. Generally speaking, government-licensed sportsbooks set the juice at around 20%, while illegal underground sportsbooks usually charge a juice between 5% and 10%.

Having the underground sportsbooks as a benchmark allows us to assess fairness. It's simple to compare: Firstly, it's commonly known that it's hard to make money from underground sports betting, and yet they only charge a 5% juice. If there's a legal sportsbook setting their juice at 20%, which is four times more, is there any hope for players to make money?

So, here arises an ironic situation. The government introduced sports betting and authorized legal online sportsbooks partly to combat illegal gambling. However, this move could very likely encourage underground betting or gambling in other countries. The reason is simple: experts are reluctant to recommend legal sites but are eager to explain how to play. Once players understand the rules, they'll look for sites that charge less "juice." So, what options are there besides legal sites that charge less juice? Aren't underground bookies the only other option? Alternatively, one might consider betting overseas. For example, in Singapore, they only charge 10% juice. If you want to make a big bet, buying a plane ticket to Singapore might be more cost-effective. As per current rules, the emergence of legal sports betting sites might actually boost other gambling industries. For more thoughts on these matters, please refer to the "Concepts" section.

However, don't be too disheartened. The above is just what the media reports. In reality, things aren't as bad as they say, and legal sports betting sites are not unplayable, as many claim. The reason is simple.

Underground bookmakers don't always charge a 5% "juice" or commission, as often reported in the news. There's a "tiered bookmaking system" in place, meaning the commission rate varies from player to player—some are charged more, and others less. In extreme cases, this rate can even exceed 10%.

On the other hand, legal online sportsbooks are managed by very shrewd business people. They aim to reduce the juice and offer better odds to attract players, ensuring that they don't suffer significant losses. Many strategies can achieve this, but dynamically adjusting the juice rate is the most convenient. Some games might have higher commissions, and others lower.

So, the juice difference between legal and underground bookmakers is not as exaggerated as the media suggests. That also means the odds that matter most to everyone won't differ much. The key takeaway here is that you need to understand how to read the juice. If a book has high juice, avoid it. If it's low, then the opportunities for everyone are greater. This is the unique characteristic of sports betting in different regions—you need to get used to situations where some betting sites make more money and some are less greedy.

Usually, the website will explicitly state how much juice they intend to take, clarifying their profit margin. Sometimes they forget to mention this, or they might decide to change the juice without notifying you. Note that if there's no explicit prior agreement on the amount of juice, the website can adjust it at any time.

| | Odds |
|---|---|
| Team A | 1.50 |
| Team B | 2.30 |
| Total Odds | 3.80 |

So how can we determine the juice ourselves? Here's a back-calculation method: Add the odds for both teams in the book; in this example, the total is 3.8. The formula for calculating the website's juice is:

**1 - (Total Odds / 4) = Juice**

Applying the formula, we get:

**1 - (3.8 / 4) = 5%**

In this example betting line, the website takes 5% as juice. What's the purpose of this juice? Generally speaking, this 5% is a watershed. For professional players, this is fairly reasonable and there's potential to make money. If it goes any higher, say 10%, it's not necessarily profitable. This would reduce your chances of getting high odds significantly, and if it goes even higher? You're almost guaranteed to lose more than you win.

**Advice Two: Watch More Sports and Keep Detailed Records**

The title is borrowed from the widespread advice found on the internet. Apparently, to make money from sports betting, one should follow this advice? The theory is as follows: watching more games can increase your chances of predicting the outcome, and there's a direct correlation between prediction accuracy and player returns. So, watching more games equates to increasing player returns. Moreover, keeping records helps you understand your actual return on investment (ROI). Logically, after understanding your own performance, you should be able to identify ways to improve.

However, we have some reservations about this theory. There's no concrete proof that watching more games will increase the chances of predicting the outcome accurately, especially when you're betting with your own money. To put it bluntly, how many people who bet on sports don't actually watch the games? Here, there's no computer-generated random selection, and while some people might buy betting tickets on a whim, not everyone ends up winning, right?

Nevertheless, keeping records is beneficial. This way, you can understand what your actual ROI is. Let's see the best way to maintain these records. One method is the simplest form of a table: just record all the betting tickets you've purchased in the past and sum them up to determine your ROI.

| | Purchase Amount | Odds | | Winnings |
|---|---|---|---|---|
| | | | | |
| Team A | 100 | 1.8 | | 180 |
| Team A | 100 | 1.6 | | 160 |
| Team B | 100 | 1.8 | | |
| Team A | 100 | 1.75 | | 175 |
| Team A | 100 | 1.8 | | |
| Team B | 100 | 1.75 | | 175 |
| Team A | 100 | 1.8 | | |
| Team C | 100 | 1.9 | | 190 |
| Team A | 100 | 1.52 | | |
| Team A | 100 | 1.61 | | 161 |
| | | | | |
| Total | 1000 | 1.73 | Total Winnings | 1041 |
| | | | | |
| | | | Rrofit | 41 |
| | | | ROI | 4.10% |

In this table, the fields we need to record are:

- "Team" - This is the team we bet on with our betting ticket.

- "Purchase Amount" - The amount of money wagered on the betting ticket.

- "Odds" - The odds secured on the betting ticket.

- "Winnings" - If we win in the end, this is where we record the money we retrieve; if we lose, no need to fill this in.

- After recording, we can then compile statistics based on this data:

- "Total Amount" - This is the sum of all the amounts wagered.

- "Average Odds" - This is the average value of all the odds.

- "Total Winnings" - This is the sum of all the winnings.

- "Profit" - By subtracting the "Total Amount" from the "Total Winnings," we get the actual profit earned.

- "Return on Investment" - This is calculated as "Profit" divided by "Total Amount."

We recommend using Excel to implement this table. That way, whenever you all purchase a betting ticket, you can come here and record it. After some time, you'll have an idea of what your return on investment is— whether you're making or losing money. If you find that your return on investment exceeds 1%, then congratulations are in order. You've outperformed the majority in this game and can consider yourself a savvy player. However, if you find that your return on investment is negative, meaning you're losing money, there's no need to panic. This is completely normal. After all, the game relies on the majority of players losing money for it to function smoothly. You're just an average participant in this regard.

**Advice Three: Don't Place Bets Lightly**

There is a notion circulating online that actually advocates the opposite of this advice: it encourages people to place bets frequently, and ideally, to bet on every game. The rationale behind this is that the more you watch sports, the more money you will win over time. This idea is similar to the theory that watching more sports games will increase your chances of winning. Because frequent betting supposedly keeps you interested in watching games, the theory suggests that you must keep placing bets to increase your odds of guessing correctly, thereby making big money in the future.

We strongly disagree with this for three reasons:

- The relationship between frequently watching games and your odds of guessing correctly cannot be proven. And even if you have high odds of guessing correctly, it doesn't mean you'll have a high Return on Investment (ROI). So, watching more games does not equate to making more money.

- After placing a bet, you have to pay the bookmaker a juice, regardless of whether you win or lose. So, the more bets you place, the more juice you'll owe to the online sportsbook. If you're placing bets on every game, you're paying the juice every time. This can add up to a significant amount over time. Even if you win more by placing bets frequently, it's unlikely that these gains will offset the juice you've paid.

- The theory that you have to place bets regularly to keep watching games seems a bit backward. It suggests that sports betting is so lucrative that you must force yourself to watch more games to make easy money. This is flawed logic; there's no big money to be made in sports betting. If you're looking to force yourself to learn something, you're better off investing in stocks or funds, where the ROI is generally higher than sports betting. We believe that you're already interested in sports and watch games regularly, so there's no need to place bets just for the sake of betting.

Based on these points, we advise against placing bets frequently and impulsively. If you're not passionate about sports and can't watch games regularly, that's fine. There's no law saying you have to make money from sports betting. You have other investment options like stocks, funds, or real estate. Why insist on betting?

So, you shouldn't buy betting tickets casually. When it's absolutely necessary to buy one, you need to pay attention to the odds. We're familiar with the formula for player's return rate, which is directly impacted by the odds.

**Player's Return Rate = (Average Odds * Probability of Winning) - 1**

Improving your odds of winning is difficult, but you can easily adjust the odds. When you place a bet, simply opt for higher odds to effectively improve your return rate.

However, a question arises. Everyone talks about getting higher odds, but what exactly constitutes "higher odds"? For this, we have a method that can clarify this question for everyone: the Balanced AB Table.

Assume you've been buying betting tickets for some time now and have a pile of expired ones—some winners, some losers. This is the time to analyze whether you've been selecting tickets with sufficiently high odds. To do this, you first need to categorize your betting tickets based on their odds. If the odds on a ticket are higher than the average odds on the line, classify it as Category A. If the odds are lower than the average, place it in Category B.

For example, let's say we have a line.

|  | Odds |
|---|---|
| Team A | 1.70 |
| Team B | 1.90 |
| Average Odds | 1.80 |

The average odds would be (1.70 + 1.90) / 2 = 1.80. Therefore, if the odds on a betting ticket are greater than 1.80, it falls into Category A; if they're less than 1.80, it's Category B.

After categorizing, we can proceed to fill out the following table.

| Group A (Not following the crowd) | | | Group B (Following the crowd) | | |
|---|---|---|---|---|---|
| | | | | | |
| Total Bets | Winning Ticket Odds | | Total Bets | Winning Ticket Odds | |
| 5 | 2.2 | | 5 | 1.6 | |
| | 2.5 | | | 1.7 | |
| | | | | 1.75 | |
| | | | | | |
| | | | | | |
| | | | | | |
| Win Rate | Average Odds | | Win Rate | Average Odds | |
| 40.00% | 2.35 | | 60.00% | 1.68 | |
| | | | | | |
| Return Rate | -6.00% | | Return Rate | 0.8% | |

First, we count how many betting tickets each group has (regardless of win or loss) and then fill in the total bets column. In this example, our Group A has 5 betting tickets, and Group B also has 5.

Next, we pick out the winning tickets from all the bets and fill in the odds in the "Odds of Winning Tickets" column. In this example, Group A has 2 winning tickets with odds of 2.2 and 2.5. Group B has 3 winning tickets with odds of 1.6, 1.7, and 1.75.

With this basic data, we can now proceed with some statistics. There are three main metrics here:

1. Win Rate: This is the "Number of Winning Tickets" divided by the "Total Number of Bets". For instance, Group A has a total of 5 tickets, but only two of them are winners. So, the win rate is 2/5, which is 40%.

2. Average Odds: This is the average odds of all the winning tickets. For Group A, it's 2.35, and for Group B, it's 1.68.

3. Return on Investment (ROI): The formula here is (Win Rate * Average Odds) - 1.

In this case, Group A's ROI is (40% * 2.35) - 1 = -0.06, which translates to -6%. For Group B, it is (60% * 1.68) - 1 = 0.008, or 0.8%.

**Analysis of Betting Preferences Balance Sheet**

We have now completed the balance AB sheet, which is specifically designed to analyze betting preferences. From this chart, one can discern whether you like to bet with the crowd or not. In the A group of betting tickets, what you've bought is actually the team that is less favored by most, which is why the odds are higher than the average. Whereas, in the B group, you're betting on the teams that are popular, resulting in lower odds. From this example, it seems you do prefer to bet with the majority.

However, whether you like to bet with or against the majority isn't the main point. The crucial insight is that once we segregate the bets, we can offer two specific improvement suggestions:

Firstly, in Group A, when you're not betting with the majority, you're actually losing money with a return rate of -6%. In the future, if you wish to go against public sentiment, you should aim for even higher odds. Ideally, they should exceed 2.5, otherwise, you'd end up in losses.

Secondly, in Group B, when you're betting along with the crowd, you're making a profit with a return rate of 0.8%. You can continue with this approach, but it would be better to be selective about the odds, ideally looking for ones exceeding 1.68 to maximize your return rate.

Our previous advice about aiming for higher odds was based on this logic. By analyzing past betting ticket records, it becomes relatively easy to identify a benchmark. This can make future betting decisions much more straightforward.

However, the Balance AB sheet isn't only useful for analyzing betting preferences. With some modifications, it can also help analyze which teams you prefer to bet on.

## Analyzing the Balance Sheet of Preferred Teams

This time, we won't categorize based on the odds shown on the betting ticket. Instead, we will classify by teams. With this method, it becomes easier to discern which team we are more likely to win by betting on?

| Group A (Team A) | | | Group B (TeamB) | |
|---|---|---|---|---|
| Total Bets | Odds of Winning Tickets | | Total Bets | Odds of Winning Tickets |
| 5 | 1.92 | | 5 | 1.9 |
| | 1.73 | | | 1.6 |
| | 1.4 | | | 1.3 |
| | | | | |
| | | | | |
| | | | | |
| Winning Percentage | Average Odds | | Winning Percentage | Average Odds |
| 60.00% | 1.68 | | 60.00% | 1.60 |
| | | | | |
| ROI | 1.00% | | ROI | -4.00% |

In this example, it's evident that when betting on Team A, we are more confident, and the return rate can be 1%. However, for Team B, it's not feasible as it results in a loss. In the future, if you aim for a higher odds, then for Team A, please place your bet when the odds are 1.68 or higher. For you, odds of 1.68 and above are considered high. For Team B? The odds should be 1.68 or higher.

## Advice Four: There's No Teacher in Sports Betting

Every profession has teachers who teach you how to make money, but not in sports betting, and that's common sense. If a teacher always had the knack for guessing right, there wouldn't be a need to teach others how to buy betting tickets to make money. The odds in sports betting are high. They could just buy betting tickets and get rich without the hard work.

So, never be superstitious about the "renowned masters," especially those on the internet, claiming to have unparalleled insider tips. They are 100% fake. Remember, our website offers high odds. If that gentleman was so accurate, he should directly place a parlay of eight matches. One bet could turn his fortunes around. Why would he bother earning a living online?

Sports experts also shared the same sentiment with us. When predicting game outcomes, those who can guess seven out of ten matches correctly don't exist. And those who can guess six out of ten matches? There's only one among a hundred. Hence, most teachers are not reliable.

From this, we can deduce that joining paid memberships from these so-called experts in the future is pointless. Thus, everyone can save that money. However, if we only stated this, some would say we are being irresponsible.

Because we have generalized and dismissed all the teachers and experts. Among them, there might be individuals who are impartial and don't charge for their advice. On the other hand, players consult experts simply because they don't know how to choose. Now, if there are no experts, then how are players supposed to play the betting ticket? So, let's go back to our balanced AB chart. From now on, if people decide to place a bet based on the advice of experts, at least they'll know how accurate these experts truly are.

**Analyzing Expert Opinions with a Balanced Chart**

We all know that before placing a bet in sports gambling, everyone first checks the newspapers, listens to the experts' opinions, and then decides which team to bet on. Under such circumstances, we can analyze their past performances to determine whether or not to continue following their advice in the future.

| Group A (Orange Daily) | | | Group B (Banana Daily) | |
|---|---|---|---|---|
| Total Bets | Winning Odds | | Total Bets | Winning Odds |
| 5 | 1.9 | | 5 | 2.2 |
| | 1.7 | | | 1.9 |
| | 1.5 | | | |
| | | | | |
| | | | | |
| | | | | |
| Win Rate | Average Odds | | Win Rate | Average Odds |
| 60.00% | 1.70 | | 40.00% | 2.05 |
| | | | | |
| ROI | 2.00% | | ROI | -18.00% |

In the example above, the Orange Daily is clearly more accurate than the Banana Daily. However, the odds we selected were not good enough, resulting in a poor return rate. In the future, we can follow the Orange Daily's bets, but when buying, we should aim for odds above 1.70.

**Advice Five: Our Recommended Betting Strategy**

When recommending a betting strategy to everyone, we believe it must adhere to three main principles:

- The bookmaker should find it challenging to profit from this strategy. This implies that not only is the line difficult to control, but ideally, they should also frequently bet against the player.

- Players must be able to effectively apply their sports knowledge. It's not beneficial if you watch games frequently, yet it doesn't aid in making money.

- Ideally, this strategy should also offer some advantage to the player.

After filtering through these three principles, we have only one recommendation, which is "money line" combined with "live betting".

First, the money line, also known as the "win" or "Money Line", is the point spread line without any points given. Players only have to guess the outcome. It's a method where even with your eyes closed, there's a ½ chance of guessing correctly. This is because without the interference of giving points, your judgment tends to be more accurate.

Please note, some matches can end in a draw, such as soccer and baseball, and you should avoid these. We always need that ½ probability of guessing correctly. Sports like American basketball and baseball are ideal because they always play until a winner is determined.

Next, live betting, everyone agrees that the chances of guessing correctly in this method increases. Your passion for the match, your experience, and your courage can all be effectively reflected in this method. What's even better is that sometimes you can take advantage of the online sportsbook's mistakes, and if they make an error, your chances are even greater.

Live betting also gives us an opportunity to hedge our bets. If during the match you see the tide turning against your bet, you can quickly place another bet to avoid a total loss. This hedging method can be very helpful for long-term profits.

Furthermore, the "money line" and "live betting" are the bane of Asian sportsbook websites. Both betting types are notoriously hard to manage and profit from, often forcing the bookmaker to bet against players. So, combining these two betting methods maximizes our advantage. It's crucial to note that combining them means placing bets on the money line during live games.

Apart from this scenario, we don't recommend any other betting methods. Whether it's point spread, over/under, exact score, total goals, championship games or whatever, none are advisable. Especially the method we call "not profiting from the juice," is a big no-no. Engaging in it is like being on bad terms with your own money.

However, some might argue that the money line is hard to find in Asia, and that sports betting websites in Asia don't use this system extensively. Moreover, sports betting in Asia primarily revolves around the point spread. In our view, first and foremost, while it's true that the money line is harder to find, many websites still offer it because it's simpler. Furthermore, although Asian sports betting is predominantly about point spread, remember that not all games have a spread. When a point spread game doesn't offer any points, it essentially becomes a money line bet.

Additionally, let's mention the parlay strategy. We have discussed this strategy in a dedicated article before. Essentially, the return on investment for this strategy is quite poor. If you're betting on the same number of games, it's better to place individual bets on each game rather than combining them into a parlay. This will result in a much higher overall return on investment. The only suitable scenario for placing a parlay is if you didn't bring enough money. For instance, if you only have $100 left in your pocket but you really want to bet on two games, that's when you should consider a parlay. Remember, parlays are not a cost-effective strategy. If you place too many parlays, you're just making it hard for yourself to make any profit.

There's also a trend on online sportsbook where they offer parlays for bets that don't earn them any juice, such as combining a point spread bet with a total goals bet. The odds for such combinations can be shockingly high. However, we have to say, if you truly place such combined bets, the chances of you winning would be so low that you wouldn't believe it.

Lastly, we must emphasize that our recommendation of the money line combined with live betting is not because you can make money from it, but rather because we believe that if you can't win with this strategy, you stand even less chance with other strategies.

### Advice Six: Look to the methods of Wise guys.

In the Wise guy chapter, we detailed the arbitrage techniques of players. It's a highly effective mathematical approach and is the biggest gift this game offers to players. So after you've placed a bet, if you have some free time, pay attention to the changes in the line. If an opportunity for arbitrage arises, don't hesitate. Every dollar you make counts, and this method can help make up for losses and assist in long-term profitability. However, be wary of the rules, because online sportsbooks really despise arbitrage. Sometimes, they might stipulate that if you bet on both teams in a line, your winnings will be halved. This situation would be disadvantageous for you. But if there's no such rule, then go ahead without reservation.

### Advice Seven: Beware of the "Patriotic Line"

What is the "Patriotic Line"? When a team has a vast number of fans, or there's a particularly beloved star player in the lineup, bookmakers become especially cautious when setting the odds. To prevent one-sided betting by fans, they might lower the odds or increase the point spread. Such betting lines, crafted meticulously by bookmakers for the fans, are termed as the "Patriotic Line."

The "Patriotic Line" is a unique form of betting line, often found in sports events that involve national or cultural pride. This term is mostly used within Asian gambling culture. In these betting lines, the odds are intentionally biased towards the home team or the side that's backed by the majority of the nation, enticing more people to place their bets.

For instance, if there's a baseball match between Taiwan and China, betting sites in Taiwan might deliberately raise the odds for a Taiwanese victory, even if, based on actual skills and statistics, Taiwan might not be the most likely to win. This is done to draw Taiwanese people to bet out of national pride.

You can think of "patriotic line" as an "emotional trap". It's a strategy employed by betting sites to lure you in because of your strong feelings for your country or team, even if it might not be the wisest bet. Under such circumstances, the odds and payouts often don't accurately reflect the actual chances of winning. Instead, they reflect people's emotions and preferences. As a result, it's usually a profitable method for bookmakers since many people bet based on emotions rather than logic. Thus, if you want to stay calm and objective in gambling, it's best to steer clear of these patriotic lines.

For instance, consider a popular star team playing a match. This team is widely adored, so regardless of which team the star team is playing against, when the bookmaker sets the line, the star team might start by giving away a point or two. This doesn't mean the star team is objectively stronger than other teams. It's just that people are patriotic, and when buying betting tickets, they tend to support their own. Following the principle of "prevention is better than cure", bookmakers adjust the line and odds in advance to effectively balance the betting pool.

What does this teach us? It's best to avoid betting on teams that are too popular. The more popular a team is, the worse the odds are, making it harder for us to profit. If you truly want to make money, you need to do the opposite and stand on the other side. This is the so-called "If everyone agrees, we oppose, and if everyone opposes, we agree."

The patriotic line is one of the distinct features of sports betting. Regardless of whether a team is objectively easy to win, as long as it's a favorite, the odds are certainly low.

**Advice Eight: It's challenging to pinpoint the right moment to bet at betting sites.**

This is to advise everyone to avoid purchasing betting tickets at betting sites and instead opt for online or mobile betting. There are three main reasons for this:

- We all know that online sportsbooks adjust odds and point spreads frequently to balance the line. At times, these adjustments can happen every few seconds. Such rapid changes present an excellent opportunity for us to capitalize on favorable odds. However, due to the instantaneous nature of these adjustments, only online betting can truly capture these ideal moments.

- As previously mentioned, players who bet online are considered "direct customers" of the online sportsbook. In the world of sports betting, there's a global trend where online sportsbooks prioritize and reward their direct customers. So, once you become a direct customer, there might be special promotions or benefits waiting for you.

- If you're accustomed to purchasing your bets at physical betting sites, you might be tempted to buy a ticket whenever you pass by. However, the chances are slim that you'll always encounter high odds during such impromptu visits. Over time, this means your average odds will be lower, leading to poorer returns on your bets.

If online betting is not an option for you, at the very least, check the lines at the betting site first. Don't rush to buy a ticket from the proprietor the moment you arrive

**Advice Nine: Try to avoid betting on outcomes with a probability of less than 1/2.**

In the article "No Profits from Juice", we've repeatedly discussed that these lower probability bets are not financially viable in terms of overall return. However, it's essential to emphasize this again.

In this game, bets with lower chances of winning tend to offer high odds. And human nature is such that we can't resist the lure of these high odds. Thus, when people see the potential payouts, they're often tempted to try their luck.

So, we'd like to remind you once more: if you genuinely feel very lucky today and believe that your bet will surely win, then we think you should channel that luck where the returns are genuinely higher. Consider betting on number lotteries or Power Lottery tickets. If you're really feeling lucky, those are the more appropriate venues for such bets.

## Advice Ten: Average Betting

Sports betting is not a get-rich-quick game, and it's fundamentally designed to cost you money. Hence, it's advisable to spread your bets evenly. This concept is akin to the diversified investment commonly seen in the stock market. Suppose you have a thousand dollars. Instead of placing a single bet of a thousand dollars on one game, it would be better to bet a hundred dollars on ten different games. There are two advantages to this approach:

Firstly, when betting on just one game, luck plays a significant role. How will a player perform on the day? Will there be unexpected mistakes? Such unpredictable factors, heavily dependent on luck, can significantly impact the game's outcome. If we aim for long-term profits, we must try to minimize the influence of these unpredictable elements.

Secondly, the more games you bet on, the closer the outcomes will align with statistical predictions and expert forecasts. A strong team won't always make mistakes, and a weaker team won't consistently outperform a stronger one. Thus, the more bets we place, the higher the probability that our predictions will be accurate.

We strongly support the concept of average betting. This is because it doesn't conflict with any of the rules within sports betting. However, it's important to note that "average betting" means you have already set aside a specific amount of money each month for betting. You simply distribute this sum over multiple bets instead of using it all at once. Please do not confuse this with frequently buying betting tickets.

Furthermore, we would like to mention the rumors or gossips that often circulate before a match. Some claim that these tidbits can help people win money. We won't comment on the accuracy of these sources. Even if we advised everyone to ignore such rumors, it would likely be difficult to follow.

But if you decide to place bets based on gossip, remember to utilize average betting. This way, you can effectively mitigate risks and not jeopardize your entire savings due to blind faith in rumors. Naturally, if the rumors often prove to be incorrect, one would likely stop following them, further reducing risk.

In sports betting, there are numerous rules. However, no one says you must rigidly adhere to them. Some of these restrictions can be broken, while others can be avoided. We've discussed many of them already, and you've seen how other players navigate them.

So, while enjoying sports matches, consider challenging these rules. Creativity can be applied to sports betting just as effectively as in other areas.

**Overcompensation**

On the internet, there are often concepts shared with players. These concepts aren't necessarily wrong, but they often come with subtle hints. This is an ancient practice, implying that some secrets shouldn't be revealed. These ideas can't be stated too directly and can't be explained entirely.

This ambiguity is quite intriguing. Regardless of whether these hints are right or wrong, because they are merely hints, we can neither agree nor disagree, leaving us without a clear opinion. Yet, we can't help but point out the issues for the players.

Let's just translate it for them, explaining the concepts thoroughly. By doing so, we can turn the deer into a horse, overcompensating in our corrections. Firstly,

They say, "Isn't this a game where you can't get rich overnight?"

Regarding the notion that one cannot get rich overnight through sports betting, many people are already aware. After seeing the formula for player's return on investment, one can essentially understand that

**Player's return = Principal * Odds.**

The amount of capital you have determines how much money you can win. And there's a limit to how high the odds in sports betting can be. So, given that everyone has limited capital, it's tough to win big. Moreover, the higher the odds, the lower your chances of guessing correctly. This means if people spend a lot of money chasing high odds, hoping to get rich overnight, there's a high chance they could lose everything.

However, if you flip the approach and aim to increase your chances of guessing correctly to secure safer profits, you're essentially minimizing risk. Then, the odds you can choose won't be high, probably not exceeding 3.00. So, you can't win big, and naturally, you can't get rich overnight.

Undoubtedly, the above concept is very accurate and widely circulated online. But we must point out that this concept carries a suggestion. It hints that while you might not become wealthy overnight, there's a possibility of amassing wealth over time.

We often mention the idea of "getting rich overnight". Let's delve into this phrase. "Getting rich overnight" refers to becoming wealthy in just one evening. As many would attest, this is an unattainable dream. So, we take a step back and ask, "What about getting rich over multiple nights?" With many nights at your disposal, is it possible to gradually amass wealth?

This question receives far less attention. Once people hear that getting rich overnight is improbable, they seem to accept it without further thought, which puzzles us. Another vital question is whether it's feasible for individuals to accumulate wealth bit by bit over time.

If no one else is addressing this, let us be the ones to say it: "Getting rich overnight is impossible." The emphasis of this statement isn't on the "overnight" part, but on "getting rich". In essence, sports betting isn't a game that lets players earn money. Whether it's one night or several, the outcome remains the same.

We have two main pieces of evidence to support this:

1. There are many individuals who make their living through sports betting. As mentioned earlier, there are online sportsbooks, agents, Wise guys, and even our previously discussed friends from Hong Kong who primarily profit from the juice. The way they earn money is genuine and sincere. Their goal isn't to get rich overnight but to accumulate wealth over time. The crux here is that the money they earn comes directly from the players. Thus, while they are amassing wealth, it means the majority of players aren't.

2. Based on the total payout principle, if an online sportsbook receives $100 in bets, they pay out at most $80 to the players. For players, this is a losing proposition. So how can they possibly get rich?

Not bad. As we've discussed, the "juice" or vigorish is dynamically adjusted. You won't always be charged such a high vigorish every time, but the longer you play and the more types of bets you place, the closer the vigorish you'll be charged will approach this number.

Time is not on the player's side. And the more a player follows the rules, the less likely they are to break this limitation. So, while "getting rich overnight" is certainly impossible, "getting rich over many nights" is also out of reach. Players will not only fail to become wealthy but will undoubtedly lose money.

In summary, if someone is emphasizing that you can't get rich overnight, they are often subtly suggesting you gamble regularly to achieve wealth, which we disagree with, as there's no evidence that you can win money this way.

They ask, "Isn't a 50% win rate good enough?"

This is a fundamental concept in sports betting. Because the online sportsbook takes a cut or "juice," if everyone's betting tickets only have a 50% win rate, they'll still lose money.

Let's do some calculations using the player's return on investment (ROI) formula:

Player's ROI = (Average Odds * Probability of Correct Prediction) - 1

Assuming that everyone gets very high odds, say an aspirational 1.97:

**1.5% = (1.97 * 0.5) - 1**

But we calculated a return on investment (ROI) of a negative 1.5%, meaning for every $1,000 wagered, there's a loss of $15. And this is under the intimidating situation where the average odds are high.

Thus, the notion that a 50% win rate in sports betting isn't enough is entirely accurate. Every seasoned player emphasizes this concept when guiding new players. However, there's a hidden implication here: if everyone just improves their win rate, can they all profit?

## We Argue That the "Win Rate Doesn't Matter at All."

When beginners start in sports betting, every expert will advise you to increase your win rate, that is, to enhance your prediction accuracy. According to the ROI formula, you must improve; otherwise, losses are inevitable. Not only do they say this, but earlier sections of this book also mentioned the same.

But the above reasoning is for beginners. If you've read up to this point, you now understand the rules of how online sportsbooks operate, so we consider you an advanced player. Since you're advanced, there's no point in hiding the truth from you. Let's be straightforward: urging everyone to improve their win rate is meaningless.

First, the "majority" cannot improve their "win rate".

Second, even if the "majority" truly improves their "win rate", it doesn't help the Return on Investment (ROI).

Let's discuss the second point first. The logic here is simple. If the "majority" truly enhances their "win rate", then most players win money, and a small portion lose. We also know that online sportsbooks always use the money from losers to pay the winners, so they always aim for balanced betting lines to profit from the juice.

Therefore, adding one and one together, if everyone is winning and the betting lines are balanced, there can only be one conclusion: the odds offered would be extremely low. This is because, at this time, a small number of players are paying the winnings for the majority. We can imagine that the amount each winner would receive would be pitifully small. In other words, the odds would be very low.

However, the formula for ROI has two main factors affecting it: the probability of guessing correctly and the odds. So, while the majority might have increased their win rate, it affects their odds. In the end, your ROI remains the same. Thus, we believe that even if the "majority" could genuinely improve their "win rate", it would not benefit the ROI.

Going back to the first point, this is even simpler. Think about it: is it possible for a small portion of players always to be paying the winnings for the majority? This absolutely cannot happen. Who would want to run a losing business? If such a situation existed, the small portion of players would quickly deplete. And if these small portion players were all gone, who would foot the bill?

Fundamentally, sports betting is not inherently a game where everyone can win. It's impossible for everyone to increase their odds of winning. But some will argue that the increase in odds can be individualized. Doesn't this mean that a small portion of players, by diligently watching matches and conducting statistics, can eventually outperform the majority and make money? Doesn't this kind of odds increase have significance?

Indeed, if we narrow the scope and allow only a segment of people to watch the games and research the sporting events, then this advice would be helpful. However, there's an issue here. Do people just randomly buy betting tickets? Most, if not all, will watch some games and do some homework. At the very least, they might listen to the recommendations of those who have done their homework or seek the opinions of renowned sports experts in newspapers and magazines.

So, if you aim to be the minority that outperforms the majority, you are essentially trying to outdo all the experts. While it sounds easy to say, doing it is virtually an impossible task. These seasoned sports experts are authoritative figures that we deeply respect. They have exhaustive statistical information, access to real-time news, and extensive experience in watching games.

Here's the crux: unless you also pursue a decade or more as a sports journalist or broadcaster, there's no reason to believe you can surpass them, let alone defeat them. Unless, of course, you have some unique insider information. Even if you did, the average person wouldn't be able to access or learn from it. So, advising you to watch games and compile statistics still holds little merit because, even if you could improve your odds, you couldn't outperform the majority.

It's like someone telling you how to win the world championship in a 100-meter sprint, "As long as you can run 100 meters in under seven seconds, you're guaranteed to become the world champion." Tell me, does anyone give advice like that?

They suggest increasing your winning rate, which also implies encouraging you to bet frequently. Because if people don't bet regularly, how can they increase their winning rate? So we believe there's an issue with this perspective.

In fact, we think that instead of increasing the winning rate, it's better to enhance the odds. In the return on investment formula, odds are just as important as the winning rate. However, the cost of improving odds is much lower than that of increasing the winning rate. The logic behind this is straightforward. There are mainly two ways to improve the odds:

First, carefully select the odds. If the odds aren't favorable, it's better not to place a bet.

Second, try to reduce the juice of the online sportsbook. As long as the juice is low, the odds are high.

From the very beginning, we can see that to increase the odds, you will reduce your bets. Consequently, fewer betting tickets will be purchased. This is the exact opposite of trying to increase the win rate. So, looking at the juice from the online sportsbook, the commission you pay now is reduced. Isn't that a decrease in costs? On the other hand, choosing better odds doesn't require any technical skills, research, or homework. Unlike the immense effort required to increase the win rate, raising the odds is much easier.

Similarly, both odds and win rates are constrained by the factor of "everyone." If "everyone" can't achieve a high win rate, naturally, "everyone" also can't get high odds. However, it doesn't matter. When you can't get the odds, you simply won't place a bet, ensuring no losses. But if you can't achieve the desired win rate, you're in trouble because you've already bought the betting ticket. And to raise the win rate, you often have to bet.

They want you to increase your win rate so you'll buy more betting tickets. We advise you to increase the odds so you'll buy fewer betting tickets. This is the biggest difference. As for who's right and who's wrong, I'll leave that for you to decide.

They ask, "Is the juice from online sportsbooks always mandatory?"

When beginners start, everyone teaches that sports betting is a game where the online sportsbook takes a cut, and they take it from the winners. So, if the sportsbook is certain to make money, then if you can win, paying a bit of juice is expected.

After all, everyone knows about the sportsbook's cut, and they still play. This indicates fairness. Hence, you come to accept the idea that the sportsbook's cut is akin to a tax. And you continue to play your betting tickets, focusing on studying the sports matches, hoping to increase your win rate and make money.

We argue, "In sports betting, it might not necessarily be the case."

But since you've advanced, we can talk about it. First off, in this game, every sharp player

makes a big fuss about the juice. No one listens to what the online sportsbook decrees. The reason is simple: the impact of the juice on your rate of return is much more significant than you might think.

We've mentioned that the 5% juice is a significant threshold in this industry. Nearly every online sportsbook starts their discussions from this point. So, let's see how much impact there would be if this juice is raised by one percentage point or reduced by the same amount. Suppose a website charges a 5% juice, and we assume that you have a hit rate of about 55%. Thus, your return on investment would be (1.90 * 55%) -1 = 4.5%. This means if you bet $1000, you can earn $45.

However, if the website claims that due to a downturn in the economy, they need to charge an additional 1% juice. Your return on investment would then become (1.88 * 55%) -1 = 3.4%. Now, if you bet $1000, you can only earn $34.

So, what does the difference in these two return rates tell you? In this example, an increase in the website's juice by 1% results in a 24% decrease in your return on investment. Think about it; when we invest in stocks, we stress so much over a surge or plunge of merely 7%. Yet, just a 1% adjustment in the website's juice leads you to lose more than three times that amount. Hence, there's no denying that the topic of juice is one of great contention.

In sports betting, the juice is actually dynamic. It varies depending on the particular game. For instance, the juice for American basketball might not be the same as that for American baseball. Even within American basketball, the juice can differ between more popular and less popular games.

We can also say that for online sportsbooks, each betting line for a game is like an individual product. Some games are popular, attracting many bets, while others aren't as favored. So, just like other businesses, sportsbooks must also run promotional campaigns or create buzz to stimulate sales. One of the best promotional strategies is to lower prices. In this context, the sportsbooks intentionally reduce the juice they take for certain games, encouraging more people to place bets.

Apart from the games, every agent and player also has a ranking. Players with strong skills pay less in juice, while those less skilled pay more. We've detailed this further in the section on agents.

Therefore, the amount of juice is negotiable and can be fought for. Given its significant impact, you should also negotiate and fight for a better rate. Otherwise, even if you work hard to increase your winning rate, a slight adjustment in the juice can still lead to losses. Strangely, very few discuss this, which is perplexing to us.

Some might ask, is it easy to negotiate with these online sportsbooks? If you're asking this, you're hitting the nail on the head. Naturally, sportsbooks won't negotiate with every individual. With so many sports betting players out there, it's impractical to negotiate with each one. Besides, what's there to discuss with a minor player? Your impact on the sportsbook's profits is minimal at best.

However, there are many ways to negotiate. So, at the beginning of our advisory section, we teach you how to spot the juice. First, you need to be able to see it, and once you notice that the juice is set too high, then you shouldn't play. Simply choose the ones with lower juice to play. This way, not only will it be easier to select higher odds, but it will also greatly enhance your returns. Using the previous example, by just reducing the juice by one percentage point, your profits can increase by 20%. This is what we refer to as "negotiating."

Moreover, from the beginning of this book until now, we've introduced many roles in sports betting, such as agents, representatives, Wise guys, etc. Each has their own way of making money, but they all have one thing in common: they're trying to "steal" the juice from the online sportsbook. So, from a certain perspective, this can be seen as a global trend.

Therefore, you should strive to prevent your own juice from being set too high. Remember, the juice taken by the online sportsbook is never a fixed value.

# Other Characters

In this extensive section, we're going to introduce the two most crucial roles within the online sportsbook: the Traders and the computer system they use, the Betting Transaction System. When these two pivotal roles work flawlessly together, they form the online sportsbook that players have a love-hate relationship with

## Traders

In the "Online Sportsbook Section," we've discussed that online sportsbooks need to balance the betting lines for every match. Only when the lines are balanced can the sportsbook earn the most juice. Hence, it's conceivable that there's a team within every sportsbook specifically responsible for balancing these lines and safeguarding the website's interests.

The official title for these individuals is "Risk Traders." Every sportsbook establishes positions for this role. In industry jargon, they are also referred to as "Line Controllers," essentially the hands that control the betting lines. They determine the fate of the sportsbook, which is why in this article, we are going to delve into this mysterious yet pivotal role.

By definition, Risk Traders are those in charge of managing the sportsbook's risks. For simplicity, let's just refer to them as "Traders" from now on.

First and foremost, we need to understand that "Traders" is not just one person but a team. Smaller websites might have five to six, while larger ones could have dozens. This is because the offerings of the sportsbook span globally, encompassing Japanese games (Japanese Professional Baseball and Football), American games (NBA, NFL, MLB), and European games (European soccer), along with local matches from various regions.

To accommodate this international business, online sportsbooks must operate 24 hours a day. In the morning, they feature American professional baseball and basketball. In the evening, it's Asia's turn with Japanese and Korean baseball and soccer. Late at night, European soccer takes the stage. There's also a limit to the number of betting lines each trader can handle, which typically ranges from five to ten games. However, this can be adjusted based on various factors, such as the popularity of the match or if it's being played live. This is why online sportsbooks require so many traders.

## Job Posting

What are the requirements to be a trader? Let's refer to some job recruitment conditions on the internet:

"Proficient in English, knowledgeable about sports events and interested in them. Core job responsibilities are stressful, requiring high stress tolerance, and flexibility to work in shifts or flexible hours."

Job Responsibilities:

- Assess, monitor, and analyze odds for different sports betting lines.

- Set odds for various events.

- Evaluate and analyze bets for different events, and suggest future pricing (odds) strategies.

- Must be available to work in shifts.

Let's elaborate on this. Firstly, having an interest in sports matches is fundamental. Traders must be well-acquainted with games and teams. They would often read newspapers and websites, absorbing related information. This way, they would generally have an idea about the strengths and weaknesses, victories, and defeats of various teams. Moreover, they need to know which team is popular? Which has a large fanbase? And which one is always at the bottom with very few fans? Additionally, this job also requires watching sports news and televised broadcasts during work hours. So, not liking sports is definitely a no-go.

However, personal preferences for a particular sport or country don't matter much. Whether you like basketball, baseball, or soccer, and regardless if you specialize in watching games from the US, Europe, Japan, or China. The bookmaker can arrange it, and mostly they'll assign the sports events based on the trader's own preferences. For instance, if you're fond of the American NBA professional basketball, you would be primarily responsible for the NBA betting lines.

Next, we delve into the job description. This role demands a strong sense of statistics and numeracy. Essentially, every trader's daily tasks are executed by computers. Once the betting line is set, their computer screens display real-time updates such as how many betting tickets have been accepted, the total revenue, the projected payout for both teams, and the odds offered by other online sportsbooks. All of this is presented in a sea of numbers.

Based on these numbers, the trader draws from their experience and past statistical data to make swift judgments. How should they adjust the odds and point spreads? What magnitude of adjustment is needed? How quickly can they influence players to balance out the betting line? Once decided, they need to promptly configure the computer to make the necessary adjustments to the betting line. Hence, without a solid grasp of numbers, this job would be incredibly challenging.

Then there's the issue of "English". The majority of online sportsbooks, both aboveboard and underground, are in fact international entities. Their members hail from around the globe, possibly from countries like the USA, China, Europe, Hong Kong, Singapore, and even Malaysia. While this might be hard for the average person to fathom, it's the reality.

I believe this global mix stems from the unique nature of the sports betting industry. It's not easy for just anyone to break into this field. Consequently, the number of professionals each country can groom is limited. Therefore, for an online sportsbook to grow and thrive in this industry, it needs to harness talents from all corners of the world.

This requirement is not exclusive to traders. Other roles within the website, such as customer service and IT personnel, also need to possess this quality. Additionally, in the chapter "Laying Off Bets on Websites," we discussed that every website must connect with websites from other countries to "lay off" or essentially buy insurance, so the international language "English" becomes a basic mode of communication.

Furthermore, English has a unique purpose for traders. We all know that before players place a bet, they would look into related pre-match reports, analysis forecasts, and other news. The savvy players would constantly be on the lookout, keeping up with any potential changes leading up to the match. For instance, are there last-minute changes to the starting lineup? Has a key player gotten injured during practice? Even accidents or injuries need to be monitored.

These factors might significantly influence the match's outcome. If players can grasp this information a step ahead, they would have more confidence when placing bets. Naturally, traders would be concerned about this news, and in fact, they might be even more so. This is because if any explosive news regarding a team emerges, players will place their bets in large volumes. The betting line would then lean heavily in one direction, making line control exceedingly difficult.

So, in line with the principle of "prevention is better than cure", traders need to access the information in advance. By doing so, they can make early preparations on odds and point spreads. This helps prevent the betting line from tilting too drastically in one direction, which could lead to difficult adjustments.

To obtain information ahead of time, websites often purchase real-time news information at a high cost. This information is provided by professional sports news companies from abroad. The content is mostly in English, offering timeliness and expertise that general news media can't match. Moreover, it's quite concise; it might be just a headline, such as "Starting pitcher of a certain team injured during pre-game practice today." Upon receiving this news, the traders must immediately react to it.

Lastly, resilience under pressure is vital for traders. The primary pressure on traders comes from their profitability. Realistically speaking, training a trader is challenging, but if a seasoned trader constantly incurs losses, no website would tolerate that. In this industry, evaluating a trader's performance is relatively straightforward. By simply checking the computer reports, one can instantly determine whether they made a profit or loss for the day, if they were able to balance every betting line, or if they consistently placed the website in direct bets against players. This industry isn't about long-term investment. The performance of a trader is immediately evident. Therefore, every trader must meticulously control the odds and point spreads to ensure maximum profits for the website.

But controlling the lines, while sounding simple, is incredibly challenging in practice. Once the odds are set, players begin placing their bets freely. And during this process, various unexpected news events can influence the situation, especially during the last hour before accepting bets is stopped. At this time, betting tickets flood in. If a trader cannot identify trends and take action within seconds, the balance can be lost, leading to potentially significant losses for the online sportsbook.

Moreover, traders can make mistakes, and the pressure from such errors is immense. Let's talk about a simple example. Say while setting up a game's information, a team name "Team A" was mistakenly typed as "Team X". This creates a problem. When it's time to pay out the winnings after the match, players will have complaints.

Firstly, players who lost their bet will request a refund, wanting their initial bet returned. Their reason is simple: there isn't a "Team X". So, on what grounds can it be claimed they lost their bet on a match that never existed? Hence, the sportsbook has to cancel these players' bets and return their money.

However, for players who won their bets, they won't be so understanding. The mistake was clearly made by the online sportsbook, and it's unreasonable for players to bear the responsibility for this error. Therefore, the sportsbook still has to pay out their winnings. This is what we call "a costly typo". A simple mistake can lead to substantial losses. The sportsbook can't use the money from losing bets to pay the winners, so they have to dig into their pockets and accept the loss.

That's an explanation of the job conditions. However, we also need to look at it from the website's perspective. If a website hires an incompetent trader, the consequences can be disastrous. For example, in a match, if the trader misjudges the situation and ends up accepting $10 million on one side and only $1 million on the other at the last moment, the website might lose several million dollars in that game. Given the huge risks the website is taking, it's not hard to understand the strict demands they place on traders.

## Junk Games

We've mentioned before that a sportsbook might offer hundreds of games for players to bet on in a single day. With so many games available, it's necessary to employ a large number of staff to manage the betting lines. But if you think about it, you might wonder, are there really that many games to bet on?

Let's explain. Essentially, a sportsbook is like a business, and the betting lines are their products. As any business would, they prefer to offer as many products as possible. So, apart from major leagues like American basketball and Japanese baseball, sportsbooks also want to provide betting options for smaller leagues to increase their profits.

These minor league games are colloquially referred to as "junk games." In our opinion, this term is quite apt. Junk games are typically matches that most people aren't familiar with; many might have never even heard of them. Given that, the actual number of players who would place bets on these games is likely limited.

However, don't underestimate the significance of these "junk games." They play a crucial role. One of the main features of junk games is their ability to fill up the sportsbook's offerings. A well-operated online sportsbook could offer several hundred matches a day, creating an impressive array that could leave you dazzled. There's an old saying, "there's beauty in numbers." Some players are particularly drawn to this abundance.

With such a grand setting, whether it's on the website or at the betting sites viewing the lines, the website feels prestigious and utterly professional. Therefore, players are more inclined to place bets. Moreover, major matches don't occur throughout the year. There are times within a year when there are breaks without any games. During these periods, "junk matches" carry the responsibility of generating profit and provide those eager players an opportunity to place a bet.

However, the existence of these "junk matches" also signifies something: traders often have to handle matches they've never even heard of. But this isn't a major issue. The operation principle of online sportsbook lines is primarily based on mathematical statistics. It doesn't matter if it's an obscure match or even if what's being bet on isn't a sport; it's all feasible. So, being a trader, while sports knowledge is crucial, understanding mathematical principles is even more essential.

A good online sportsbook can offer lines for any match, be it a televised NBA game or a basketball match at the park near your house. For these websites, all matches are the same. As long as someone wishes to bet, the website has a way to earn juice. And these are the tasks that traders have to accomplish.


**Trading Room**
The risk control traders are the soul of a sportsbook website. Their workspace, commonly referred to as the "trading room", is also colloquially

known as the "line room" in places like Hong Kong and Macau. A distinctive feature of these trading rooms is the abundance of

televisions and computers. TVs are used to broadcast news and various major sports events. If you're a sports enthusiast, this place is a paradise. Countless televisions display sports events and news from around the world, with some even featuring huge screens broadcasting live games.

However, the other side of this environment might not be as pleasant. The multitude of computers symbolizes endless work. Speaking of the workload of a trader, the computer setup typically consists of at least four large monitors and two computer systems. Note that this is the setup for just one individual. Some might have even more, with a few opting for an entire wall of TVs.

Within a trader's screens, you'll find real-time bet intake, up-to-the-minute sports news, odds from other websites (used for arbitrage, as discussed in the section on online sportsbooks), and various professional sports discussion platforms. From this, we can gauge the vast amount of information a trader has to simultaneously process in order to effectively manage the "line".

## Sales Department

From the above description, we can see that a trader's job is closely tied to numbers, and it might seem not very interesting. However, this impression is not entirely accurate because there's another vital role in this department, the "Sales Department."

The "line" is the product of the online sportsbook. Since the price and product sales are inherently linked, these traders, who control the price, naturally have to take on the responsibility of sales. They might raise the odds or lower the juice to stimulate sales. While we often discuss risk management, one might think that online sportsbooks aren't willing to take any risks?

In reality, these websites don't aim for zero risk. If they were entirely risk-averse, their offerings wouldn't be very appealing. Therefore, each trader is given a certain amount of authority. They set aside risk concerns initially, focusing solely on boosting sales. They might offer high odds, generous handicaps, and deep discounts on specific teams to generate buzz. Once the sales targets are met, they then aim to stabilize the situation and regain control over the risks.

We can use stocks as an analogy for this situation. When everyone sees a stock that fluctuates significantly every day, either hitting the upper or lower limit, such a stock easily piques interest. But if a stock's price remains consistent, and the price three months ago is almost the same as three months later, it won't grab as much attention; people might just give it a cursory glance. This is the same principle traders use to stimulate sales. They can set odds with stark contrasts, and drastically change these odds in a short time frame, creating the effect of dramatic price changes. This naturally makes it more intriguing for everyone.

Additionally, just like salespeople in every industry, traders also need to "know" their customers. But don't get it wrong; they don't know you personally. On the online sportsbook, players are just computer codes. They don't even know your names or whether you're male or female. However, when it comes to your betting habits? Favorite teams? How much you win or lose? These minute details, which you might not even remember, are well-known to them. As a result, they can use this information to entice everyone to place bets. And if players lose too much, they have to find opportunities to offer some form of compensation. Otherwise, if players lose a lot and stop playing, then the traders will be out of a job.

## VIP

Traders also keep an eye on so-called "VIP" players. First and foremost, the term VIP isn't a compliment on these betting sites. When a VIP logs onto the website and checks out the lines in preparation to place a bet, there's usually a trader watching closely.

Of course, you would never realize this. When you're browsing the site, you might assume you're the only one viewing the odds. However, the site's computer system will report every move you make to the traders in the control room, keeping them updated in real time. They will know which teams you're watching, which bets you're considering, how much money you've won recently, and your win rate.

Yes, there are countless players, and no shortage of VIPs. It's not feasible for websites to monitor every single VIP given the manpower required. But it's safe to say, if a player consistently predicts outcomes accurately, has a high win rate, and likes to place substantial bets, then such a VIP will always have traders paying attention to their every move. You might wonder, what exactly do these traders want to achieve by monitoring VIPs so closely?

Of course, the aim is to prevent. VIP players who place accurate and substantial bets can lead to other players losing money. Or to put it another way, if this fellow constantly places large bets, he at least poses a challenge in maintaining a balanced betting line. Therefore, a trader would first review past betting records to determine his preferences and habits. Then, considering the teams and betting methods the VIP is currently interested in, they anticipate which team he might bet on and how much he might wager. To forestall any potential issues, they adjust the odds in advance of his bet to reduce his interest. Even if they can't deter him entirely, a proper reduction in the odds ensures that the betting line won't be too imbalanced. This makes it easier for the trader to restore balance later on.

This practice is common across all online sportsbook sites. Thus, many seasoned players complain that the odds they want are visible but unattainable when they place bets. Everyone should be assured about this point: this gentleman might have been targeted, and the trader might have altered the odds even before he decided to bet, leading to this situation.

However, the average person shouldn't be overly concerned about this, as reaching the level of a "betting god" is challenging for most. Yet, in the sports betting industry, such "betting gods" genuinely exist and can influence the betting line just by "watching". As legend has it, some can make the odds jump with just a glance.

This is a bit exaggerated, but it's not entirely baseless. For these types of players, traders often regard them with a mix of respect and fear. Typically, once they see such players placing their bets, traders will rush to "lay off" those bets, spreading the risk to other online sportsbooks. However, while some of these "betting gods" might be genuine, the majority are likely cheats. Later on, when we delve into the betting transaction system, we'll discuss this in greater detail. It's worth noting here that apart from their regular duties, traders also have to collaborate closely with the IT department, constantly verifying certain players to determine whether they truly have a "divine foresight" in their predictions.

## A Day's Work

Being a trader is never a nine-to-five job. Instead of detailing a typical day at work for them, it's better to describe the tasks they handle. But first, let's address a common misconception.

Many people assume that 24 hours before the start of a game, traders begin their work, opening the betting lines for wagering, and continue until the lines close. In reality, it's the exact opposite. Opening the betting lines is the last task traders do before clocking out. Once the lines are open, they are taken over by computers.

The reason for this is straightforward. Players tend to place their bets in the few hours leading up to a game. Very few start wagering as soon as the lines open. Typically, the highest volume of bets comes in about an hour before the game starts. If you're betting on local football, baseball, or basketball, this usually happens in the evening, after most people have finished work. If it's American baseball or basketball, it's in the morning, before the typical workday begins. And if it's European football, it's deep into the night, when most are asleep.

This is easy to understand. Most local matches are scheduled in the evening when people are off work or during weekends when people are seeking entertainment and leisure. This ensures that there's an audience for the game. Therefore, evenings and weekends are the most popular times for local players to place bets. However, for foreign matches, due to time zone differences, the game might start during the daytime or early morning local time. That's when local players would usually place their bets.

When the odds are first set, there are no players betting yet, so there's no need for the traders to closely monitor. They can even go home and rest. By the time they return to work, it's usually 2 or 3 hours before the start of the match, and players' betting activities gradually pick up. That's when the traders take over the management of the betting lines and start the crucial task of balancing the lines.

This management continues up until shortly before the match starts. At this point, they close the betting, settle the accounts, and begin the process of "arbitrage," spreading the risk. If the match is being broadcast live, they might also need to offer in-play betting, continuing their work until the match is nearly over.

Once the match concludes, they input the results, and the computer starts to settle all the betting tickets, calculating the wins and losses for each player. As mentioned before, the website can roughly calculate how much they've earned once they stop accepting bets after closing the lines. However, the actual wins and losses for each player can only be determined after the match ends.

When the betting lines close, traders then know how they performed that day. Following the schedule, they set the lines for the next day's games. Once the lines are posted, they can pack up and head home.

That concludes the discussion about risk management traders. Essentially, everything they do is to control the risk for the online sportsbook. I can't tell you what makes a good trader, because the job relies heavily on intuition. Especially when it comes to stimulating betting sales, it goes beyond mathematics and enters the realm of art.

This is also the main reason why computer systems can never fully take over the role. Another thing to note is that those in this position usually have to sign a confidentiality agreement. But this contract is not what most people think. The agreement stipulates that you cannot disclose to anyone that you work as a risk management trader. This is mainly for safety reasons. If someone finds out you're in this role, it might invite trouble.

## Betting Transaction System

The computer system used by online sportsbooks, commonly referred to as the "Betting Transaction Management System", plays a pivotal role in the sports betting industry. It could be said that what most people envision as a website is indeed this computer system. Moreover, the efficiency of this system has a direct impact on the profitability of each online sportsbook.

It might be hard for the average person to fathom the immense power of this computer system. However, it's true. We've witnessed how a sportsbook can experience meteoric growth and success merely by switching to a new computer system. Conversely, we've also observed sportsbooks that had to exit the business due to repeated system glitches.

The high level of immediacy inherent in this industry requires us to encode all game rules, business models, and profit control mechanisms into the computer. Only by doing so can we ensure the smooth day-to-day operation of the online sportsbook. Hence, when a sportsbook updates its computer system, it signifies that they're experimenting with new operational models, new rules, and novel management methods. The significance of such a computer system goes beyond what most people typically encounter.

Building such a system is challenging, and the knowledge involved could fill several books. If you're interested, we could delve into this topic in the future, teaching you how to design a betting transaction system – it's quite an intriguing subject.

However, I believe that most people are likely to be curious about only two topics:

First, how exactly does the website's software monitor players?

Second, can we hack into the website's computer system?

So, let's primarily discuss the above two points. But first, let's provide an overview of the website's computer system.

Most of the software systems used by websites are self-designed; few opt to purchase off-the-shelf software from the market. This is because each website has its unique perspective when handling business, making it challenging to have unified rules. Using someone else's packaged software feels like trying to fit a square peg into a round hole, making the business feel restricted. The system is also of paramount importance. Whether a system is well-designed directly influences if a website can make money. Relying on generic packaged software would make profiting very challenging.

Thus, the systems each website uses vary widely, and we don't have a universal standard to discuss. We can only approach this from a general perspective and see the common features of these software systems.

Let's look at the five main functions of the system: event editing, line management, online betting, player monitoring, and prize settlement. Essentially, every website's computer system can handle these tasks. Let's briefly explain.

1. **Match Editing** allows you to create matches in the system based on the schedule, enabling players to place bets.

2. **Odds Management** is used by traders to control the betting lines. Here, you can view the betting conditions, and operators can adjust the odds or point spreads in real-time.

3. **Online Betting Interface** is primarily for players to place bets online.

4. **Player Monitoring** enables you to view past betting records and credit status of the players.

5. **Payout Settlement** involves entering the match results and settling all betting tickets after the match ends.

Essentially, any betting transaction system must have these features. Some might argue that the system should also include a mobile betting interface and features for managing agents. True, but we consider these advanced features. Even without them, a site can still operate and do business with just the above five features.

Having these functions means the system is set up. But can it be termed a "good system"? That depends on individual proficiency. We mainly focus on two points. First, whether the system can quickly correct human errors. And second, if the system can properly monitor all personnel.

Talking about human errors, it generally refers to any data input mistakes, such as errors while inputting a betting ticket at betting sites, traders entering wrong odds, or errors in entering match results, and so on.

Because sports betting is a fast-paced game with significant fluctuations, if manual errors cannot be quickly corrected, it can lead to player dissatisfaction at best, and at worst, the entire accounting process can be disrupted. Let's take a common error as an example: entering the wrong game result. For instance, if the actual game result was 99:88, but an employee mistakenly inputs it as 88:99, which is the exact opposite, then all betting tickets related to this game would be calculated incorrectly.

However, mistakes in entering game results can't be entirely blamed on the website's internal staff, as it might not be their fault. If a game isn't broadcasted live, getting the immediate final result relies on online news and official reports. But these sources aren't directly affiliated with the betting website and might not be as attentive to the scores. If they make an error, they might think it's no big deal since they can correct it later. But for the betting website, it's a significant issue. Sometimes when checking online, two websites might report completely different game results. Or several sites might report the same score, but they all sourced their information from the same incorrect source. In such cases, errors will inevitably occur on the betting website.

Human errors in this industry are commonplace and inevitable. So, the quality of a system can be determined by how quickly it can rectify its mistakes. For instance, if there's an error in the input of a game's result, the system must be capable of accepting corrections to the score from the online sportsbook and immediately recalculating the results for that game's betting ticket.

We've also seen poorly

designed systems. Every time there's an input error, it takes the website several days to reconcile its accounts. However, the nature of this industry is unique. If a betting site cannot pay out winnings promptly, players might start questioning the fairness of the games. This could influence their future buying intentions. Thus, if a website's financial transactions are too slow, taking days to dispense winnings, players will likely abandon the platform quickly.

## What Is the System Monitoring?

Just as we often hear the phrase in casino movies, "In the casino, the house is always watching everything," the same applies to sports betting. Generally speaking, the system will monitor at least the following three targets:

- Monitor players

- Monitor traders

- Monitor the system itself

The first target is the players. Although we've emphasized that the interests of the online sportsbook do not conflict with those of the players, the website still does not wish for certain players to "always" win money.

People always winning is usually due to cheating, and the most likely method is that the player is colluding with the internal staff of the online sportsbook. They win jackpots by modifying data.

People might wonder, how could this happen? Do the internal employees of the website have such immense power to alter the bets placed by players? We can say that a well-designed system would never allow such an occurrence. Even engineers who are responsible for maintaining data can't do it. However, not all website computer systems are designed so perfectly.

We discuss "cost-cutting websites" in detail later on. Some website systems are quite flawed, leading to the drawback of internal staff having too much power. Let's take an example: a common function used by website customer service personnel is the ability to cancel betting tickets. This function was designed with good intentions, as players occasionally place bets on the wrong team. With the cancel ticket function, customer service can help everyone cancel wrongly placed bets, offering a chance to rethink. However, this function can be easily misused. For instance, by simply canceling losing betting tickets for certain players after the match ends, it ensures these players always win money.

The computer systems of online sportsbooks are vast and intricate, with many aspects relying on human operation. If a system is not comprehensive, cheating methods like those mentioned above can easily take place. There's another tactic that can always let a player win: finding loopholes in the game rules, ensuring a risk-free and consistent victory. For instance, as we discussed in the "live betting" section, some players would go directly to the game venue. By leveraging the few seconds delay in satellite broadcasts, they can see the game outcomes before the website updates, thus placing their bets ahead and increasing their chances of winning.

Both of the cheating methods mentioned are a major concern for sportsbooks. Some directly affect the profit margins of the websites, while others compromise the fairness of the game. If some individuals keep winning, it could make it easier for others to lose. Hence, it's vital for the system to monitor all players, observing their bets and the payouts they receive. This serves as a starting point to review the website's management. Are there any issues?

Recall our discussion on the so-called "betting gods" in sports gambling. If someone is found to be consistently winning, the computer system needs to kick in, meticulously investigating every detail of that player's activities. For instance, are the betting tickets they've purchased legitimate? Has any system data been modified? Is there a chance they breached the system? Did they place their bets only after the game concluded? Beyond this, other detailed information must be pulled up, such as their computer IP, their current geographical location, and the status of their computer, among other details.

Regarding geographical location, this is a critical aspect. Let's take an example. Suppose a website opens a live betting line for an NBA game in the U.S., and upon investigation, it's found that the computer the player used to place the bet is also located in the U.S., and precisely in the vicinity of the game venue. Then this "betting god" becomes very suspicious.

A good system should always be able to monitor its players properly. Some might wonder, if players place bets through phone or online, it's feasible to monitor them, but what if everyone buys betting tickets from betting sites?

We all know that buying betting tickets from betting sites is anonymous. How do you monitor that?

To be frank, websites are not that concerned about betting sites. When players buy from betting sites, they can't take advantage of the timeliness and can't break the game rules. We've always emphasized that savvy players should opt for online betting. On the other hand, getting high odds from betting sites is relatively challenging, and in the long run, it's still favorable for the website. So, for betting sites, the website only needs to have a general grasp of each betting site's betting situation.

Everything discussed so far pertains to monitoring players. This topic is actually very broad, and every website has its own approach. However, what's common is the need for a sophisticated computer system to achieve this. Up to now, there's still significant room for improvement, and every website is striving for it. What's certain is that in the sports betting industry, it's possible for a player to cheat and take advantage of a website, but it's challenging for them to do so for long without being detected.

**Monitoring the Trader**

Moving on to the topic of "Monitoring the Trader." We've previously discussed traders, whose primary role is to manage risks and ensure profits for the online sportsbook. But is a trader professionally competent enough? Can they withstand immense pressure? Is their daily performance up to par? These aspects are crucial. If a trader falters, it can easily result in significant financial losses for the online sportsbook.

Hence, it's imperative for computer systems to record the working conditions of every trader. Through these records and subsequent analysis, the sportsbook can evaluate the competence of a trader. This evaluation mainly encompasses two dimensions.

Firstly, it's viewed from the profit perspective. As we all know, the more balanced the betting lines managed by a trader, the more money the website can earn. Thus, looking at it from the money-making perspective is the most direct way; a good trader will undoubtedly generate more profits.

Secondly, it's about assessing the trader's skills. This part is more intricate. It requires the system to produce integrated reports, tracking every command they've given, evaluating the frequency of odds changes, and the magnitude of these changes, to determine if the trader has undergone comprehensive training.

Therefore, a sound system will always record every command of the trader. This also has an added advantage—it can prevent any collusion between the traders and players, making it a fundamental feature for many online sportsbooks.

## Monitoring the System Itself

Lastly, the system must be able to monitor itself. Some may wonder, why does the system need to watch over itself? This is because the betting system is vast. Establishing such a system requires many software engineers, and we can't guarantee that every engineer's work is flawless. As many know, a perfect computer system is fundamentally nonexistent.

Therefore, a comprehensive system must have its independent monitoring system and log files. These logs include changes in odds, accepted betting tickets, actions taken by various personnel, and more. Moreover, these records are stored in various places within the system.

The above approach also answers some people's questions, such as, is it possible to breach the website's computer system? Can one change a lost ticket to a winning one?

The answer is evident: it's utterly impossible. Because as soon as a betting ticket is entered into the computer system, several log files will simultaneously record its content. Even if a genius intruder could breach the database and change the ticket, they couldn't alter all the log files.

It's important to understand that these log files are managed by different engineers, each having their unique formats and placement. It's almost impossible to modify all the log files at once, even for the internal engineers of the website. If there's any discrepancy between the betting ticket and the log files, the system can alert the website. This ensures that even if someone breaches the system, they can't claim the winnings.

From the above, it's evident that the websites trust no one, not even their computer systems. This skepticism has led to the creation of a nearly impenetrable system. However, it's worth mentioning that the systems described above are well-designed and sophisticated. Following the principle of "you get what you pay for", the cost of setting up such systems can be quite high, making it unaffordable for some websites. Consequently, in reality, many websites have to rely on simpler computer systems. This simplicity provides some players with exploitable loopholes.

## Computer Attacks from Players

Speaking of infiltrating systems, I believe most people would be quite interested in this. In this industry, an online sportsbook's computer database can be likened to a vault. Although there isn't actual cash inside, it's filled with betting tickets. If one can gain access, even just changing a single digit can turn a loss into a win, or make a win even bigger. It's akin to directly taking money home.

So, if any of you are into sports betting and have some knowledge about computer networks, wouldn't you want to sneak into the website's database? It's this very mindset that results in relentless cyber attacks, computer viruses, etc., targeting these websites daily without rest.

There was once a specialized engineer who, unknowingly, was called to inspect the firewall of an online sportsbook. Upon checking the logs, he immediately turned around and asked, "Is this place some sort of secretive government intelligence agency?" The log displayed an enormous number of cyber attacks. A closer look was like a comprehensive guide to internet viruses, including every virus one might or might not have encountered.

This presents the biggest challenge in designing or maintaining transaction systems. It's also the primary reason for the high costs of construction.

As for the burning question many of you might have: can one really breach the computer databases of these websites? Can an average player succeed? As previously mentioned, it's indeed possible, but it's unlikely that most of you will ever encounter such an opportunity.

The logic is simple. Indeed, some online sportsbook systems are quite vulnerable. However, once such vulnerabilities are discovered, a swarm of people rush in to exploit them, leading the websites to immediately face data tampering and massive financial losses. This eventually forces them out of business, leaving us with nowhere to bet. In the sports betting industry, everything happens swiftly, including the shutdown of these sites.

But be cautious. Sports betting is an industry that demands real-time reactions. If a website detects an issue, they address it on the spot. So, when you attempt to attack a site, be prepared for retaliation. These online sportsbooks have top-notch engineers ready to pinpoint your computer's location and identify the type of malware or attack you're deploying, allowing them to neutralize your efforts. It's entirely feasible. There have been instances where attackers not only failed in their attempts but also found their own computers crippled in return.

**Computer attacks from other websites:**

The attacks from players are merely minor inconveniences to the betting transaction system. Over time, one gets used to them, and they really don't cause much trouble. The real nightmare, however, comes from malicious attacks by other websites. Ever since the internet and sports betting perfectly combined, players no longer need to be confined to their geographic location when placing bets. A player from Hong Kong can place a bet in the UK, and a player from China can purchase a betting ticket in Vietnam. With the internet, credit cards, and Alipay, these actions have become easy and are no longer news.

However, this "globalization" phenomenon means that every website has to compete with others from around the world. Naturally, there will be winners and losers in this competition. But aside from regular business competition, some websites inevitably resort to underhanded tactics. Through computer attacks, even if it's just paralyzing another site's business for a few hours, they can effectively damage the reputation of that website. Consequently, players might migrate and look for other websites to place their bets.

In this industry, players' loyalty to a particular website is not particularly high. If a site's computer system frequently crashes, hindering everyone's ability to make money, then players will quickly move on to another site. After all, with profits in mind, no one wants to miss out on opportunities to earn.

And these cyberattacks coming from other websites are organized, funded, and technically sophisticated. The damage they can inflict is far beyond what regular players can cause. Another characteristic of these attackers is that they strike swiftly and leave just as quickly, making it nearly impossible to trace them back to their origins. Why is this the case?

It's because the attackers are also insiders in the industry. They specifically choose to strike during the prime time for online sportsbook websites to accept bets, which is usually the 2 hours leading up to a sporting event and throughout its duration. If they can cause a system crash during this window, players will undoubtedly become furious. But outside of this period, there are fewer users online, making any attacks less impactful, so the attackers happily take a break.

So, when websites see these types of cyberattacks, they are both frustrated and amused. There's hardly any sign of an attack during off-peak hours, but as soon as the rush starts, the attackers seemingly clock in for their shift. The tactics they employ vary widely, making them incredibly hard to guard against. Many websites, in the end, find it intolerable and choose to relocate their servers or rebrand to escape the constant threat.

Falling victim to cyberattacks is a characteristic of this line of business and a critical consideration when designing systems. A well-designed system can withstand cyberattacks over the long term, but a slightly inferior one might force the website out of business. ›

## Budget-Friendly Small Websites

In previous chapters, we discussed the challenges of running an online sportsbook. Given the earlier discussions, one might now envision these websites as strictly organized entities, comprised of brilliant traders, meticulous computer engineers, and state-of-the-art computer systems. Such an elite group of experts, communicating in English, each excelling in their respective roles, tirelessly playing the role of the online sportsbook day in and day out, ensuring everyone can enjoy the thrill of sports betting.

Regrettably, the reality is not exactly as such. Or perhaps we might say, not entirely. While some powerful and sustainably-operated websites do function this way, with actual situations not deviating much from what most imagine, many more websites don't. Maintaining the aforementioned vision can be quite costly, and not every website can afford it.

So, in this chapter, we'll delve into how these smaller websites employ cost-saving philosophies to conduct their business. We'll explore the peculiar phenomena that arise from their practices and ultimately, what leads to the downfall of these small websites.

First, let's clarify the topic of discussion. This chapter focuses on small websites that are severely lacking in manpower, financial resources, and materials. The various methods discussed below are not what they genuinely want to use, but they are forced into these methods due to their circumstances.

Within the various money-saving tricks for small websites, the first to be introduced is the "line-following intern." Those who have read the previous articles would know that there is a group of "risk control traders" inside the website, also known as "book controllers." They are responsible for setting odds and balancing the betting lines.

However, such talents are firstly hard to discover. Even if they are discovered, training them is challenging. After being trained, they may not necessarily be usable. Once a competent person is finally trained, their salary will not be cheap. Hence, the first cost-saving target for small websites is directed at them.

Now, websites no longer use traders. Instead, they look for a group of interns, have them turn on a computer, connect to other websites, and then tell these interns, "Whatever they open, we open. If they change the odds, we follow." In short, they completely copy the betting lines. In this way, opening a betting line becomes effortless. While risk control for a betting line is challenging, copying is easy for everyone. This job is even simpler than working at McDonald's. Plus, by hiring interns, they can be paid hourly, maximizing savings for small websites.

What's even more significant is the betting lines that this group copies seem quite authentic. Not only do the odds fluctuate, but they also update in real-time. Compared to major websites, there's barely any difference. And since these part-time workers only need to adjust the odds in line with other websites and don't have to handle anything else, we call them "Line Following Interns".

However, the problem with this approach is quite evident. These "Line Following Interns" merely emulate others, copying their odds. This entirely negates the purpose of balancing the betting lines. It's easy to imagine—if we continually copy someone else's odds, how can our own betting lines possibly be balanced? Instead of painstakingly plagiarizing, might as well arbitrarily set some odds; the outcome might even be better!

But let's consider the position of these smaller websites. Hiring a skilled "Risk Control Trader" can be costly. To quickly get into the business and make money, it's more expedient to employ part-time workers than to invest time in training a trader. It's a makeshift solution. Moreover, some small websites only have a rudimentary understanding of the purpose of odds, let alone grasping how the "juice" functions.

Nonetheless, there is a silver lining to the simplistic "line following" approach. At the very least, the odds won't be set outrageously. Just think about it—if a part-time worker haphazardly set the odds like "Team A at 2.50,

Team B at 1.90", with a total payout ratio exceeding four and entirely devoid of any juice concept, wouldn't that be laughably amateurish?

However, it must be clarified here that "following the line" is ultimately not the same as "controlling the line." Without risk control, and operators who haven't undergone professional training, this approach is bound to create significant chaos eventually. This is the primary reason small online sportsbooks go out of business. Sooner or later, there will be an imbalanced betting line, leading to the financial collapse of the small site.

Earlier, I introduced the concept of "line-following interns." This cost-saving method, although astonishing, is hard to believe. Most people would find it difficult to imagine that there are websites so frugal that they're unwilling even to hire a risk control trader.

Yet, this isn't even the most extreme cost-saving measure. The real penny pinchers don't even want to hire interns. This ultimate money-saving technique involves replacing human labor with computers: evolving the "line-following intern" into the "line-following robot."

Websites capable of creating a "line-following robot" typically have a robust team of computer engineers. These engineers can analyze the websites of other bookmakers, identify patterns, and then design a program to collect their betting lines, integrating them into their own systems. This programmatic and periodic fetching of betting lines becomes the line-following robot.

Not only can computers fully replace interns, but as long as the internet connection is fast enough, a website's betting lines can be synchronized and updated alongside other sites. Moreover, this approach is even more powerful than manual updating. When humans are tracking, fatigue or human errors can lead to incorrect odds. Computers don't have this problem, and they can execute tasks faster and more efficiently.

Therefore, with the introduction of these "line-following robots," websites can completely eliminate the manpower costs required for line tracking. However, it's worth emphasizing again that, whether it's a "line-following intern" or a "line-following robot," they both serve the purpose of line tracking. And as with all line-tracking methods, they come with similar issues. Ultimately, this is not a permanent solution.

Perhaps some may wonder, is it possible to use computers for genuine line control?

This question has long been discussed in the industry. Many websites have experimented with it. Frankly, theoretically, computers can definitely observe betting patterns and then adjust odds to balance the betting line. However, in practical execution, there's a parameter model that needs to be established. This model includes questions like: How much imbalance is required before adjusting the odds? You can't possibly adjust the point spread just for a difference of one dollar, right? Then, what should be the magnitude of adjustment? Should it decrease by 0.01 or 0.02? Should the point spread be adjusted by 1.5 points or 2.5 points? And how long should the adjustments be sustained?

All these parameters determine the effectiveness of computer-controlled lines. To my knowledge, the parameter models available currently aren't detailed enough to compete with humans. As for another kind of AI, artificial intelligence, it's even less mature. As a result, all major websites still rely on traders for risk management.

## Leasing Systems From Computer Companies

Having reduced labor costs, the next step is to save on computer expenses. We've previously discussed the significance of the "betting transaction system," emphasizing the essential role of computer systems. For most, their idea of a website is essentially this computer system. However, developing a comprehensive computer software system demands a lot of time and incurs high costs.

Moreover, once the software system is complete, you need a server room, internet, computer hardware, and dedicated computer engineers to ensure smooth operations. These considerable investments aren't affordable for every website. As a result, smaller websites might opt to forego these investments and instead "rent" to cut costs.

Within the sports betting industry, there are two concepts of "system leasing." Let's start with the first one. This service is provided by certain computer companies. They might have previously been commissioned to design betting transaction systems. Possessing these systems, these computer companies naturally aim for volume over high margins and rent these systems to other websites on a monthly basis.

The leasing of this type of service is straightforward. The entire system is designed as a website, which is divided into front-end and back-end. The front-end is for players to place bets, while the back-end allows websites to set up betting lines and handle accounting and settlements. And because it's a web-based service, these computer companies often take care of the server room, internet, and maintenance as well.

Basically, once a website pays, it can start operating immediately without any preparations. The prices for these types of services are generally affordable, ranging from fifteen to thirty thousand dollars a month. The more comprehensive the system's features, the higher the monthly rental fee. From the perspective of smaller websites, the advantage of using such services is that the entry cost is quite low, affordable for almost everyone. Therefore, many websites choose this method when entering the industry.

However, there are also numerous downsides to using such rental services. First and foremost is the system functionality. As we've discussed, many in this industry have only a superficial understanding of sports betting. These computer companies might fall into this category as well. Furthermore, most of them have never operated as websites and lack hands-on experience. Systems in this category are typically developed based on the website's requirements and specifications. The computer company then embellishes and adds computer reports and analytical functions before selling it.

Regrettably, the issue lies here. There can be conceptual errors. For instance, I once saw a system's line control interface. The information displayed to the trader was as follows:

**"Team A Odds 2.20 Total Bets $100,000, Number of Betting Tickets 5, Average Amount $20,000"**

**"Team B Odds 1.60 Total Bets $100,000, Number of Betting Tickets 4, Average Amount $25,000"**

At first glance, it seems quite detailed. Not only can you see how many betting tickets have been collected, but you can also calculate the average purchase amount of the tickets. However, those who have read the previous article on "online sportsbook" would realize that this kind of information isn't that useful. Firstly, what truly matters in a line is the payout on both sides. To determine if the tilt is excessive, one needs to look at the total bets accepted.

In this incorrect demonstration, the information that should be displayed isn't, and a bunch of unnecessary details are shown. Frankly, regardless of who is in charge of this line, they would be clueless about how to proceed.

Let's look at the correct example:

"Total bets accepted $200,000"

"Team A current odds 2.20, projected payout $210,000"

"Team B current odds 1.60, projected payout $180,000"

This is a standard betting balance sheet. After the trader looks at this table, it's easy to see that the odds have tilted excessively towards Team A, and the projected payout amount has already exceeded the total bets of $10,000. If adjustments are not made, there would be a need for arbitrage. So, the appropriate action at this point would be to lower the odds for Team A.

The misconceptions mentioned above are often made by computer companies in collaboration with websites. The root cause is their lack of understanding about the sports betting industry and not knowing the principle behind how these websites make money. With half-baked knowledge, it's easy to produce such strange trading systems.

It's not that these computer companies are incapable; they simply don't have enough understanding. On the website's side, it's possible that they too aren't entirely clear, or perhaps the website has some tricks up its sleeve, not wanting the computer company to fully understand all the intricacies. As a result, numerous systems with flawed concepts continue to flood the market.

When a small website rents one of these systems, it's quite risky. On one hand, they don't know how to operate these systems, and on the other, their understanding can be misguided. In the end, they might just gamble directly against the players. This is potentially the second reason why smaller websites might go bankrupt: they "don't know how to manage the odds."

## Renting Systems From Other Websites

Earlier, we discussed the downsides of leasing systems from IT companies. However, there's another form of "renting" available in the market. This involves smaller websites approaching larger websites to rent their existing systems.

The primary motivation behind this approach is to counteract the possibility of a custom-designed system (made by hiring an IT company) not being suitable for one's needs. Systems used by large websites must be flawless. Moreover, since the large website's system is already operational, setting up a separate platform for a smaller website can be done effortlessly. As a result, these large websites are often willing to lease their systems at extremely low costs or even for free.

Yes, free rental. But there's no such thing as a free lunch. Although the monthly rent might seem ridiculously low, the large websites charge another type of fee known as a "commission." This commission is the same as the one discussed in the previous "agent" section.

To put it plainly, when a large website rents its system to a smaller one, it essentially views the latter as its agent. And there are many benefits for the smaller website in leasing the system of the larger one. There's no monthly rental fee, no need for traders, and essentially, all they need to do is bring in the players.

When smaller websites lease this system, a certain percentage of the bet amount from each betting ticket they accept goes directly to the larger website. Let's illustrate this with an example. Let's say the agreed commission is 30%. If a player places a bet of $100 with the smaller website, then:

The larger website receives 30%, which is $30.

The smaller website retains 70%, which is $70.

If the player eventually wins this bet and the odds are set at 2, then the payout will be divided as:

The larger website pays out 30%, which is $60.

The smaller website pays out 70%, which is $140.

Of course, players don't notice these commission splits. They'll receive their winnings no matter what. But for the websites, the difference is substantial. The profits they make from the "juice" depend on the total bets they accept. Now that the larger website takes 30% of the total bets, it means they are taking 30% of the smaller website's juice. This 30% commission can be much higher than the monthly rental fee charged by software companies.

Another aspect worth discussing is the balance of the betting lines. Both small and large online sportsbooks must balance their betting lines to earn the juice. The best way to manipulate the betting lines is by utilizing point spreads and odds. Ideally, large online sportsbooks should set their own set of odds to control the balance, while small online sportsbooks would have a different set of odds to manage their equilibrium.

However, a problem arises due to commission structures. When a player places a bet, it is allocated across two betting lines based on a certain percentage. If a large online sportsbook sets the odds and point spreads, it wouldn't want the small online sportsbook to change them. Because if the small online sportsbook controls the odds, then the large online sportsbook can't manipulate the players, and they might not earn the desired juice.

Therefore, both small and large online sportsbooks would want to influence players to see their odds. Otherwise, they cannot balance their own betting lines. But there's only one set of odds. If they are set according to the large online sportsbook, then the juice for the small online sportsbook could be significantly impacted. If they are set according to the small online sportsbook, the large online sportsbook wouldn't agree. So, when there's a commission structure involved, which online sportsbook sets the odds becomes crucial.

However, there isn't a proper solution to this issue. Although there are two betting lines balances, there can only be one set of odds. Thus, in these types of rental services, the odds and point spreads are mostly determined by the large online sportsbook. However, small online sportsbooks can still negotiate slight adjustments to the odds to protect their interests. After all, completely losing the ability to control odds is not acceptable.


Therefore, the two parties usually negotiate. The odds from the larger website are the primary reference, but the smaller website can slightly adjust these odds. The adjustment range shouldn't be too large, possibly within 3% to 5%. Let's take an example:

For Team A, the odds on the larger website are 1.95.

However, the smaller website can offer odds of 1.98 or 1.92, which is a 3% range. Both sides will have some influence over the players. Although it's not perfect, it's something both parties can accept.

However, this is also the third reason why smaller websites might go bankrupt: "Not being able to fully control the betting line."

Lastly, there's a flaw that can arise when renting any system, and that is "collusion and cheating." If anyone has visited websites that specifically explain betting techniques, they would have come across advertisements called "ticket modification collaboration." They claim to have cooperative relations with some large websites or computer companies. Together with the player, they can modify the bets, changing a loss into a win, targeting smaller websites.

Here, we don't need to discuss the authenticity of such advertisements; to be frank, most of them are false. However, the message revealed behind these ads is quite alarming. If a small online sportsbook rents a system, they are essentially handing over the most crucial betting ticket data to someone else. If the person in charge is incompetent, leading to the loss or alteration of the betting tickets, or if their intent is to maliciously scam the small sportsbook, then the resultant loss could be substantial.

Furthermore, with the entire database in someone else's hands, if the betting tickets within it were altered, it would be impossible to detect. This is the fourth reason why a small online sportsbook might go bankrupt: "Improper database management."

Having discussed potential approaches for budget-conscious online sportsbooks and their respective pros and cons, one can see that there are no shortcuts in this industry. If you try to save money in areas where you shouldn't, it will inevitably lead to problems. This aligns perfectly with Murphy's Law: "Anything that can go wrong, will go wrong."

Lastly, we'll touch upon the final and most common reason why online sportsbooks might face bankruptcy.

Actually, online sportsbooks are just like everyone else; they too enjoy watching games. Of course, they have their own opinions on the outcomes of the matches. However, a good online sportsbook knows how to control its emotions, focusing on the juice and balance, and not letting the outcome of a match dictate its betting actions.

But some online sportsbooks can't resist the urge. They'll place bets themselves. In other words, when they're almost certain that a team is bound to lose tonight, they might think, "Why earn from the juice when you can earn faster by betting against the players?" So, they abandon their usual practice of maintaining a balanced line and arbitrage. Instead, they significantly increase the odds for that team, hoping to attract more players to place bets, and then they take on all the bets themselves.

This is known as the online sportsbook betting against its players and taking on the full risk. Of course, if the online sportsbook's judgment is right and the supposed losing team indeed loses, then it's a huge win for the sportsbook. The money they earn this way can be much more than what they earn from the juice.

However, the risk here is, what if they judged it wrong? The ball is round, and anything can happen. If the supposed losing team ends up winning, the online sportsbook could face a disaster. A single wrong judgment could lead to the loss of their entire business. And that's what we'll discuss next. As the saying goes, "Even gods lose if they gamble for too long," and online sportsbooks that bet themselves are no exception.

# Concept

In every article discussing sports betting, it's inevitable to mention the topic of "match-fixing." The public's interest in the relationship between rigged games, teams intentionally underperforming, and sports betting has always been intense. In fact, there have been numerous online rumors suggesting that online sportsbooks secretly collude with teams to rig games and trap players. So, in this article, we will explore the question: Do these sportsbooks really manipulate match outcomes? How does "match-fixing" affect everyone? Does a rigged game make it easier for uninformed players to lose money?

Let's first understand how, if a sportsbook were to profit from manipulating matches, it would specifically go about it. Firstly, the sportsbook would have to strike a deal with one of the teams involved in a match before it starts. This would typically be the team that's expected to win. This team would intentionally lose the match. Following this, when the sportsbook opens the betting lines, they would offer very high odds for the team they've made the agreement with. Of course, the other team would then have extremely low odds. As a result, players would rush to buy the high-odds betting tickets, essentially betting on the team that's agreed to lose.

At this moment, the website will abandon all the principles of acting as a bookmaker, accepting bets without any limits. Furthermore, after accepting the bets, they do not engage in "arbitrage" or any other insurance buying methods. Thus, this one-sided betting situation eventually results in the website taking in all of the players' bets, creating a scenario where the website is gambling directly against the players. If everything goes smoothly and the team with the high odds deliberately loses as agreed, then the website essentially wins against all the players who bet on that team.

However, a team intentionally losing a game does not necessarily have anything to do with the website. In the methods described above, if we replace the word "website" with "agent", "player", or "some wealthy individual", it would still work practically. Other roles can also profit from this. So, why do online rumors always assume that teams must be colluding with websites to fix games? Based on observations, there are three main reasons:

Firstly, websites have the means.

Secondly, websites have the motive.

Thirdly, websites have the methods.

Firstly, the online sportsbooks have the means. We all know that the turnover for a single match can easily range from tens of millions to hundreds of millions of dollars. Hence, every sportsbook needs to have enough manpower, resources, and financial strength to run a betting line and accept bets from everyone. With such abundant resources, they naturally have the means more than anyone else to influence a match, making teams deliberately lose. Thus, we say that the sportsbooks have the means.

Next, the online sportsbooks have the motive. We are also aware that sportsbooks make money from the "juice." So, how much can they earn from the "juice" of a match? After being exploited by layers of agents, earning 1% to 3% of the turnover is already quite good. However, through a rigged match, the sportsbook's revenue can reach 90% to 99% of the turnover, which is almost like pocketing all the winnings. This figure is dozens of times that of the "juice." Hence, based on the money-can-do-anything theory, we say that the sportsbooks have the motive.

Lastly, the online sportsbooks have the methods. To maximize profit from a rigged match, there's one essential condition: they need to find people to bet against. Otherwise, even if the match is rigged, and you can't find someone willing to bet against you, there's still no way to make money. Finding people to bet against is easiest for sportsbooks. The existing players are there, and by using high and low odds, they can easily create situations where they bet against the players. This is something ordinary people can't achieve. Thus, we say that the sportsbooks have the methods.

After a detailed analysis, this website has the conditions, the motive, and the methodology. Therefore, it naturally emerges as the primary suspect. Hence, it's not surprising to find such rumors circulating online.

Even more specific details are associated with these rumors. Allegedly, some "veteran" players have begun to share insights on "how to detect a fake website." There are also self-proclaimed "mentors" openly recruiting members with the promise that after joining, one can receive immediate, firsthand information about website manipulations, claiming this could assist members in winning money with greater ease.

## How To Identify Websites Rigging Matches

Let's delve into two renowned methods on the internet to identify websites involved in match-fixing.

Firstly, this involves observing the odds. According to traditional beliefs, strong teams have lower odds while weaker teams possess higher odds. From this, they advise people to monitor how websites set odds for each match. If you detect that a match involving a traditionally strong team that always had lower odds suddenly has higher odds, then there's an "issue" with that match.

Secondly, it's about observing the spectator stands. Some anonymous players online claim to have entered the so-called "mysterious trading rooms". To clarify, the trading room refers to the office where the "trader" we discussed operates. They've noticed some traders using instant messaging software like Line or WeChat, continuously exchanging information with individuals at the game venue. Given that online sportsbooks don't typically send representatives to the match venue without good reason, they conclude those matches also have an "issue".

Therefore, before a match starts, it's essential to pay attention to the spectator stands. Check if there are unidentified individuals with laptops nearby. Moreover, by observing where they sit, you can infer

How to Detect Match Fixing by Websites

Let's delve into the two prominent methods found online for detecting website match-fixing.

Firstly, it's about observing the odds. Conventionally, stronger teams are associated with lower odds, while weaker teams are pegged at higher odds.

Hence, they teach others to carefully observe how websites set odds for every betting line. If it's noticed that a traditionally strong team, which always had lower odds, suddenly has higher odds for a particular match, then that game is deemed "suspicious."

Secondly, it pertains to the spectator stands. Some anonymous online players claim to have been inside the so-called "mysterious trading rooms". To clarify, these "trading rooms" refer to the offices where the "traders" we've previously discussed work. These individuals have reported seeing some traders using instant messaging software like Line or WeChat to communicate with people on-site, continuously relaying messages. Since websites don't usually send representatives to the venue without good reason, they conclude that such matches are also "suspicious."

Therefore, before the game starts, we should pay attention to the stands to see if any unknown individuals with laptops are around. Moreover, we can deduce which team the website is in contact with based on where that individual is seated.

So, we have discussed two common observation methods. Why do we need to know if a game site is faking a match? The reason is simple. If we know how the website intends to manipulate the game, we can obviously take advantage of it. All you have to do is buy along with the website, that is, to buy the team with the "low odds" or the team without the men in black in the audience.

While the odds may not be high, at least you can win money. Besides, those who think the win is too small can place larger bets, and thus earn more. Because of this, rumors of website cheating spread far and wide, and various judgment methods have emerged.

Now we can get to the main point and discuss the truth of these rumors. First, let's see if the website truly meets all the requirements to be a culprit?

Firstly, the website has the means, and there's no doubt about that. To say a website doesn't have the manpower, resources, and financial power would be unbelievable to everyone, so we don't have to doubt this. However, it's worth mentioning that not only do websites have the means, but players or agents do too. As mentioned earlier, the turnover of a single match can range from tens of millions to hundreds of millions. Those contributing to this turnover also have considerable financial power, so they could also influence a game if they wanted to.

Next, when it comes to websites having a motive, from the numbers we just discussed, it's indeed hard work for the online sportsbooks to earn their "juice". However, just because it's strenuous doesn't mean they would manipulate matches. This "hard work" is relative. If we consider a match with a turnover of $100 million, even earning just 1% would mean $1 million. And that's just for one match in a day.

Considering this turnover and profit, think about how many industries can compare to this. For these websites, the "juice" they earn is by no means insignificant. Moreover, from another perspective, these websites are well aware of the proverbial story of "killing the goose that lays the golden eggs". If they scam players in just one match, players will be deterred from continuing to bet. Then what will the website earn from in the future?

Therefore, scamming players is not a wise move. Even from a profitability standpoint, websites wouldn't want to manipulate matches. We can observe that many mechanisms are designed by these platforms to compensate players who frequently lose, ensuring they don't get frustrated and quit. The rationale behind this is that scamming players in one match is akin to shooting oneself in the foot. Such a foolish act is something the websites wouldn't engage in. Hence, I argue that the websites lack a motive.

Finally, there's the theory that online sportsbooks manipulate games. This perspective is often supported by proponents of the "websites are rigged" argument. Indeed, in a rigged game, online sportsbooks, by accepting bets, don't have to invest any capital. They can maximize their profits just by manipulating odds to influence player bets. Meanwhile, other agents and players have to invest some money to buy betting tickets to profit from the rigged games. So, it's true that online sportsbooks have a more convenient path. However, manipulating odds is the nature of this industry. We can't assume that those who manipulate odds will also manipulate games. Just because someone has an easy way to make money doesn't mean they'll exploit every opportunity to do so.

In my view, while online sportsbooks have the means and the methods, they certainly lack the motive to manipulate games. In fact, as we'll discuss later in this article, game manipulation can be hugely detrimental to online sportsbooks. But I must emphasize, this is just my perspective. Given that there are thousands of online sportsbooks worldwide, we can't guarantee that every one of them operates honorably.

Next, we'll discuss two common perspectives from the public about online sportsbooks and their potential involvement in game manipulation. Regrettably, we can already state that both of these perspectives are baseless.

First and foremost, looking at the odds is correct. With long-term observation of the betting lines, we will certainly notice that some betting lines are quite odd, where a strong team is given unreasonably high odds. Such odds appear without any nationalistic sentiment influencing them, nor are there any tabloid reports of player injuries.

Moreover, no matter how one looks at it, it doesn't seem likely that anyone would bet on the weaker team. So, even those who are familiar with the principles of sports betting and understand the balancing of online sportsbook odds, will think that this betting line doesn't make sense. Therefore, the natural conclusion is that this game "has. some. issues."

However, everyone forgets the principle of sales. We've said before that online sportsbooks are also salespeople, and they apply marketing concepts.

For instance, when we go shopping, we all exhibit a certain "inertia." Let's say you go shopping and see a product in one store priced at $10. You might inquire and then continue shopping. In the next store, you see the same product still priced at $10. After asking, you might move on. If the next shop again offers it for $10, you might not even bother asking and just move on. If every store on the way offers it for $10, you might not even bother looking and just walk by. This is the human nature of "inertia." However, if one store suddenly puts up a promotional sign offering it for $5, whether or not you decide to purchase, you will at least stop and take a look.

And this sales principle is something online sportsbooks have no reason not to use. Constantly sticking to the formula "strong team = low odds" makes players get used to it over time, and once they're used to it, they tend to lose interest in placing bets. Hence, from time to time, sportsbooks need to break this norm by offering odds where "strong team = high odds" to capture everyone's attention. Of course, this approach carries risks, and there's a high chance that the sportsbook might not make any profit or even suffer losses. But sometimes, for the sake of creating a buzz, sportsbooks are willing to intentionally lose on one or two games. Moreover, once this topic becomes the talk of the town, it can benefit the odds set for subsequent games.

So, when we see unreasonable odds, it doesn't necessarily mean that the sportsbook is being deceptive. In fact, it's often just a marketing strategy. If everyone assumes that when a "strong team = high odds", it means the game is rigged and the strong team will deliberately lose, and then rushes to bet on the weaker team hoping for an advantage, the usual outcome is that many end up losing alongside the weaker team.

## Websites Send People on-Site

Now, let's delve into the matter of players who have been inside the so-called "trading rooms" and have seen websites sending people to the scene. What's this all about?

Firstly, the term "trading room" refers to the office where traders work. Although it's not a place that just anyone can walk into, it's not some "mystical" location. There are no ancient wizards performing rituals, nor are there schemers plotting secretive plans. The working environment there is similar to a regular stock exchange. Due to the concentration required for their job, outsiders are not typically allowed in.

Furthermore, it is indeed common practice for websites to send people on-site. These are often traders as well. Once on-site, these traders do indeed communicate with their office using apps like WeChat or Line during the game. However, these traders are not manipulating the games. What they're focused on is what they're best at: "manipulating betting lines."

This is because websites have the "live betting" option, allowing players to place bets even as the game is ongoing. To operate this live betting platform, websites usually rely on TV broadcasts or radio transmissions to get the latest updates on the match, in order to adjust the point spread and odds in real-time. However, TV or radio is not always reliable. They might experience interruptions, or even signal delays due to weather conditions.

Therefore, websites send traders to the actual game venue. These on-site traders, with their computers and wireless internet, can control the betting lines directly, thus avoiding risks like TV signal delays or interruptions. But there's another issue here: the equipment of these on-site personnel, including their computers and wireless connections, might crash.

If the on-site computer breaks down and the website's office is unaware of it, that could be disastrous. Therefore, on-site staff must constantly communicate with the office staff via WeChat or Line. If there's an issue like a computer malfunction or a lost connection, the office-based traders would immediately take over the betting controls.

Sending personnel to the venue and having constant monitoring in the office is a method to control the betting lines. It's a sort of insurance mechanism and showcases the website's careful approach to its operations. It's crucial not to interpret this practice as websites manipulating matches or sending people to monitor teams throwing games. Such assumptions would be incorrect.

In conclusion to the above points, setting aside the possibility of match-fixing, what can be affirmed is that the methods of judgment found online are utterly unreliable. Hence, if anyone is thinking of placing bets on websites based on the premise of "match-fixing" to make money, solely relying on these online judgments will not work.

However, there might be a lingering question: If we don't want to profit from fixed matches, does the issue of "match-fixing" still concern us?

Before answering this, we first need to examine the attitude of online sportsbooks towards "match-fixing".

## Websites Are Actually Afraid of Match-Fixing

Essentially, websites are very fearful of "match-fixing." Not only do they have no incentive to manipulate matches, but they also strongly avoid the possibility of match-fixing. First and foremost, if one website can manipulate a match, then other websites can as well, and even the players can. Hence, "match-fixing" is uncontrollable, and no single website can control a team for an extended period.

Moreover, from a business perspective, if a match is fixed and the website is kept in the dark, launching the betting lines without knowledge, the website might suffer significant losses. However, when discussing losses, we need to distinguish between two aspects. We know there are two main ways websites operate. One is the "juice-making" method, and the other is the "non-juice-making" method.

In the juice-making method, where the odds of guessing correctly can reach 1/2, the website relies on balancing the bets and earns a percentage of the total wagered as "juice." In these methods, if match-fixing occurs, i.e., players collude with teams to let them win, it generally doesn't directly affect the website's profits. This is because the website will balance the bets before the match ends, so no matter the outcome, the website just has to pay the winners with the losers' money, without any loss. However, while there might not be a direct impact, there is still an indirect one.

The principle is simple. The total payout in prize money is fixed; the pie is only so big. So, if some players consistently win money using certain tactics, it means that the share of the pie available to others becomes significantly smaller. This uneven distribution over time leads to other players losing more and more, and their desire to play diminishes. As a result, the online sportsbook sees a gradual loss of customers. Naturally, the daily revenue will decline, reducing the website's profits.

Next, we discuss the betting methods that do not rely on "juice." The characteristic of these methods is that the probability of guessing correctly is much lower than ½. To attract players to bet, the sportsbook must offer high odds. Since the players' odds of guessing correctly are not high, most of these bets are pocketed by the sportsbook. It's a situation where the sportsbook and players are in direct competition. The sportsbook, backed by statistics and odds, can achieve stable profits. However, if "match-fixing" occurs in these types of bets, it spells trouble. Because it's a head-to-head bet, the sportsbook stands to lose, directly affecting its profitability.

This concept is also straightforward. Firstly, players who manipulate matches have already predetermined the outcome, rendering the sportsbook's statistics and odds less reliable. In these head-to-head betting methods, the sportsbook starts off on the losing side. Next, there's the issue of the odds.

Let's take the "Correct Score" betting method as an example. In this method, players must guess the final score of the match, whether it's 1:1, 1:2, 2:1, 2:2, and so on. Just by looking at this, one can tell it's hard to predict accurately. Therefore, the online sportsbook needs to offer high odds to attract bets. The odds for this type of bet can go up to hundreds. This means if you place a bet of $10,000 and guess correctly, you can win millions of dollars. So, with these high odds, if there's match-fixing, the online sportsbook would be in deep trouble. Just one rigged match guessed accurately can bankrupt the sportsbook. One can imagine, no one would like to be this kind of bookmaker

Considering the above, the stance of the online sportsbook is very clear. They are extremely wary of "match-fixing" and go to great lengths to avoid it. They fear match-fixing even more than the players do. Therefore, most betting sites usually offer odds on renowned sporting events where the chances of teams or players fixing matches are minimal.

So, discussing the players' attitude becomes simpler. Since the sportsbook selects their offered matches carefully, it's less likely that players will encounter fixed matches. Hence, players can bet with confidence. As for the rumors on the internet, it's best to just hear them out and not take them seriously.

However, let's discuss this: if a match really is fixed, what impact would it have on unsuspecting players?

## If Match-Fixing Were To Occur, What Would Be its Implications?

Let's hypothesize for a moment. If a small group of people manipulated a match and the team played a "fixed" game, what would be the impact on the unsuspecting online sportsbooks and the majority of players?

First, let's assume that tonight's match involves two teams. One team is widely recognized as powerful, a traditional top-tier team, while the other team is known for frequently losing matches, being a traditional underdog. So, when the online sportsbook sets the odds for such a match, it would initially present a typical betting line: the "strong team with low odds, weak team with high odds" to balance the bets from players.

Those who manipulate the match would have an agreement with the strong team before the match, ensuring they would lose that night. Given the anticipated loss of the strong team, these manipulators would place hefty bets on the underdog before the match. When the underdog eventually wins, they walk away with their winnings.

However, the issue is, before the game, the underdog team received a large amount of bets, causing the betting line to lean towards their side. Because of this, the online sportsbook had to take immediate action by reducing the odds for the weaker team and increasing the odds for the stronger team. This adjustment is based on the principle of keeping the betting line balanced; otherwise, the accepted bets would be unbalanced in the end.

This situation then creates a peculiar scenario where the "stronger team has higher odds, and the weaker team has lower odds." It's crucial to note that this situation arises solely due to the fundamental principles of line control.

It's an instinctual response and doesn't indicate that the sportsbook is aware of any "match-fixing" taking place.

So, what kind of effect does this betting line create? We've discussed that high odds are fatally attractive to players. Those who understand the game will place their bets on the stronger team because they're aware of the team's capabilities. But those who don't know much about the game will also bet on the stronger team simply because the odds are enticing. However, neither group is aware that the match has been manipulated and that the stronger team will lose in the end.

Looking at it from another perspective, these uninformed members of the public, unknowingly, end up placing themselves on the losing side.

Whenever there's match-fixing, this situation is bound to occur. That's because those manipulating the game will place significant bets. Websites must balance the betting lines, and players will always be enticed by high odds. This chain reaction results in the equation: "Match-fixing = Unaware individuals losing money." Thus, match-fixing inflicts significant damage on the average player.

Moreover, this damage has a more profound effect on more seasoned bettors for two primary reasons. Firstly, those manipulating matches often struggle to orchestrate precise outcomes. It's already quite an achievement to get a strong team to lose, let alone arranging for a specific final score like 2:3. This would be nearly impossible. As a result, those manipulating matches would mainly bet on the point spread line, neglecting other types of bets. Consequently, the only odds genuinely affected on betting sites are those of the point spread.

This method is precisely the one that savvy players would bet on. As we've discussed, in the long run, it's primarily this betting method that can be profitable. Other bets with lower odds of winning are much harder to profit from. While average players diversify their bets, trying their luck with various methods, hoping to gain some compensation, astute bettors put all their eggs in one basket, only betting on the point spread. This means they stand to lose much more than the average player.

Secondly, match fixing can result in an odd betting line, which is "strong teams with high odds and weak teams with low odds". Such a betting line is very appealing, especially to savvy players. As we've discussed throughout this book, to achieve long-term profits, one must seek high odds in every game. Therefore, players need to constantly monitor the odds and buy at the peak.

So, when savvy players notice this peculiar betting line, they can't resist. With both a strong team and high odds, it's an opportunity they'll want to seize, so they'll eagerly place bets, and in the end, they tend to lose the most. On the other hand, casual players who are unaware of the importance of high odds might not notice anything unusual about the betting line, so they are less affected.

Thus, when match fixing occurs, the betting line becomes especially appealing to everyone. The more experienced the player, the more they are drawn to it, much like "moths to a flame". Moreover, when players purchase betting tickets, they often end up betting on the losing team. This is precisely why everyone in sports betting dislikes "fixed matches".

So, what attitude should players adopt towards "fixed matches"? Firstly, don't believe in rumors or be superstitious about online sportsbooks manipulating matches. Especially be wary of offers that require joining a membership or paying fees to get insider information. Such offers are, without a doubt, 100% fake.

In the world of sports betting, regardless of how websites select unbiased matches, and no matter how fair the game is, rumors will always arise. There might even be some bizarre observational rules. Just listen to these rumors and don't take them seriously. Certainly, don't place your bets based solely on these rumors. Doing so might be even worse than betting blindly.

In conclusion, it's always best to place average bets and maintain a statistical table to monitor your long-term investment returns. Don't make sudden large bets just because of a superstition about "fixed games". We've detailed all of this in the "Player's Guide". I believe that if players follow these principles and have an investor's mindset, even if they encounter a "fixed game", the damage they suffer would be minimal.

Additionally, when you engage in sports betting, you're dealing with both gambling and investment returns. Relying solely on sports knowledge is not enough, especially when "fixed games" occur. Those who understand the game best often lose the most. Therefore, it's essential to also understand the principles behind how online sportsbooks operate and familiarize oneself with common investment risk management theories. Relying solely on sports expertise when placing a bet can lead to significant losses.

## Discussing the Legalization of Sports Betting

Most countries and regions around the world already have legal sports betting websites. For those interested, it's easy to apply the advice from this book into practice. Given this context, isn't discussing whether sports betting should be legalized a bit too late? Moreover, throughout this book, it's rather straightforward for readers to deduce which side we are on regarding this issue. So, do we still need to discuss whether sports betting should be legalized?

Of course, we should, because it's a fascinating topic. Additionally, even after many countries legalized sports betting, opposition to it has never ceased. And if you guessed right, I indeed support the legalization of sports betting. However, supporting the legalization doesn't mean you endorse betting. In fact, even if everyone despises sports betting and wishes to eradicate it entirely, the only way to achieve that is through its legalization.

Today's media oversimplifies the issue. They either argue that sports betting is gambling, and the government shouldn't promote gambling, hence it should be banned. Or they argue that since gambling can't be stopped, it's better to legalize it to increase tax revenue.

Making things black and white leaves people with only two choices, forcing them to pick a side. However, as the saying goes, "outsiders watch the fun, insiders understand the intricacies". Let's discuss from an insider's perspective:

Why should underground sports betting be banned?

Why can't governments across the world enforce the ban effectively?

Why is the only way to ban it, ironically, to legalize it?

Why, after legalizing sports betting, some countries succeed in curbing underground sports betting while others don't?

Why does underground sports betting still find space to thrive even after sports betting is legalized?

Firstly, sports betting is an impressive invention. It's definitely gambling, but it doesn't appear to be so. It possesses all the downsides of traditional gambling, yet many fail to realize this! What's worse is that sports betting has a self-replicating mechanism, making it spread and evolve like a computer virus. Even without any promotion by its designers, the number of players continues to grow, and the system becomes increasingly refined.

The true essence of sports betting is, when stripped down, simply wagering on the outcome of sports games. Since it's about predicting wins and losses, the odds are 1/2. Furthermore, those who watch the games tend to predict more accurately than those who don't, making it unlike traditional gambling. Or, to put it another way, winning in this game doesn't rely solely on luck. It depends on knowledge, research, and objective forecasting.

Furthermore, this game allows a small percentage of players to consistently make money. There are three ways to profit, but let's discuss the first two.

First, players can win fair and square. By precisely understanding the odds and the probability of guessing correctly, it can be achieved. The formula for players' return on investment is as follows:

**Return on Investment (ROI) = (Odds x Probability of Guessing Right) - 1.**

Secondly, players can earn "juice" or commission. This refers to profiting from the difference in odds by betting on both teams, ensuring that regardless of the game's outcome, they make money. This requires understanding the relationship between odds and time, but it's unrelated to the probability of guessing correctly. In other words, players can make money no matter what. (For a detailed method, please refer to the "Wise Guy" section of this book).

Thus, this kind of game is vastly different from traditional gambling as we know it. If you tell a newbie that gambling is bad, they'll respond, "This isn't gambling." If you tell them they'll surely lose money, they might retort, "Some people just always seem to be making money."

## In Essence, It's Still Gambling.

Traditionally, what are the downsides of gambling? Essentially, it's losing money. The bigger the bet, the more one stands to lose. In the end, when someone loses to the point of bankruptcy, it poses societal issues.

Even though sports betting might not seem like gambling, it undoubtedly possesses these negatives. The basic rule of sports betting is that the majority of players must lose money; it's imperative for the continuity of the game. Moreover, we can directly deduce the rate of return for most people's investments.

Assuming everyone hasn't read this book and doesn't understand the principles, blindly placing bets, then your annual rate of return ranges from -3% to -100%. This figure varies across online sportsbooks and is related to the "juice" or commission they wish to charge. If they take a 5% commission, then playing on that platform would result in an annual rate of return of -5%.

Yes, the return rates are all negative. This means that if people just play casually, the more they play, the more they lose. What's even more regrettable is that this figure is very accurate. The longer people play, the closer their return rate will be to the aforementioned figure.

However, the greatness of sports betting lies in the fact that if you don't keep track with charts or accounting, it's not easy to realize that you're actually losing money. The principle of this game is designed to let players lose slowly. But a slow loss is still a loss, and if players become impatient, they'll bet even more. Thus, it still causes social issues, just like traditional gambling.

**Personal growth, self-improvement, and comprehensive career planning:**
In sports betting, the third way to make money is to act as an intermediary and earn a "commission." This can be achieved by running a betting site or, as introduced in our book, "raising funds to buy betting tickets." By purchasing tickets on behalf of others and conducting private transactions, you can keep the money for yourself. By leveraging the balancing principle of the websites, you can earn the "juice" that would typically go to the website.
In this approach, if you want to earn more, you need to have many friends and handle large betting amounts. Hence, an experienced player will proactively seek to introduce more new players. And as these newcomers become veterans, they too will seek to bring in even more participants. Consequently, this game is self-sustaining and never lacks players.
Moreover, a seasoned player, once they start earning "juice", will soon realize something: as their income grows, the matters they need to manage become increasingly numerous and complex. Soon, this player will face two choices. First, to scale down and casually help friends buy betting tickets. Second, to compromise with this game, join the industry's food chain, and share their profits. Starting as an agent, they can gradually climb the ladder:
Agent -> Main Agent -> Shareholder -> Small Online Sportsbook -> Large

Online Sportsbook

This career progression is similar to working in a large corporation. With time and their own capabilities, a player can slowly climb to higher positions, gaining more power and reaping greater profits.

But in every upward development process, the player will also find that the competition has become more intense, and the money is harder to earn. Therefore, they must further perfect all the systems of the game, continually innovate to reduce costs or increase revenue. This has led to the emergence of modern systems such as the "grading system for betting lines" and the "commission-based system." The pace of such innovations never stops, making the game even more detailed and robust.

Once we understand the nature of sports betting, we can comprehend why it has developed so rapidly. Why does it bring so many social problems? However, with these issues, solutions are required. So the media offers everyone two choices. Should sports betting be banned? Or should it be legalized?

Starting with the ban on sports betting, since sports betting is such a formidable game and its vitality is so strong that it can become its industry, the simplest solution is, of course, to legislate its prohibition, asking the public not to engage in this game. Moreover, we can even add supplementary measures to ensure its completeness. These complementary solutions can roughly be divided into three categories.

Firstly, strong advocacy. Informing everyone that gambling is harmful and strengthening moral education to encourage people to voluntarily distance themselves from this mentally and physically damaging activity.

Secondly, utilizing police force for crackdowns. Strictly punishing those involved in gambling and also addressing the issue at its root, isolating it so that the general public cannot access this game.

Thirdly, promoting milder games as alternatives. Diverting the public's attention and providing those who wish to gamble with an outlet to vent.

Overall, those in favor of banning sports betting are quite visionary. They recognize the social problems brought about by sports gambling, and not only talk about it, but also propose a comprehensive plan that the government can implement to eradicate the negative impacts of sports betting on the nation.

Their intentions are good, and objectively speaking, the above plan is well-reasoned. It covers all bases and is highly operational. Specific implementation plans can be set out for every stage. We have to admit, this is an excellently designed approach. However, it's unfortunate that it's ineffective!

Yes, this entire approach is not only theoretically unfeasible, but also impractical in reality.

Let's take an example. In China, due to the public's passion for soccer and the prevalence of underground betting, the government has long legislated against sports betting and has implemented all accompanying measures.

**China Promotes the Dangers of Soccer Betting**

First and foremost, the Chinese government makes extensive use of influential media platforms such as television, newspapers, radio, and online sportsbooks to disseminate moral messages. They specifically inform the public about the dangers of gambling. Within televised news reports, there are also frequent segments that highlight cases where gambling has caused harm. For example, reporters conduct on-site interviews with victims who, with tears in their eyes, recount their stories of how soccer betting led them to lose their life savings, culminating in broken families and personal ruin. These reports deeply affect those who see them.

Moreover, the police prioritize underground soccer betting as a major case. Once they crack such a case, they immediately notify the media and take the opportunity to educate the public on a grand scale. Major media outlets cooperate fully, devoting large sections to detailing the circumstances surrounding the cracking of these soccer betting cases. For example, in Shaanxi Province, a report might detail the dismantling of an underground soccer betting ring, the amount of money seized, and the heavy sentences handed down to the main culprits, sometimes involving many years of imprisonment. These intimidating reports are frequently found in the news, serving as cautionary tales.

Some newspapers and websites go as far as to fight fire with fire, creating false rumors that accuse underground soccer betting sites of greedily collecting ill-gotten gains and colluding with foreign teams to fix matches, thereby exploiting the good-natured and ignorant rural population. Among these are purported "reformed" insiders from the online sportsbooks, who expose how they used to manipulate lines, contact players, and collect "juice" at rates even more extortionate than loan sharks.

Of course, these are nothing but baseless rumors. As we've said before, there's no reason for a betting site to fix matches, and the "juice" they collect can't be more than what's levied by loan sharks. If that were the case, sports betting wouldn't be as popular as it is.

However, from the standpoint of public advocacy, spreading such rumors may be understandable; after all, the deterrent power of rumors often exceeds that of bland propaganda.

So, regardless of the methods they employ for deterrence, it's undeniable that the Chinese government has made its utmost efforts in moral education and public advocacy. And it's also true that the intensity of this campaign is something other countries likely couldn't replicate, even if they wanted to.

## Eliminating the Root Causes of Gambling

Next is the eradication of underground sports betting sites, cutting off the gambling activities at their source. Those who are well-acquainted with the sports betting industry know that this activity has seamlessly integrated with the internet. All a player has to do is go online and through a sportsbook, they can view betting lines and place bets by buying betting tickets. Therefore, the real source is not a physical location, but the ubiquitous internet. This makes it incredibly difficult to crack down on underground gambling and prevent players from accessing these games.

The Chinese government is well aware of this. To stop underground sports betting, internet regulation is essential. Fortunately, they are well-equipped for this task. China not only has a national-level firewall, but they also have the strictest internet regulatory measures and a massive cyber police force to prevent citizens from accessing various harmful websites. Due to this, tracing domestic underground sports betting sites and blocking foreign legal sports betting is much easier for China than for other countries. Through online investigations, they can identify criminals and effectively root them out. So, when it comes to eliminating the root causes of gambling, other countries, limited by manpower or privacy concerns, simply can't achieve this level of internet regulation.

Finally, the Chinese government has also introduced its state-sponsored "football lottery" as a legitimate outlet for the public. Although both the "football lottery" and the "sports betting" we discuss in this book involve betting on the outcome of football matches, the details between the two are worlds apart. However, we will discuss this further later. We all know that mainland China is incredibly passionate about football, and the emergence of this kind of lottery offers a legal avenue for the public to place bets and win prizes. The football lottery is a rather humane arrangement; after all, gambling is human nature. Carefully designed by the government, this type of betting is fairly mild, making it unlikely for bettors to lose all their assets, thereby minimizing social problems. Since its launch, the football lottery has indeed caused a buying frenzy and continues to be a trend in mainland China.

The Chinese government's measures have been in effect for several years, making this case a prime example for the ineffectiveness of banning sports betting. Firstly, we should recognize that the Chinese government has been uncompromising in implementing these plans, essentially exhausting all avenues. Lack of efficacy should not be attributed to poor implementation. As mentioned before, although the plans are sound and thoroughly executed, they simply do not work. China remains the largest underground sports betting market in Asia, with an estimated daily turnover of billions of RMB. Even if you're not an insider and unaware of these statistics, it doesn't matter. We can see it from another angle. If these plans were effective, their news media wouldn't be busy reporting an endless stream of major cases. Logically, once the plans are implemented and sports betting eradicated, society should be harmonious.

So where exactly is the problem? To understand this, we must first comprehend the nature of sports betting. Our conclusion is that sports betting as a game is inherently resistant to sweeping crackdowns by the government.

Firstly, the game doesn't look like gambling, so your advocacy won't work. When a victim appears on television detailing how they got hurt by sports betting, people may sympathize but also think that this individual must not really understand the sport and made inaccurate guesses. When we place bets ourselves, we think we're pretty accurate. Even if we take a step back, we can at least get six or seven out of ten games right. So, while the person in the news is gambling, we don't see ourselves as doing the same when we participate.

Secondly, the industry is incredibly resilient and capable of self-healing. When law enforcement busts a sports betting operation, it may temporarily impact underground sports betting, causing them to lie low for a while. But quickly, new players will be attracted and old players will evolve into agents, who will then get promoted to the role of online sportsbook operators.

The organization quickly recovers and even learns from its mistakes, altering its systems, which makes it harder for the police to bust another operation next time. To give an example, after repeated busts, underground sports betting websites now know to periodically change the location of their servers, encrypt all transmitted content, and even add elements of sports discussion forums to disguise the website as a regular online forum. This is an evolutionary strategy, and it's why, despite China's strict internet regulations, underground sports betting websites still manage to survive.

## "Mild Version" of "Soccer Betting

Finally, let's discuss what is known as the "mild version" of "soccer betting tickets." In China, these legal betting tickets do indeed allow you to place bets on the outcomes of soccer matches. However, there are two major issues with this type of game. Let's go over them briefly.

First, players can't bet on single games; you have to play 14 games at a time. In other words, you have to predict the outcome of 14 matches and get them all right to win the prize money. This method is what we refer to as a "parlay" in this book, specifically a 14-leg parlay. So what are the odds of correctly guessing 14 matches? Assuming you're betting blindly and each match has a 1/2 chance, then the odds of guessing all 14 right would be 1/16,384. Yes, you read that right; our chances of winning the prize money are about one in 16,384. These odds aren't exactly low, but they're not high either. Compared to the traditional number-guessing lottery tickets with a one in 13 million chance, the odds for these soccer betting tickets are actually reasonable. But think about it: you'd have to buy 16,384 tickets just to win one. I suspect that not many people would be keen on playing under these circumstances.

Second, even if you do guess all the matches correctly, the amount of prize money you'll receive is still uncertain. It depends on how many other players also guessed correctly because the total prize pool has to be divided among everyone who won.

Here, the prize distribution is the same as that of lottery tickets. Once we confirm that we've won, we must quickly check how many other people have also won. For instance, if three people guess correctly, then we'll only get a third of the total prize money. This practice is known in the industry as

"Jackpot Splitting." The most notable feature is that the odds disappear. When we buy this type of ticket, it's like buying a lottery ticket. The ticket costs $2, and there are no odds listed. Everyone eventually splits the prize money.

So, this is a mild form of betting. With such low odds of winning, people are unlikely to place large bets, and all the betting techniques discussed in this book become irrelevant. Naturally, it becomes difficult to consistently make money. As you can imagine, it's hard for this kind of ticket to generate "frenzy" among players. However, it's this very "mildness" that becomes the fatal flaw of the game.

Boring, hard to win, and lacking social engagement, these football betting tickets have earned a reputation for being dull. Although they don't create significant societal issues, these games lack vitality. People who have tried them are quickly lured into underground betting systems that use "Fixed Odds," thereby ironically promoting the growth of underground betting.

Here's a quick note: the term "Fixed Odds" refers to the standard practices discussed in this book. The word "fixed" doesn't imply that the odds are static, but rather that odds will consistently appear on the ticket.

In sports betting, "Fixed-Odds Betting" and "Parimutuel Betting" are the two mainstream systems. However, it's easy to see that there is a skill and mathematical theory behind making money in fixed-odds betting, while parimutuel betting relies purely on luck. Therefore, fixed-odds betting is the mainstream method within the sports gambling circle.

Another crucial point to consider is the probability of winning. When you engage in parimutuel betting, you'll quickly realize that your friends are also losing, similar to your experience. Anyone who has purchased a lottery ticket knows this feeling since the odds of winning are one in ten thousand, making it very difficult to win. On the other hand, with fixed-odds betting, you can place bets on single games, and the probability of winning is 1/2. So even if you keep losing, you'll find that some of your friends are still making money, which encourages you to keep playing.

Whether we discuss it from a practical or theoretical standpoint, banning sports betting cannot prevent the growth of underground gambling, and uncontrolled underground gambling can lead to numerous unpredictable societal issues, such as websites shutting down or refusing to acknowledge that a player has won money.

So let's explore another option: government-operated sports betting. The theoretical basis for this is that the vitality of sports betting is too strong to eliminate. The best way to combat sports betting is through another form of sports betting. Here's a real-world example: Singapore officially launched its government-run sports betting in 1999 and focused on two key points.

First, they adopted the "Fixed-Odds Betting" system. With fixed odds, the government-promoted betting system is completely in line with underground sports gambling, and all standard techniques discussed in this book are applicable.

Second, they offer a payout rate of up to 90% of the total prize money. From a purely commercial perspective, this allows the official system to compete with underground gambling, a topic we will discuss later.

So, how effective has this been? We can't claim that underground sports betting has been completely eradicated in Singapore, but it is safe to say that its harm has been greatly reduced. The general opinion towards the Singaporean government is more positive than negative in this regard. However, we need to discuss an issue first. When the government operates sports betting, it often has two missions that underground sports betting does not face. The first is, of course, to combat underground sports betting. The second is to promote public welfare, which includes increasing government revenue, taking care of the disadvantaged, and subsidizing the sports industry to boost everyone's enthusiasm for sports activities. Simply put, the two objectives are **first, to combat underground sports betting, and second, to increase government revenue.**

Regrettably, these two objectives are in conflict with each other. Why do we say that? The main reason lies in a term we mentioned earlier: "Total Payout Ratio." The Total Payout Ratio, or the total payout, is a ratio set by the government. By setting this ratio, the government can determine its own profit. For instance, if we set the total payout at 75%, this means that when a player bets $100, they can only win back a maximum of $75. In this case, the government's net profit would be $25. If we raise the total payout to 90%, then when a player bets $100, they can win back a maximum of $90, leaving the government with a net profit of just $10.

So how effective has this been in Singapore? We can't say that underground sports betting has been completely eradicated there, but what is certain is that its impact has been greatly minimized. Public opinion about the Singaporean government's efforts is more positive than critical.

However, we need to discuss an issue. When governments run sports betting operations, they usually have two missions, neither of which underground betting faces. The first is to curb underground betting, and the second is to benefit public welfare, such as increasing tax revenue, caring for the disadvantaged, and subsidizing the sports industry to boost public interest in sports. To put it simply, the objectives are: First, to combat underground sports betting. Second, to increase government revenue.

Unfortunately, these two goals are in conflict. Why do we say that? The main reason lies in a term we discussed earlier: the "Total Payout Ratio." The Total Payout Ratio, also known as the "total payout," is a rate set by the government. By setting this rate, the government determines its own profit. For instance, if the total payout is set at 75%, this means that when a player bets $100, they can only get back a maximum of $75, leaving a net profit of $25 for the government. If the total payout is raised to 90%, players betting $100 can win back up to $90, reducing the government's net profit to just $10.

In the sports betting industry, one of the government's most convenient tools is setting the total payout ratio to control actual profits. Let's look at it from the opposite perspective: If sports betting generates $100 million in daily revenue, and the government sets the total payout ratio at 90%, then the government's daily profit would be $1 million. With such a large sum, it becomes quite easy to either fill the national treasury or sponsor public welfare projects. If that's not sufficient, the total payout ratio can be further reduced to make even more money.

However, this total payout ratio is closely related to the players. Essentially, the total payout ratio is the odds that everyone sees when they place a bet. Once the government sets the ratio, online sportsbooks adjust it into odds that everyone can bet on. The higher the total payout ratio, the better the odds that everyone can get, and vice versa. Players are very particular about these odds. As we've mentioned, the formula for a player's return rate is:

**ROI = (Online Sportsbook's Odds x Player's Probability of Guessing Correctly) - 1**

So, from the player's perspective, the higher the odds, the better, as this would lead to a higher return rate. To get high odds, a high total payout ratio is necessary.

In summary, we can conclude:

For the government, lowering the total payout ratio as much as possible is ideal for maximizing tax revenue.

For players, increasing the total payout ratio as much as possible is the key to making money and is more attractive.

Unfortunately, the interests of the government in terms of tax revenue and those of the players are in opposition. If the government wants to increase tax revenue, the game becomes unattractive to players. On the other hand, if players love the game, then the government won't generate high tax revenue. Underground sports betting also has this kind of total payout ratio, and, of course, they set this number themselves, generally ranging between 90% and 95%.

## To Combat Illegal Sports Betting or To Increase Government Revenue

This is a dilemma. We have previously mentioned that the only way to challenge sports betting as an activity is through another form of sports betting. Now the problem is that underground sportsbooks have set a standard, fixing the overall payout ratio at around 90%. This means that the government must follow suit. Ideally, their ratio should be even higher, or at least not much lower. Otherwise, players will not accept it and will turn to underground sports betting. After all, nobody wants to turn down a better deal when it comes to money.

However, we have also discussed that the government, when operating sports betting, often takes on another responsibility—that of increasing tax revenue to provide for public welfare and care for the disadvantaged. As a result, the payout ratio cannot be set too high, otherwise the government won't make much money, and consequently won't be able to provide for the disadvantaged.

So, achieving these two objectives simultaneously is impossible. If you aim for both, chances are you won't achieve either. The root cause of this phenomenon is psychology, not limitations imposed by the government or the rules of the game.

Let's now take a look at how other countries handle this. In Singapore, their overall payout ratio is 90%. This suggests that the government aims to completely eradicate underground sports betting. A 90% ratio is not much different from that of illegal sportsbooks, and since the government is credible, players no longer need to deal with the underground market. If one still seeks to make a quick buck through illegal betting, they risk encountering issues such as website shutdowns or disputes, which is certainly not worth it.

The total payout rate in China is 65%, which tells us that not only is their betting style uninteresting, but the total payout is also not enticing. It's no wonder they can't curb underground sports betting. However, looking at it from another angle, such a low payout rate results in significant revenue for the government. Their real aim seems to be to focus on increasing government tax revenue and promoting public welfare. We can't say that's wrong; it simply means they can't combat illegal sports betting effectively.

We have counter-evidence: if a total payout rate of 75% were effective, the Singapore government wouldn't need to set their rate as high as 90%. So, if after the legalization of sports betting, underground betting still exists, don't be too surprised. It's a natural outcome caused by mathematics and player psychology, and it relates to the general belief that sports lotteries should increase government tax revenue. We could say that people, with good intentions, want to use sports betting to help the disadvantaged but end up not being able to counteract underground sports betting.

Therefore, legalizing sports betting is only the first step in eradicating underground betting. Whether it will be effective depends on whether the government can earmark the revenue exclusively for this purpose. If the government could forgo the tax revenue and give the highest rewards back to the players without generating surplus or helping the disadvantaged, eradicating underground sports betting would be as easy as flipping a switch. However, this idea is not only difficult to implement but also hard to even discuss, as most people would not accept it. Unfortunately, that's the reality of the situation.

Whether it's the government acting as the bookmaker or private companies, sports betting remains sports betting, and gambling often leads to losses. Losses in turn can lead to societal issues. As we've mentioned before, in sports betting, the majority of people are destined to lose. Critics of sports betting often accuse the government of exacerbating social problems rather than solving them by legalizing sports betting. The government's credibility attracts even more people to participate, increasing the societal burden. Even if the government gains tax revenue, it can't possibly care for everyone or offset the harm caused by gambling.

To put it bluntly, the government's approach to legalizing sports betting amounts to the majority of citizens losing 20% of their bets each year, while the government takes a 10% cut. When social problems emerge from gambling losses, it's left to the government to sort them out with that 10%, although it's uncertain whether that will be sufficient.

While it's an uncomfortable truth, many argue it's still a better approach compared to China's complete prohibition, which not only incurs significant social costs for enforcement but also perpetuates underground sports betting and related social issues.

Proponents of legalization argue that prohibition only brings more harm, something we've discussed before. However, when it comes to the damage caused by gambling, they are at a loss. The common fallback is moral education. The government tries to teach citizens about the dangers of gambling, hoping they will choose to gamble less, thus partially alleviating social issues.

However, this approach is unrealistic. If moral education were effective, outright prohibition would suffice. The very reason sports betting proliferates is that the majority of people don't see it as gambling but as a way to make money. After legalization, relying solely on moral education to reduce betting doesn't seem plausible.

To truly address the societal problems caused by sports betting, education is key. However, the education we are referring to is not moral education, nor general public awareness campaigns. What we need to focus on is teaching people how to make money.

- How to engage in sports betting.

- What is the "juice" on sportsbook websites, and how do they make money.

- How players can calculate their return on investment.

- How players can make risk-free investments through arbitrage.

- Other money-making tips, such as "pooling funds to place a bet."

- Teach everyone how to build such a website.

This type of education differs from moral education; you teach people how to make money, and they'll listen. For example, let's directly calculate the return on investment. After calculating for a while, you'll find that the appeal of sports betting is far less than that of stocks, time deposits, funds, and even real estate. Why isn't it attractive? First, even if we use all the techniques, the expected rate of return on sports betting is still lower than 10%. This is much lower than the expected rate of return on stocks. Second, sports betting is not as safe as a bank time deposit. If you really want to win without losing, it's better to deposit your money in the bank.

If people are still skeptical about the return rate, that's fine. We can teach more exciting ways to make money and directly help them earn through sports betting. Indeed, sports betting is a skillful game. At its core, we see that the game genuinely allows a small portion of people to make money. So why not aim to make everyone part of this profitable minority?

Ideally, if everyone is making money, then naturally, there won't be significant societal issues, and the harm of gambling will resolve itself. This would be a situation everyone would love to see. However, unfortunately, that can't happen. The foundation of the game only allows a small portion of people to profit. Once everyone knows how to make money, the game's lifespan will be short.

The opaqueness of information is what sports betting relies on. The less you know, the more you're inclined to believe rumors or untrue methods circulated online. Because, after all, some people are making money, and ignorance will make things worse. On the other hand, if everyone understands how online sportsbooks operate and knows the skills required for players, the game would be over, even if only more than half of the players know.

Let's take another example. In the "Agent" chapter, we mentioned how to buy betting tickets on behalf of others to embezzle the "juice" that should go to the online sportsbook. This is a risk-free way to make money. If everyone adopts this method, no online sportsbook will survive. It's simple: without the "juice," there's no profit. And no one wants to be in a business that doesn't make money. Without online sportsbooks, the game of sports betting can't exist, relying solely on players.

So, either way, as long as we promote the economics of sports betting and educate the public, the outcome is precisely what those opposing gambling hope for. Either everyone makes money, or the game ceases to exist.

Sounds paradoxical? To eliminate sports betting, we need to promote it? That's why we say this game is indeed a magnificent invention. To reform it, you'll need the proverb "push something to the extreme, and it will turn the other way."

### Support for Legalizing Sports Betting

Whether you like gambling or not, and regardless of the social issues it may bring, you should support the legalization of sports betting. This is the first step, and only after taking this initial step can subsequent measures follow. The ultimate solution to the gambling issue lies in education, specifically financial education rather than moral lessons. Once we teach people how to make money properly through sports betting, it becomes just a game that does no harm. If such education reaches its pinnacle, it will lead to the collapse of the entire sports betting industry, which is what we infer and the only way to tackle sports betting. Don't believe it? That's because you don't know how much online sportsbooks fear the so-called "Wise guys."

## Sports Betting and Export Markets

In 2006, the U.S. Congress passed a bill prohibiting American banks and credit card companies from processing payments for offshore online gambling. Following this, WTO members led by the European Union and including India, Japan, Costa Rica, Canada, Macau, and Antigua, sequentially demanded consultation and compensation with the United States. The EU also stated that it would pressure the U.S. for non-discriminatory treatment for European gambling companies.

This news is intriguing, especially when viewed from an outsider's perspective. However, the first thing to mention is that this U.S. action targets all online gambling, not just sports betting. It includes other games like poker and online roulette. Despite that, it does primarily affect sports betting due to its inherent fairness and the fact that it doesn't seem like gambling. It has long been the dominant force in online gambling, attracting more players and larger bets than any other games.

So why are we discussing this news? This book has already discussed how online sportsbooks make money, how players make money, and even how agents make money. Now, of course, we need to talk about the pinnacle of profitability, which is how a country can profit from the sports betting industry.

Many people might find our discussion on this topic distasteful and unethical. The government legalizing sports betting is already a reluctant move. It's a compromise because prohibiting it would make things worse and will still bring social issues. So, why are we trying to capitalize on this situation, giving the government an opportunity to rake in even more money?

So, the article starts by referencing news about the European Union and the United States for a reason. The key focus of our discussion is solely on the export of sports betting, not domestic sales. Moreover, we are not discussing how the government can make more money or what additional social costs need to be borne. What we're discussing is beneficial for the nation and advantageous for everyone.

Allowing sports betting will indeed bring issues to society, but it is a better solution compared to banning it. Furthermore, these issues can be mitigated through economic education—not moral education—to help people understand sports betting and reduce social problems. We can't deny that both allowing sports betting and educating the public will incur social costs. But since these are unavoidable, why not look at it from a perspective of maximizing the benefits for everyone using the existing social costs.

Taking a step back, the impact on society from legalizing sports betting has already occurred. Regardless of how we increase profits or how the government increases tax revenue, there will be no further impact on society. However, if we allow the country to fully develop the sports betting industry and use the tax revenue gained from exports to benefit the public, this will contribute more to social welfare, or even to the development of our sports activities.

Next, we will discuss the entire industry chain and export competition of sports betting. This is not something any company can easily do. This is a highly knowledge-intensive industry that requires advanced software and hardware technology, along with talented individuals for development. It's not like traditional gambling, where you can just get started with a bowl and some dice.

Don't believe it? Consider the example of Taiwan Sports Lottery's development. Taiwan didn't have the sports betting industry, so they had to import relevant software, hardware, and talent from the Hong Kong Jockey Club to issue lottery tickets. This serves as the best example of Taiwan legalizing sports betting while Hong Kong reaps the benefits. The export of technology to Taiwan didn't cause more damage to Hong Kong; on the contrary, the Hong Kong Jockey Club gained more benefits to contribute to their government, creating more foreign exchange.

I believe this factor is the primary reason we advocate for the development of a national sports betting industry. We will also argue that once the government develops an export industry for sports betting, the negative impact of gambling on the country will be minimized, far better than the situation where only one company dominates the market.

## What Should We Export?

After discussing why we should get into exports, let's talk about what exactly we intend to export. Generally, there are four major categories that can serve as the goods a country wants to export:

Online betting, Technology exports, Professional operations, and Website trading centers.

Starting with the first category, as we could discern from the news earlier, legal gambling companies in Europe are conducting business globally. Through the internet, they attract bettors from around the world to engage in legal sports betting on European websites. This is something we can do as well.

I believe that this kind of export might easily meet with public disapproval. Traditionally, gambling is considered bad. If we are already partaking in it behind closed doors, exporting it to other countries would seem even worse, wouldn't it? On this issue, we have three points to consider.

Firstly, gambling is not necessarily a bad thing. In fact, it's only bad if you lose. In many countries, local casinos are allowed but only foreign passport holders can enter to gamble. South Korea operates under such a rule; its own citizens are strictly prohibited from gambling, but it's fine for foreigners. So, the idea that it's bad for locals to gamble, but fine for foreigners, is a widespread concept. Our desire to export sports lottery tickets aligns with mainstream thinking; it's not a significant wrong.

Secondly, both the United States and Europe have legal casinos that attract tens of millions of tourists for gambling each year. Las Vegas in the U.S., for instance, is a renowned gambling hotspot. So, why should they be allowed to invite us to gamble but we can't invite them?

Thirdly, when it comes to gambling, it's a consensual activity. We are not holding a gun to anyone's head and forcing them to gamble. Whoever decides to participate does so willingly. So, why feel guilty for them?

Therefore, we are already in the process of exporting betting tickets abroad; it's not just an idea but something we are actively doing. The realm of sports betting has always emphasized the importance of opening virtual channels, right? This is precisely what online betting is. Once a foreigner opens a bank account, they can start placing bets online. Even if they return to their home country later, nothing stops them from continuing to place bets and winning money online.

So, exporting betting tickets is already a practical action we are taking, albeit quietly and on a small scale, so it doesn't qualify as an export industry as such.

Next is technology export, which is less controversial as it doesn't invite foreigners to gamble. This is a labor-intensive avenue. What do we mean by technology export? We've seen this before, like when Taiwan needed help from the Hong Kong Jockey Club to issue its own Taiwan Sports Lottery. Similarly, we want to offer our technical expertise if other countries wish to develop their sports betting platforms in the future.

The concept of technology is broad and includes talents familiar with sports betting, such as risk traders, computer engineers, and management personnel. It also covers practical experience in website operations, management skills, and even computer hardware and software required for the betting system and betting sites.

Sports betting is an industry that demands a high level of technical expertise, talent, and hardware and software. These crucial elements are not only difficult to obtain but also quite expensive. Therefore, we can also choose to export specific talents and technologies to supplement the deficiencies of other countries.

In summary, if a location wants to develop its betting tickets, whether they lack the entire technology or just a small part, we can provide them with the required personnel, experience, or hardware and software.

Lastly, there's the concept of trading platforms for the sportsbooks, but this is more complex. We will skip it for now and discuss it in later chapters.

## Why Is There no Country That Has This Industry?

When looking at the items intended for export, we can already see the foundations of the sports betting industry. What makes up this industry? In a nutshell, it's about talent, experience, and both hardware and software. Only when these resources are abundantly available can an industry be formed.

So, is there any country currently possessing such an industry? We can say with certainty that there isn't. The reason is straightforward: anything related to sports betting—whether it's talent, experience, or hardware and software—is incredibly expensive, not just costly, but exorbitantly so. Such unreasonable prices wouldn't exist in a mature industry.

Only when there is a shortage of resources do prices get pushed up. Therefore, globally, whether it's legal sports betting above board or underground websites, none can form a mature industry, or rather, cannot nurture a sufficient number of talents or technologies.

So, let's discuss why no country has been able to form a mature industry. Currently, the world generally views sports betting as gambling. Either it's entirely banned, or it's entirely open. Both approaches fail to offer sufficient incentives to drive online sportsbooks to invest heavily in technology and fortify the entire industry chain.

The reason is simple: state-owned websites don't need it, and private websites don't want it.

Why don't state-owned websites need it? Because they often receive exclusive permission, completely monopolizing the market. Profits are already state-determined, so they have no need to strive for higher profits. They also have no incentive to develop further human and technological resources, as long as they have enough to get by.

As for entirely open, private operations—this is when the government issues licenses to private companies for legal operation—this approach also fails to fortify the industry chain. That's because their pursuit is profit, and the most significant profit in sports betting comes from "juice," a percentage of the turnover. Hence, technological development is undoubtedly unimportant, or at least, we can say it's far less critical compared to market advertising to attract new players.

So, although they have developed internal talent and technology within the company, they will certainly protect it rigorously to prevent it from leaking out. This is because they are the online sportsbook themselves. If their technology gets out, making other websites more competitive, it would be disadvantageous for them. Think about it, which licensed website would be willing to sell their own system for others to use?

To sum up, we can conclude that the main reason the industry can't flourish lies in the rules of the game. And the rules adopted by countries at present, either complete monopolies or complete openness, aren't particularly helpful. For a nation, building an industry can't be just for the purpose of increasing tax revenue. Otherwise, it loses the meaning of government support. To develop an industry, it must be able to increase domestic employment opportunities, enhance national competitiveness, and have a positive impact on citizens. Of course, the most important thing is that both the government and private enterprises should be able to make money; you can't let everyone run at a loss.

Sports betting indeed has these characteristics, but the prerequisite is that the government has to regulate it appropriately. We'll discuss the methods of regulation later, but it is definitely not about complete openness or monopolization. Sports betting is currently authorized by the state and is monopolistic; this cannot promote the sports betting industry. On the contrary, because the license is only valid for six years, this actually causes the operators to be shortsighted and to bring in foreign expertise, thereby losing the opportunity for us to develop the industry. But business people are naturally profit-oriented; we can't blame them for that.

A government-supported sports betting should be an open market, freely competed in by private enterprises. As long as any company wants to enter this market, they can do so legally by applying for a license. But their competition with each other is not about grabbing players; in other words, they don't want to engage in vicious price competition in the market. What they want, instead, is to allow technical talent to circulate to a limited extent, and to broadly recruit talent to develop more advanced hardware and software. The primary source of profits would be to export these high-end talents and technologies or to attract foreign bettors.

Moreover, for the citizens, having more websites means there are more new jobs, and these jobs are high-intellectual jobs. Not only do they offer high compensation and a sense of accomplishment, but the entry threshold is also very high. The talent nurtured by one website is not easily replaceable by just anyone.

Suppose we want to get into the sports betting industry now. What should we do to get the best results? For those with an economic background, you've probably realized that yes, we need new rules for an open market.

Some might argue that isn't the market already open? Even before the opening, we had countless underground websites operating according to market competition rules.

Firstly, what we want to discuss is that the purpose of the country's development of sports betting is not to nurture the entire industry. It is mainly to curb underground sports betting and increase government tax revenue. For easier management, the government uses a franchise system, allowing only one major player. With just one online sportsbook, there's no need to spend heavily on developing a better system or mastering all the technologies. The government has already set their profits at 15% of total revenue. All they have to do is focus on advertising to attract players to place bets. This is not what you call an open market.

Next, we have so-called underground websites. Many people say that our legal online sportsbook has to compete with them, right? This is true, but to be honest, this is not competition at the same level. Underground sites, being illegal, find it difficult to attract good talent, and therefore cannot develop technology and hardware. Cases where they have money but cannot find people are common.

Even if they are in competition, the competitors are the players; it's about capturing market share or developing new player groups. This kind of competition is malignant from a national perspective and unhelpful for the industry.

So, if we want to shape the sports betting industry and make it competitive at the national level, there's only one way. We need to open the market and allow more legal online sportsbooks to coexist; there's no other way around it.

## New Game Rules

In order to grow the industry, the only way is to open up the market, which means allowing more legal online sportsbooks to compete. At first glance, this approach appears to be radical and will undoubtedly face opposition from moral conservatives. The reason is simple: even one legal online sportsbook can disrupt social norms and potentially create societal issues. What chaos would ensue if multiple sites were legalized?

This concern is valid. An entirely deregulated market would undoubtedly lead to cutthroat competition and not achieve the desired effects. So let's discuss our main topic now: we want to open up the market, but not rigidly. We aim to flexibly delineate the rights and responsibilities of these online sportsbooks to facilitate their healthy development.

So, what are these rights?

Firstly, delineate between domestic and international sales.

Secondly, distinguish their scale of business.

What about responsibilities?

Firstly, categorize the amount of taxes to be remitted.

Secondly, specify the locations of their operations.

Essentially, the government should issue more licenses, and these licenses should be flexible and open to adjustments in their limitations.

Many countries currently adopt a rigid approach by granting a monopoly to a single online sportsbook. Its rights? It has the exclusive privilege of dominating the entire market and can also accept bets from abroad. And its responsibilities? Naturally, it has to pay taxes. The stipulation here is that 10% of the turnover goes to the government as tax. So what are the constraints? Two: firstly, the license period is only six years, and secondly, 15% of the turnover is their fixed profit.

This kind of liberalization is actually problematic. Because the profit margin is already fixed, there's only one way to make more money: boost the turnover and enlarge the market to attract more players. And this is precisely what moral conservatives vehemently oppose.

We also oppose this because once the profits are fixed, the online sportsbooks have to expand their market and cut costs as much as possible to recoup their initial investment within six years. This often leads them to source technology and manpower from abroad, minimizing local employment and talent development. While the government's regulatory approach is often based on precedents from other countries and isn't inherently flawed, we believe there's room for improvement—specifically, more flexible licensing systems.

Firstly, licenses could be categorized based on whether the online sportsbook focuses on domestic or international markets. Those focusing solely on international players should not be allowed to accept bets or transfers from domestic players. In contrast, those with domestic licensing would have no such restrictions and could freely accept bets from both domestic and international players. Such categorization would prevent an oversaturation of domestic-focused online sportsbooks, thereby mitigating social issues at home.

Secondly, separate licenses could be issued for big and small sportsbooks, each with its own set of daily betting volume restrictions. For example, a small sportsbook could apply for a license that limits them to $10 million in bets per day, whereas a larger one could apply for a $100 million per day license. If the day's volume exceeds these limits, they would not be allowed to accept any more bets for that day. This approach allows the government to implement volume control, further reducing societal issues. Unlimited expansion and lack of volume restrictions only incentivize these platforms to acquire more new players, increasing the number of potential victims.

With these differentiated license types, the government could also flexibly adjust taxes based on the sportsbook's volume. Smaller businesses would pay less, encouraging more competent firms to enter the market. We support the emergence of smaller online sportsbooks. Large sportsbooks rely on the "juice" to survive, but that's not necessarily the case for smaller ones. They could be technology-driven, mainly profiting from exporting talent and technology. For them, operating a book is merely a means to accumulate practical experience. The size of the sportsbook isn't as crucial as having hands-on experience, which can enhance their reputation.

Finally, it's important to differentiate based on geographic location. In other words, since we've opened up the market and are accepting license applications from various companies, naturally, foreign companies may be interested in applying. We've seen this happen in Vietnam as a precedent. However, their approach has a flaw; many foreign companies simply take the license and leave, which doesn't help the local industry.

We're not saying that issuing such licenses is unfeasible. In fact, it's a way for the government to generate revenue, and there's nothing inherently wrong with that. What we're suggesting is that licenses should be tiered. If a company operates locally, has a research and development center here, and employs local staff, the license fee should be lower. However, if they just take the license and leave, we should charge a higher fee for that license.

Is there a need for further restrictions? Actually, there's no need, as long as the rights and obligations are clearly delineated. The rest can be determined by market mechanisms. It's senseless to set operational years or limit online sportsbook profits.

So, what impact will this diversified licensing have on the sports betting ecosystem?

First, online sportsbooks lose the incentive to expand their market. To do bigger business, they'd have to buy a more expensive license. This limitation means they don't need to advertise to attract players—there's no point, as they can't accept bets beyond a certain daily turnover.

Second, with the removal of operational years, sportsbooks can adopt a sustainable business model. They don't have to recoup their initial investment within six years, encouraging them to think proactively. Is it more cost-effective to cultivate local talent? Should they develop their own systems to reduce costs? Or perhaps export this talent and technology for additional profits?

Third, because domestic turnovers are limited, the societal impact of these websites can be controlled. Since there's no cap on foreign turnover, these companies will need to expand internationally.

Fourth, this opens the door for companies from other sectors to enter the industry. For example, traditional software companies or emerging websites with internet technology can obtain smaller licenses to join the industry and bring new perspectives. As we've said before, a website without a reputation cannot export any technology. However, with a cheap, small license, these software companies gain practical experience. Having this opportunity allows them to make money by selling software to sportsbooks in other countries. It becomes easier to find buyers as long as they are actually operating.

Finally, when comparing a flexible licensing approach with a monopolistic one, it's clear that the benefits of a flexible system are numerous. Not only does it create an industry chain and increase employment opportunities, it also helps alleviate societal issues. Additionally, the government can significantly gain more tax revenue compared to a single online sportsbook. The cost of implementing such a system is also remarkably low; it merely requires changing the method of license distribution and monitoring the daily accounting of the online sportsbooks. It's worth mentioning that the financials within sports betting are fully computerized and real-time, making monitoring an effortless task.

As for the moral and ethical concerns regarding encouraging gambling, these can also be effectively managed. First, the sportsbooks will no longer need to endlessly encourage players to place bets. Also, by requiring these bookmakers to establish local operations, they would have to employ more staff, thereby increasing public awareness and understanding of this industry, which in turn minimizes societal issues.

Therefore, we believe that all countries should adopt this open system. Prohibiting sports betting is less effective than legalizing it; and legalizing it is less effective than opening up the market. Yet, an entirely open market is less effective than a regulated open market.

Having discussed the open market and its unique regulatory measures, the basic approach is to open up private companies and allow them to compete freely on an international stage, thereby nurturing a continuous flow of talent, technology, and capital at the local level. The government simply plays the role of a supervisor to prevent market disorder.

However, this approach is not the pinnacle of this industry. The ultimate method is led by the government, actively helping the market to develop steadily, and this approach is a "National Level Online Sportsbook Trading Center."

This is a public market, led by the government, specifically for the exchange and sale of betting tickets, but this market is not for players to engage in; all participants are online sportsbooks. These sportsbooks do not have a hierarchy; all are equal. They can negotiate with each other and freely exchange their betting tickets.

This concept is not new. It has existed ever since sports betting was invented and is currently practiced, albeit not so openly or systematically, by all sportsbooks. Why do sportsbooks need their trading market? The main reason is to balance the line. For example, in a game, if one team has $100 placed on it and the other has $200, the line is unbalanced and the sportsbook can't profit. Hence, it's necessary for them to take out $100 from the side with $200 and place that bet with another sportsbook to balance their line. This is a hedging strategy and is something that sportsbooks have to do daily.

Similarly, aside from laying off bets to hedge, sportsbooks will also accept bets from other sportsbooks to achieve the same hedging effect. So sportsbooks are continually exchanging their stakes to secure the most stable profits. Over time, an informal market naturally forms, and every new sportsbook must join this market to trade. Failure to do so greatly increases the risk for an individual sportsbook, which could potentially jeopardize its existence if it has severely imbalanced lines.

We cannot be sure how many such trading centers exist globally, nor can we determine the daily scale of these transactions. Most are non-public, and some large-scale sportsbooks even dominate a proprietary market for their trades. When they are poorly managed, these kinds of markets can disappear, a common issue with non-public markets. But the instability is not the only problem; these underground markets actually have many issues.

Firstly, the bigger fish eat the smaller fish in this trading market, as betting tickets have to be exchanged, creating the issue of buying and selling prices. Smaller sportsbook websites naturally have to yield to the larger ones because only the big sites have the capability to accept bets. To minimize risks, smaller sites have no choice but to be exploited, which is an inevitable aspect of business and unavoidable. However, in the long term, these small websites don't have any other options and their profits are constantly sacrificed. They will eventually be consumed by the larger sites and likely face closure.

Secondly, there's the issue of market absence. Take local small leagues as an example. Even if a legal online sportsbook does establish lines for them, the site will struggle to find partners in the international market willing to lay off these bets. The reason is simple: other countries don't offer such betting lines, so they cannot accept these kinds of bets. Thus, local sites are reluctant to open lines for local leagues. One of the reasons is the lack of a system to lay off bets, and without it, no matter how much capital a website has, it's insufficient when they have to wager against all the players.

Thirdly, there's a lack of standards. The sports betting industry is characterized by its real-time nature, meaning that odds can change at any moment. The odds are essentially the price of the betting tickets. This implies that within the trading market of a sportsbook website, the trading prices of betting tickets are constantly fluctuating. Due to the rapid changes in odds, transactions between different websites have to be fast and accurate. Otherwise, once the opportunity passes and the prices have changed, negotiations might have to start all over again. The underground market often lacks standardized price disclosure mechanisms and quick transaction processes, leading to time and financial losses for all participants.

Because of these drawbacks in the non-public markets, every sportsbook website has to participate yet wishes for a fair and open market. Only a government can assume this leadership role. Only a government-led public website trading market can ensure the healthy development of the sports betting industry. These two aspects are complementary.

Next, let's look at what a national-level sportsbook trading center can do for these websites, and what advantages it can bring in terms of national tax revenue.

Firstly, this trading center must allow legal websites from other countries to list themselves, as well as accommodate games from various regions for trading. This would offer each website the most trading options and help avoid situations where big fish swallow smaller fish, or where suitable trading partners can't be found. Secondly, the buying and selling prices and trading procedures must be standardized, so that each website can complete transactions in the shortest time possible.

Lastly, there needs to be a performance guarantee. In every transaction in this market, websites must be required to fulfill their obligations, similar to the requirements in the stock market; this is fundamental. As long as these three conditions are met, a government-led trading market can operate smoothly. This would normalize the profits for websites, greatly benefitting the industry. Moreover, allowing foreign websites to list themselves can also boost our tax revenue and internationalize our industry.

Because the benefits that this exchange market can offer websites are numerous, even if we levy a transaction tax on every deal, it won't dampen their enthusiasm for participating. This is a direct benefit that the country can reap. Opening up such an international trading market can also make other countries willing to open up their local leagues for overseas Chinese to place bets, as they can hedge their bets back to their home country. Likewise, people in the home country can also hedge their bets abroad.

In addition to this, the national credibility that the government can establish through this will bring marginal benefits that are incalculable in terms of attracting foreign investment and boosting industrial exports.

## Is There a Risk in an Open Market?

Much like other parts of this book, we must discuss the risks of an open sports betting market. One of the greatest fears a country may have when opening up the sports betting market is insufficient thoroughness and inadequate supportive measures. For example, if we open up the market without limiting domestic betting volumes, or if we make it too difficult for foreign online sportsbooks to set up shop, we risk creating a closed market, which could lead to additional problems.

Another important aspect is the necessity for rigorous regulation, particularly regarding the financial health of each online sportsbook. These platforms should be limited to doing business that corresponds to their available capital. A bankrupt sportsbook is not desirable, and while we must allow sportsbooks to close if they must, it's crucial to ensure they have the resources to pay out to players or other sportsbooks what they are due in winnings.

Lastly, there's the issue of licensing. Not everyone with the funds can enter this market; obtaining legal qualifications requires having a team of professionals on board, and the computer systems must be certified. This calls for the government to establish a certification system for both human talent and computer systems.

To minimize social issues and maximize national benefits, it's better to legalize sports betting than to prohibit it. And it's better to open up the entire market than just one sportsbook. Once the sports betting market matures, it essentially becomes another stock market. Proper regulation can create more job opportunities for the country and improve tax revenues.

This industry is highly intellectually intensive, which could stimulate industrial upgrades across society. The talent developed in this industry can also be employed in other sectors. One of the least concerns of this industry is job outsourcing because the labor cost is such a small part of the overall revenue. There's hardly any sportsbook that would move jobs overseas to save a few dollars. Also, the rise of China, which has been a concern in recent years, seems to have a minimal impact on this industry so far.

In this book, we specifically include this section to discuss the money-making rules of sports betting for nations, as the gaming industry could very well be the emerging sector that countries need next. Concerns about promoting gambling, especially after opening up the market, are mostly unfounded. Sports betting is only considered gambling when people don't understand it. Once people grasp it and calculate the return on investment, it turns into an investment and a form of entertainment that is less likely to be harmful.

To illustrate, we can look at mainland China, where underground sports betting and unreliable tips bring significant risks. Hong Kong, despite legalizing sports betting, is still rife with various strange betting techniques on the internet. For instance, some people teach how to identify rigged games, while others teach arbitrage techniques. In reality, these are incorrect approaches.

By encouraging an open market and establishing a comprehensive sports betting industry, we are indirectly educating the public. Through recruitment and training by private companies, more people can truly understand this activity. These individuals will help everyone grasp the correct concept of sports betting. Once the public understands it, they are less likely to be harmed by gambling.

Those who work in this field, whether they are risk management traders or software engineers, are not known to engage in betting themselves. This reinforces our belief that understanding is the real solution to the problem of gambling.

# Conclusion

If you've read up to this point, then this chapter serves as a conclusion. In this book, we've discussed how online sportsbooks, players, and even countries play their respective roles to maximize their benefits. We also delved into the organizational structure within the sportsbook and the unique three-tier agent system specific to this industry. Due to space constraints, we've only scratched the surface of each topic; each could be expanded into a book of its own. Since my primary expertise is still in software engineering, analytical tables and calculation tools introduced in this book will be provided later for hands-on experience.

Many principles and rules are discussed in this book, and some may contain errors or omissions. I encourage experts to correct them. You're also welcome to contact me directly for any corrections. This book is a reorganization of a publication from 10 years ago, so in the next chapter, I'll include letters and replies from readers over the years, which I hope will be helpful to everyone. Lastly, although this book discusses sports betting, it has nothing to do with actual sports events. Those who want insider information on teams will be disappointed.

To profit or lose less in sports betting, one must possess both sports expertise and gambling knowledge. You can learn about the principles of sports betting from this book, but for the remaining sports expertise, let's leave it to professional sports journalists and commentators. The operational principles discussed in this book are for research purposes only. If you're not a professional, actual implementation carries high risks, which should not be underestimated.

Additionally, in general public policy announcements, sports betting is often positioned as entertainment, and this is for good reason. Government agencies and relevant organizations also hope that people will bet within their means and simply enjoy the game without taking it too seriously. We think this is spot-on advice. Because this is a form of entertainment, try not to take it too seriously. The return rate is around -25%, so make sure to bet within your means and not lose too much all at once. This way, everyone will be happy.

Finally, let's talk about the anecdotes at the beginning of this book. "You wake up in a good mood, take a look at the sports section of the newspaper and see that your favorite team has a game today. On your way to work, you buy a cup of Starbucks coffee and, while you're at it, place a sports bet at a betting site, thinking that if your team wins, you could earn some extra money."

Here, I believe that this player has made seven mistakes, making it difficult for him to make money from sports betting.

1. He shouldn't feel compelled to place a bet; if he's not confident, he shouldn't bet at all.

2. He shouldn't bet based on his mood. Betting when he's in a good mood and not betting when he's in a bad one is a big mistake. The correct approach is to bet when the odds are good and refrain when the odds are not favorable.

3. He shouldn't only bet on his favorite team. Just because it's his favorite team doesn't mean it's the team that will win.

4. He shouldn't place bets during work hours. Odds are constantly changing, and work hours may not necessarily be the best time to get favorable odds.

5. He shouldn't bet at a roadside betting site; he should use the internet or a mobile app to place bets. This could offer bonuses or, at the very least, allow for better timing when odds fluctuate.

6. He shouldn't place a bet and then completely ignore it; he needs to keep an eye on the game.

7. He shouldn't have bought that Starbucks coffee. True gamblers use every penny for betting.

Additionally, we also talked about an outrageous election betting line. "In the recent election, a certain underground website offered an election betting line where a candidate was given a 500,000-vote handicap, with odds going as high as 8 to 1." Why is this outrageous? Because we can use Wise Guy tactics to beat this website. Here's how players use arbitrage calculations:

| Election Betting Line | | | | | |
|---|---|---|---|---|---|
| | Amount | Odds | Winnings | | Profit |
| First Bet | 100.00 | 8.00 | 800.00 | | 300.00 |
| Second Bet | 400.00 | 2.00 | 800.00 | | 300.00 |
| | | | | | |
| Total Bet | 500.00 | | | | |
| ROI | 60.00% | | | | |

This means that when the website releases a line with odds of 8:1, all we have to do is unhesitatingly buy two tickets at the same time. One ticket backs one candidate, and the other backs the opposite candidate. Doing so, our rate of return is 60%. Pay special attention: if you invest $100, you make a guaranteed $60; invest a million, and you make a guaranteed $600,000. No matter the election's outcome, we can earn this much. For those who still don't understand the details, you can go back and read the Wise guy section. That's why we say such a betting line is outrageous. How could a website release a line where they're certain to lose?

# Letters From Readers

After the release of this book, a considerable number of readers have written to me. Due to my busy work schedule, I can't reply to each letter individually. However, whenever I find the time, I make every effort to respond to each one. This section features a selection of my correspondence with readers.

**Mr. Liu,**

**Hello, I am a reader of your book "The Unspoken Rules of Online Sports Betting," and I must say that I've learned a lot. Your book unveils many facts unknown to the general public about the world of sports betting, helping those who enjoy it to bet more wisely. I am truly grateful to you. However, there are a few questions I'd like to ask.**

- **You've taught us how to calculate the juice for sports like baseball and basketball, but how is it done for soccer which has home, away, and three possible outcomes?**

- **Do Wise guy strategies also apply to soccer betting?**

**Thank you!**

**Jasper Chen, Neihu**


Dear Jasper,

I'm pleased to receive your letter, which brings up a fascinating question: How do online sportsbooks calculate the juice and ensure profit in soccer games that can end in a draw? You're quite astute. In my book, whenever juice is discussed, basketball is usually the example because a basketball game will definitely produce a winner; if not, they keep playing.

In soccer, a draw is possible. If neither team wins, the match ends in a draw, and everyone moves on. This scenario presents a unique challenge for sportsbooks. When setting up the betting lines for such games, sportsbooks offer three options for players to bet on: a win for the home team, a win for the away team, or a draw. As a player, you have to pick from these three options and get it right to win money.

Such a betting line is usually termed as "Home-Draw-Away," and it is indeed more complex than basketball lines that only offer home or away wins. Logically, one might think that sportsbooks would need more sophisticated algorithms or specially-designed software systems to monitor their juice in such cases. But, in reality, as far as I know, that's not the case. To be frank, there are no new tools involved when sportsbooks set up a "Home-Draw-Away" line, and the calculations for controlling the line and calculating the juice remain largely unchanged.

The principle is simple. Let's start with some fundamentals. The most important aspect for a bookmaker is to use the losers' money to pay the winners and ideally keep some leftover for themselves. In a basketball betting line (which only involves the home and away teams), the sportsbook must ensure that regardless of whether the home or away team wins, there will be enough money on the "other side" to pay out the winners, and some extra will be left over. That's why we go through the trouble of calculating the juice, balancing the bets from players, and ultimately ensuring a profit from the juice.

Soccer, in contrast, is less taxing in this regard. In soccer's "Home-Draw-Away" betting line, no matter who wins (be it the home team, the away team, or a draw), there are funds from the "other two sides" to pay out the winners. For example

If the "home team" wins, then we can pay out using the money lost by those who bet on the "away team" and a "draw." Likewise, if it's a "draw," we can pay out using the money lost from bets on the "home team" and "away team." It's easy to see that this kind of "home-away-draw" sportsbook has many advantages. To put it simply, there's only one winner but two losers. It would be difficult for the bookmaker to lose money in this setup. This kind of betting line inherently gives the online sportsbook an edge, eliminating the need to meticulously calculate the juice. However, it's worth noting that running such a sportsbook is not as easy as just setting up a "home-away-draw" betting line and forgetting about it.

The sportsbook still needs to manage the "home-away-draw" line and calculate the juice. But the method is straightforward: it's just like basketball betting, focusing on balancing bets between the home and away teams. The sportsbook operates as if a winner will emerge from the contest between these two teams, essentially ignoring the possibility of a draw. This approach ensures maximum profit for the online sportsbook, as draws are the least likely outcome and thus attract the fewest bets. Therefore, the focus of line management should be on balancing the home and away teams, which also forms the basis for calculating the juice. As long as the sportsbook manages the line this way, it's almost guaranteed to make money, and the book may even afford to offer slightly higher odds.

For example, in basketball, we said the total odds should never exceed four; otherwise, the sportsbook won't make any juice. But it's not the same for "home-away-draw" betting. The sportsbook can offer odds slightly above four, with the profits supplemented by the infrequent draws (which will inevitably occur and usually attract fewer bets, hence generating a large profit for the sportsbook).

In summary, there's no special line management technique for "home-away-draw" betting. It often uses the same formulas as basketball betting, which is why I didn't particularly mention this type of betting in the book. Instead, I grouped it under types of plays where the sportsbook doesn't earn juice. And as you can surely understand, being a player in "home-away-draw" betting is quite disadvantageous.

Lastly, to answer your second question: Can Wise Guy arbitrage techniques be applied to "home-away-draw" betting?

The answer is no, and the reason is simple. The principle behind arbitrage is to place bets on two teams, ensuring that one will win and one will lose. However, because you've carefully calculated the odds, you can ensure that the money you win will be more than the money you lose, allowing for a risk-free profit. This principle is essentially the "constitution" of arbitrage tactics.

But what about applying this to a home-away-draw betting line? The principle remains the same, meaning you have to buy all three scenarios (home team wins, away team wins, and a draw). Of course, you'll only win on one betting ticket while losing the other two. Unfortunately, the constitution of arbitrage dictates that the money you win from that one successful ticket must be more than the combined losses of the other two. This is nearly impossible to achieve.

We all know that the profits from arbitrage are not high, only a few percentages of the amount wagered. When even basketball, where you only lose one betting ticket, makes it hard to earn money, it's theoretically even less feasible with a home-away-draw line where you're bound to lose two tickets. However, I can't say it's entirely impossible in reality. With home-away-draw, you can place three bets, and if you buy these tickets from three different online sportsbooks and manage the odds well, you might be able to pull off an arbitrage strategy. But it's very difficult, as the profits from arbitrage are low and the odds for a home-away-draw are not as high as people would like.

Fortunately, your second question mentioned a Wise Guy, which makes it easier for me to respond. A smart bettor would choose a target that's more favorable to them when employing arbitrage tactics. With the 1/2 odds in basketball, there's really no reason to play a betting line where the odds of guessing correctly are only 1/3.

Finally, I truly hope you enjoy this book.

Regards,

**How do bookmakers identify players who are engaged in arbitrage or "water tricks"?**

Mr. Liu, Hello:

I recently purchased a book you wrote called "The Unspoken Rules of Online Sportsbooks" from Eslite. I have a technical question about sports arbitrage that I'd like to ask you. If multiple accounts are using the same PC and clear cookies and log in with different IPs, do websites have other ways to track that multiple accounts are being logged in or registered from the same computer? I've heard that websites can use digital "fingerprints" to know which accounts are being accessed or registered from the same computer. Could you please offer some advice when you have the time? Thanks!

Best regards,

Peter


Dear Peter,

I'm delighted to have received your letter, in which you posed a very intriguing question. This is indeed a significant query, and many friends are also curious about its details. My apologies for the delay in getting back to you.

To answer your question directly—yes! Online sportsbooks can still track whether you're logging in from the same computer, even if you clear cookies, use different IPs, or browse with different web browsers. They can find out!

To put it bluntly, even if it's not just one person, even if multiple computers from various locations are used, as long as you employ the tactic of Arbitrage, the sportsbook can track you. However, tracking is not reliant on just one method; we generally employ a mix of techniques to get the job done. The tracking results are not entirely accurate, though; usually, what we can conclude is something along the lines of, "We're 70% sure that these three accounts are operated by the same person."

Of course, such a report cannot be used as conclusive evidence, but for the sportsbook, it's good enough. This generally addresses your question. Still, I will go on to explain from the beginning how online sportsbooks manage to carry out these tracking activities because not everyone is that tech-savvy. Also, I'm not entirely sure if there is a "digital fingerprint" technology per se, as this term has been overused in the IT industry. Many computer technologies are named under this label. Nevertheless, I'll list all the techniques I'm aware of later.

## Background Knowledge

First, to understand how online sportsbooks track users, we need to discuss the principle of arbitrage. Sports betting is inherently a game where arbitrage can occur. The basic concept of arbitrage is simple: you buy two betting tickets for the same match, placing bets on both teams. Then, by exploiting the difference in odds, you ensure that no matter which team wins, you'll have a stable return. This is generally a few percentage points of your total wager. For example, if you've bought two tickets totaling $10,000, you could make a profit of around $700. Of course, this is just an example; the actual return on investment can vary based on the odds you get.

Compared to traditional gambling—like buying just one betting ticket—where you could potentially double your prize money (e.g., turning $10,000 into $20,000), the money you can make from arbitrage is modest. Some might even say it's pitiful. However, the key point is that when you only buy one ticket, you can't be right every day. If you lose, you could lose your entire principal. With arbitrage, since you're betting on both teams, you'll always get some money back, eliminating the risk of losing everything.

Therefore, arbitrage techniques in sports betting have long been popular and attract a lot of attention. There's even a term for it: "Arbitrage," or "打水" in the vernacular. However, executing arbitrage is not a simple task. In fact, it's easy to fail. In such cases, you're essentially gambling, just like someone who only bought one ticket. Therefore, only a small number of people manage to make a living through this technique.

The above is some background knowledge. Detailed arbitrage techniques are described in my book, and I believe you're already aware of them, so I won't go into more detail here. But for those who might be curious, you might wonder what does opening multiple accounts have to do with the arbitrage techniques discussed above? The answer is simple: if you want to execute arbitrage, you can't use the same account to buy both tickets.

Because websites worldwide are aware of this arbitrage strategy, we can assume that they are very displeased with it. Arbitrage is a no-loss technique, and no online sportsbook enjoys having customers who only win and never lose. Therefore, in their game rules, they will always include a condition prohibiting players from betting on both teams in the same game. If they catch you doing so, they will either cancel your betting ticket, give you only half of the winnings, or outright close your account.

What's more, it's quite easy for the sportsbook to detect if you have purchased two tickets for the same game. Some more direct sportsbooks can even program this rule into their system, outright blocking you from purchasing the second ticket. So, for those looking to engage in arbitrage, there are only two methods. First, buy the two tickets on two different sportsbooks. Second, use two accounts and pretend to be two different people, so even if it's the same sportsbook, they can't tell it's the same person making both bets.

Why must you open multiple accounts on a single sportsbook? Why not open accounts on two different sportsbooks? To sum it up, this explains why opening multiple accounts is related to arbitrage. These two are like twins; if you want to engage in arbitrage, you will need multiple accounts. Conversely, if someone opens more than one account on a sportsbook, you can be nearly 100% certain that they are there for arbitrage.

Some might wonder, why are we so insistent on opening accounts on the same sportsbook? Theoretically, isn't buying tickets from different sportsbooks the best solution? It could at least save us the trouble of having to outsmart their software. Indeed, most players who live on arbitrage don't limit themselves to a single sportsbook. Buying tickets from different sportsbooks not only makes it less likely to get caught but also provides better profits. Frankly, just looking at it from a profit angle, I can't think of any reason to convince people to stick to a single sportsbook.

But if we set aside profitability and look at it from a legal or economic perspective, it makes a lot of sense. In many places, people can only purchase betting tickets from government-authorized online sportsbooks. Buying from anyone else would be illegal. So, from a legal standpoint, if you're looking to arbitrage, you would need to buy both tickets from the same sportsbook.

On another note, from an economic angle that many people might not be aware of, the specialization within the world of sports betting has reached an incredibly advanced level. For instance, some online platforms only appear to be bookmakers. They look like online sportsbooks, and they act like one too, accepting bets and paying out if you win. However, they aren't actually bookmakers; they simply pass the money they collect to a larger back-end online sportsbook. This is akin to travel agencies selling flight tickets: no matter which agency sells you the ticket, the entity issuing the ticket at the end of the day is always the airline. So, in scenarios like this, you may think you're buying betting tickets from different online platforms, but in the end, they all funnel to the same larger sportsbook. Essentially, you've purchased both tickets from the same sportsbook, just through different accounts. Of course, you would be unaware of all this.

Regarding the Browser You're Using

Now let's delve into the main topic. Given that we may intentionally or unintentionally have multiple accounts on the same online sportsbook, the pressing question is: does this arbitrage strategy attract the website's attention? If so, how do they notice, and how can we prevent it?

First, let me provide some background. A large sportsbook might host tens of thousands of players placing bets during a popular sports season, like the NBA in the United States. Of these, fewer than 0.1% might be professional arbers, specifically looking to make money through arbitrage. So, the sportsbook faces the challenge of filtering out these few hundred "problem players" from tens of thousands.

Many people's first thought is that accounts are the point of vulnerability. As we've discussed, if you have multiple accounts on a sportsbook, you're already under suspicion. After all, who casually creates multiple accounts on a betting site for no reason? Especially if you're managing these accounts from the same computer, the suspicion only deepens.

Your intriguing question is: how do these sportsbooks know? This is where internet technology and web browsers come into play. Popular browsers like Internet Explorer or Firefox play a role here. Online sportsbooks generally have their platforms to accept players' bets. In theory, the technology they use to detect suspicious activity would be the same as that employed by any other website. This includes the information provided by IPs, cookies, and the browser itself.

First, IP Location: Every computer that connects to the internet is assigned a unique identifier that looks like this: "72.14.205.100". We call this an IP address. This number is visible to any website you visit. In essence, we know what your IP address is the moment you arrive on our website. Importantly, each IP address is unique to each computer. So if a website sees two seemingly different players using the same IP address, it's reasonable to assume that both accounts belong to the same person.

Second, Cookies: Every website has the ability to leave small pieces of data on your computer. These data packets are sent back to the website for reference as you browse different pages. We call this technology Cookies. They are extremely useful for identifying a user's computer. For example, the website could leave records like this in your browser:

1:30 PM - User1 arrives
1:35 PM - User1 leaves
1:40 PM - User2 arrives
1:45 PM - User2 leaves
1:50 PM - User1 arrives
1:55 PM - User1 leaves

It stands to reason that if these records are continuously sent back to the website, they would know that the computer is being shared by "User1" and "User2."

Third, the Browser Itself: Browsers also kindly provide basic information to websites, such as whether you're using Firefox or IE, whether your operating system is Windows or Mac, and whether you're browsing in Chinese or English. Even if you're using an iPhone to surf the web, the iPhone will inform the website, "I am an iPhone."

These are the standard detection techniques commonly employed by websites. It's reasonable to infer that online sportsbooks use these same techniques to identify players. After all, they have access to the same basic set of information and nothing more.

So the issue becomes quite straightforward. If you can hide these three pieces of information (IP, Cookies, Browser), the website won't be able to employ standard detection techniques, and consequently, won't be able to identify if you're using two accounts simultaneously. Fortunately, all three elements—IP, Cookies, and Browser—can be easily modified or hidden. A bit of time spent searching online will yield related guidelines, and it's not difficult at all.

Is it really safe to just hide your IP and clear your cookies? But as you pointed out in your letter, this is perhaps the most interesting part of the entire issue: "Is that all there is to a website's capabilities?" Indeed, you're correct. Websites have more tricks up their sleeves, and their thought processes might be quite different from what most people imagine. So let's discuss how websites actually deal with this issue.

Regrettably, in reality, websites don't care about IP, cookies, or browsers. In fact, they don't even care if you have multiple accounts. The reason is simple. First, "arbitrage" is a very difficult technique to execute. To successfully pull off arbitrage, you need not only boldness and meticulousness but also a good understanding of the formulas, and some luck (for detailed methods, you can refer to the chapter on arbitrage in the book). So even if you fully understand the principle, only a few can successfully arbitrage, while most people can only complete half of it, which is not much different from gambling. In such scenarios, the website won't consider you as someone who is there to "arbitrage." We have a specific term for you, called a "good customer," and you can imagine that no one cares how many accounts a good customer has.

Not caring about the number of accounts doesn't mean they don't care about arbitrage. Websites actually do more to catch "arbitragers" than you might think. So how do they catch them? It actually has nothing to do with all the computer technologies we talked about before. IP and cookies are not utilized for this purpose (although we do record everyone's IP and cookies, but that's just for customer protection. For example, there's a risk of online accounts being hacked. If you've ever used Yahoo Auctions, you'd know. So monitoring IP and cookies is just to ensure that your account is being used by you and not stolen by some high school hacker).

Back to the point, we all know that websites hate arbitragers and that tens of thousands of people place bets on each game. We also know that we need to find the very few players who are arbitraging among these tens of thousands. So what's the best way to do this? It's not the latest computer technology, but the most basic nature of this game: follow the money.

To identify arbitrage players, websites primarily rely on two tools: accounting reports and data analytics software. First, we need to understand that as soon as a player places a bet and buys a betting ticket, a record is generated in the website's computer system. This record includes who bought the ticket, which team they bet on, what kind of bet it was, how much money they placed, what the odds were, and finally whether they won or lost.

When aggregated, these records form the accounting reports that the website reviews daily. With these reports, we can determine which players are winning money and which are losing. Importantly, this report is crucial for identifying those engaging in arbitrage. The issue, however, is that this report can be quite extensive.

For instance, a medium-sized online sportsbook might receive 10,000 bets in a single day. Assuming each person only places one bet, that's 10,000 player accounts. Let's further assume that out of these 10,000 people, only you have opened two accounts for arbitrage. Now the challenge for the website is to pinpoint the problematic two accounts from among 10,000, and to establish that both accounts are yours.

You might think that sounds absurdly simple—akin to picking out two naked spectators in a stadium filled with 10,000 baseball fans. Indeed, you read the analogy correctly. Whether it's a crowd of 10,000 or 100,000, identifying those without clothing would be fairly straightforward. Why? Because accounts engaging in arbitrage exhibit very distinct characteristics in the accounting reports.

First, the teams bought by these two accounts must be different. For example, if you want to arbitrage in a game between the "Yankees vs. Red Sox," one account must bet on the Yankees and the other on the Red Sox. Second, the odds on the betting tickets purchased by these two accounts must add up to be close to or greater than 4.0. Third, the amounts wagered by these two accounts must be similar. For instance, if you bet $100 on the Yankees, the amount you bet on the Red Sox in the other account should also be approximately the same. We can even calculate that if the Yankees have odds of 1.95 and the Red Sox have odds of 2.28, then you must bet $117 on the Red Sox to maximize your profits.

With these characteristics in place, websites can use computers to examine each betting ticket individually and perform cross-analysis to identify any correlations. And computers are fast enough these days to analyze 10,000 tickets in less than a second.

But there's another crucial aspect: the rate of return on investment. Suppose you are a very skilled and professional arbitrage player. In that case, your rate of return would be a positive percentage, such as 5% to 7%, similar to fixed deposits or stock dividends. You might think that this amount is negligible compared to other players who win or lose big. But unfortunately, this is a misconception.

In the game of sports betting, if the website only takes a 5% "juice" (for a detailed explanation of "juice," refer to Chapter 1 of the book), then the average rate of return for most players would be a negative 5%. Given that most people's rate of return is negative, your positive 5% would indeed make you stand out. So now, those two spectators in the stands are not only naked but are also picking up loudspeakers to announce, "I am nude."

Yes, accounting reports can reveal much more than computer logs. Although in reality, matching algorithms may not entirely find two completely matching accounts. Perhaps the arbitrage player didn't execute this strategy in some games. Maybe they occasionally want to genuinely place bets for fun, or perhaps their calculations aren't precise enough. All these factors can affect the computer's accuracy, leading it to conclude that "these two accounts have a 70% likelihood of being operated by the same individual."

But that's okay. A 70% likelihood is good enough for websites. Often, even a 50% chance is considered too high.

What should a website do when they discover arbitrage bettors?

Moving on to our final question, what actions should online sportsbooks take when they identify players engaging in arbitrage? Should they simply cancel all of the accounts according to the rules? Or should they confiscate your winnings?

The answer varies, as each website has its own protocols. However, for larger sportsbooks, the most likely course of action is to turn a blind eye. Cancelling accounts or confiscating winnings are drastic steps that could provoke public backlash. Moreover, you may have already withdrawn your money, making it impossible for the sportsbook to recover the funds.

The best approach is to act subtly, allowing you to continue playing. Yet, behind the scenes, they may tweak the system. Many people assume that all websites operate on a level playing field, thinking that search results on Google or prices on Yahoo Shopping are consistent for everyone. This is not the case with sports betting sites, especially the larger ones. Once they identify you as an arbitrage bettor, the code you interact with will be different from that of other users. This could mean delaying your bets, making it difficult for you to wager on the team you want, or altering your odds so that they're less favorable than those of other players. They may even restrict one of your accounts from continuing to bet while you're in the middle of an arbitrage scheme.

These programmatic adjustments make arbitrage much more difficult to pull off. Keep in mind that arbitrage betting typically yields only a few percentage points in profit. If the system trips you up, causing you to place only one successful bet, and you end up losing that one, then the sportsbook can recover all the money it lost to your arbitrage bets in one go. Isn't that better for them?

Returning to the technical aspect, that's about all I know. In summary, sportsbook websites don't need to rely on IPs or COOKIES to identify arbitrage bettors. So, no matter how much you try to hide on your own computer, it's futile. But let's get back to the technical side since you asked a technical question. Let's make some assumptions:

Let's assume that the sportsbook doesn't have any financial reports or data analytics systems. Suppose you've already hidden your IP and properly managed your cookies. Assume you're using two different browsers for these two accounts. Suppose you've also paid attention to the timing, making sure to log in and log out at different times with both accounts. (We haven't discussed this before, but note that turning off your computer and going to sleep right after arbitraging is a foolish move. The timing records will attract attention because both accounts will go offline simultaneously.)

So, you've taken all of these precautions, you've added a uninterruptible power supply to your computer, and you're using a Mac instead of Windows to prevent frequent crashes that might cause both accounts to go offline. Furthermore, you've firmly decided not to install any software from these websites, eliminating any other ways they might monitor your computer. Under these conditions, do the sportsbooks still have technical means to monitor whether you're using two accounts on the same computer?

The answer is still YES, echoing Barack Obama's presidential campaign slogan, "Yes, We Can." The key depends on how skilled the programmer is. A good software engineer will know how to monitor all system events to infer user behavior. For your question, all I would need to do is monitor the mouse and keyboard. For example, you must have seen those cute little ads on some websites that follow your mouse cursor. The principle behind these ads is simply capturing the mouse's location information and moving to that spot.

This mouse location information has a critical impact on determining whether you are using two accounts. Even though you use two browsers, you only have one mouse. This mouse is either operating in one browser or moved to the other; it can't operate in both browsers simultaneously. So, that gives us a feature. Now, programmers just have to send mouse events back to the website and write a program to check whether there are players whose mouse locations never overlap. Because under normal circumstances, mouse events between different players will absolutely overlap. Only in your use case, there would be no overlap.

Lastly, aside from the mouse, programmers have many other methods at their disposal. But let's not get into that to avoid an endless discussion. For the website, the real focus is just money. As long as you closely monitor the flow of money and the players' rate of return, business can proceed smoothly. As for the technical computer details? Websites rarely pay attention to them.

However, let's get back to the point: not every website can afford expensive computer systems and advanced computer engineers. Many small websites do not have the means to detect player arbitrage (you may not believe it, but many small websites have never even heard of what a database is). So while this technique is old, well-known, and easy to catch, I believe it will continue to be passed down from generation to generation.

I hope I have answered your questions and that you'll enjoy my book.

Best Regards,

# Technical Issues in Sports Arbitrage

Hello,

Thank you for taking the time to share your valuable insights. Regarding your mention of "browsers also thoughtfully providing some basic information for each website," I would like to ask whether, besides knowing the types like Mac/IE/iPhone, websites can see the name of the computer being used. For example, the computer I am currently using was likely named "Peter" during the OS installation. If it's just the type of browser, I believe the level of distinctiveness is probably not high (for example, there may be 50% of computers in the world currently using IE 7.0). Additionally, I've found that about 50% of websites place "certificates" on my computer, so I've been deleting those certificates. I'm not sure whether these certificates would identify that multiple accounts are being used on the same computer. Could you please share your experiences on this matter?

I've noticed that websites can easily identify who is arbitraging because the occurrence of arbitrage, in terms of both "time" and "event," happens within a very short period. Accounts that happen to place bets under these specific "time/event" conditions a few times are most certainly arbitragers. Websites likely all have arbitrage software. However, each website has its own policy. The most strict one I've encountered is Bet365. They may lower the maximum betting amount on your account to less than 10 Euros in just one to several days, effectively forcing arbitrage players out.

I've had experiences where my funds were confiscated by two different websites. Another good website only gave me a warning. I got my money back from the two that confiscated it. One of them even blocked several of my related accounts. After I verified my identity by providing documents like a passport, address, and bank statement, they allowed me to withdraw my money, although they reduced my betting limit to an extremely low level. Because many websites limit the betting amount for each game, to increase profits, people generally use multiple accounts to increase the arbitrage amount.

Dear Peter,

The following is the information transmitted by my browser: Mozilla/5.0 (Macintosh; U; Intel Mac OS X 10.5; en-US; rv:1.9.0.5) Gecko/2008120121 Firefox/3.0.5. It doesn't contain the computer name or username, as that would raise significant privacy concerns. However, you can deduce quite a bit from this information. For example, you can tell that I'm using Mozilla's Firefox browser, the version is the latest 3.05, my operating system is Mac, the version is 10.5, and my preferred language is English.

You're correct that if you're using a standard Windows setup with IE, the identification would indeed be low, since at least 80% of computers worldwide would transmit similar browser information.

As I mentioned before, online sportsbooks don't need this information to identify who is arbitraging. The act of arbitrage has too many identifiable characteristics. They also don't need to be 100% sure; even a small percentage of suspicion is enough. Traditional thinking may suggest that data analysis takes a long time, like several hours or days. However, modern computers are too fast. Generally, running a report or settling a day's worth of games takes less than a second.

In other words, if a sportsbook is very concerned about arbitrage, they could do real-time analysis. They could compare each incoming bet against their entire database instantly, quickly identifying potential arbitragers without putting much strain on the system.

The bet365 website you mentioned is not to be underestimated, particularly their betting transaction system. It is outstanding, and many new competitors start by emulating their system.

I must apologize for my lack of practical experience in betting, so I'm not aware of some "tricks of the trade." But I'm curious, do you manually check the odds on each website and then arbitrage? Or do you use software for automated scanning, commonly known as arbitrage software? If it's the latter, that's a whole new issue, as they have specialized systems to deal with that.

Lastly, you made the right choice by not installing any certificates. Website programs can read the related certificate files.

Hello, thank you for reading my book and gaining an understanding of the basic concept of "juice" in online sportsbooks. You have a question about the standard formula to calculate the sportsbook's "profit margin," which is

1/HO + 1/AO - 1 = margin (Ho = Home Odds, AO = Away Odds)

**HO = Home Odds, AO = Away Odds).** You point out that my book describes another way of calculating profit margin by summing the odds of the home and away teams and using 4 for computation. This helps in understanding the sportsbook's juice setting.

You've noticed that these two approaches don't always yield the same results, especially as the odds differ. For instance, with both home and away odds at 1.6, my book's formula suggests a juice of $0.2 (or 20%). However, when using the "standard" margin calculation, the result is $0.25 (or 25%). This discrepancy seems to grow as you test different odds like 1.5/1.5 or 1.4/1.4. You're asking if this means that the general "standard" margin calculation is incorrect. Thank you.

Your question is quite intriguing, and the formula you provided has caught my attention. I'd like to ask if you could share the origin of this "standard" formula, as I don't understand its significance and am skeptical of its results. If you can provide more information, I can delve deeper into it.

I prefer to use real examples to examine issues, so let's use the 1.6 odds you hypothesized. Imagine that a sportsbook opens a betting line with both teams having odds of 1.60, meaning if you bet $100 and win, you'd get back $160. Now, let's assume two players each place a $50 bet on both teams, resulting in a total intake of $100 for the sportsbook.

Using your "standard" formula (1/HO + 1/AO - 1 = margin), we can calculate that 1/1.6 + 1/1.6 - 1 = 0.25, indicating a profit margin of 25%. According to this, out of the $100 collected, the sportsbook should earn $25. However, it's clear that this margin is incorrect; the sportsbook can't possibly make $25. From the betting line, we can see that no matter the outcome of the game, the winning player will take $50 x 1.6 = $80, leaving the sportsbook with only $20, far short of $25. The actual profit margin, considering that the total intake is $100, should be 20%.

From this example, I would conclude that the formula is incorrect. To determine the correct profit margin, you should stick to the method described in the book: using the number 4 along with the home and away team odds for the calculation. However, I'm still quite curious about the meaning behind your formula and wonder if its creator considered some unique circumstances.

**Thank you very much for your response. First, I'll list the source of the formula below.**

http://www.pinnaclesports.com/online-betting-articles/strategy/margins-1x2.aspx

**However, I also wonder if this formula is suitable for 1X2 (Money Line) odds, and perhaps not applicable for outcomes that are simply one loss and one win (e.g., Home/Away, Point Spread, Over/Under, where there is no draw or a third outcome).**

**Returning to your calculations, indeed, using the total revenue of the website for calculations, the proportion of money obtained is always the total odds divided by 4.**

**I'm very grateful for your explanation. I didn't expect a response, as I was worried that the author might not be looking at this blog anymore, given how long ago my last comment was.**

**Besides my previous comment, I'm also curious about the concept of expected value. When the odds have a probability of 0.5 for each, a total of 4 seems reasonable (or say the odds are each 2). But if you incorporate the concept of expected value, for example, if the respective winning probabilities are 20% and 80%, would the ideal odds become 20% → 5, 80% → 1.25?**

**Thank you. If my concepts are confused or misused, please forgive me.**

This blog has indeed been quiet for some time, likely because the book has been out for five years now and isn't selling as much as it initially did. Nevertheless, whenever someone pays attention to my blog, I'm always happy to hear their thoughts.

I've seen the "standard" formula you provided from the Pinnacle Sports website. First of all, Pinnacle is a well-established company in the sports betting sector, and I've heard about them for a long time. They're a very profitable online sportsbook. The formula they provide serves as "guidance" for players, allowing them to calculate and see that Pinnacle's "juice" is lower than other sportsbooks, thereby attracting players to place bets on their site.

We've previously crunched the numbers on this formula. Essentially, it doesn't reflect games with only two outcomes, such as point spread line wagers on home and away teams. So, can it accurately represent the 1x2 money line results? Let's calculate that. Assume that the online sportsbook opens a line where the home, away, and draw odds are all 2.00. If you bet $50 and win, you get $100. Now, let's assume three players each bet $50 on home, away, and draw, which means the sportsbook's revenue for the day is $150. Using Pinnacle's formula, the margin comes out as 50%, meaning the site would make $75 from the $150. However, this margin still isn't accurate; the site would only make $50. So, when it comes to home and away, Pinnacle's formula still isn't accurate, as it doesn't reflect the actual profit the site can make.

Regardless, I think it's pointless for a professional player to focus on finding the perfect formula for home and away bets. Not only are the odds of winning low, but the bookmaker's profit is also higher, making it far less worthwhile than traditional point spread betting. And, I must criticize Pinnacle's article a bit here. For any serious and responsible player, the focus should be on pursuing the highest odds available in the market at that moment, regardless of the sportsbook's juice.

To reiterate a point from the book, how much juice a sportsbook takes and the odds a player can get are two separate issues. You may get lower odds from a site with higher juice and vice versa; it all depends on the current market conditions and isn't something a formula can represent.

Finally, we come to the concept of expected value. One essential idea to grasp is that, regardless of the outcome of the match, the online sportsbook's profit is fixed. We all know that before the game officially kicks off, once the line is set, the online sportsbook can already calculate how much profit they'll make for the day. Hence, which team wins has little to no significant impact on the profit. Naturally, expected value wouldn't be included in our formula for calculating profits.

## A Strange Formula Part Three

First of all, I still want to thank you for your patient and clear answers. Moreover, since July 8, 2008, only this book in the Taiwanese market clearly explains the gameplay and spirit of sports betting, and I have gained a lot from it.

Your explanations are practically based, which makes them easy to understand and very realistic.

As for the concept of expected value, indeed, online sportsbooks really don't have to care about the odds they set.

From one perspective, each game only has a winner and a loser, and the true probability is only known to God and the final outcome.

The correctness of the concept is much more important than any formula. Formulas should only be mathematical representations of concepts.

Finally, I want to discuss the topic of margin with you.

Indeed, after repeated calculations, I finally found that the margin here can't be considered the juice that the online sportsbook earns.

However, it does represent a certain "profit ratio" for the online sportsbook.

I will present my inference below, and please provide your opinions and guidance.

For simplicity's sake, I will only use the home and away teams' win/loss outcome in the formula, although a draw can also be applied.

(Note) HO = odds for the home team winning, AO = odds for the away team winning.

$$1/HO + 1/AO = 1/(1/Hp*X) + 1/(1/Ap*X)$$

(Note) Hp = probability of the home team winning, Ap = probability of the away team winning, X = scaling factor for the odds (profit ratio for the online sportsbook).

This formula exists because the higher the winning probability, the lower the odds should be, hence it is presented as a reciprocal.

Multiplying by X (where X >= 1) is due to the online sportsbook needing a profit. If X = 1, it would mean there is no profit.

So, the above formula can be expressed as: $Hp*X + Ap*X = X*(Hp+Ap)$

And Hp + Ap = 1 (because if one team loses, the other wins, so the total probability sum is one). So, I think this formula is trying to tell the bettors that our online sportsbook has the lowest "profit ratio." However, as per your explanation, this number can't quite be equated to the juice, although the formula seems reasonable.

I completely agree with your point that bettors should only care about high odds; the juice is something that the online sportsbook should worry about. Lastly, I found that 1 - 1/X can align with what we call juice. Taking our ongoing example, where the home team's odds are 1.6 and the away team's odds are 1.6, the calculated margin is 1.25 (please do not subtract 1; subtracting 1 removes the net profit ratio after accounting for the total probability sum being one).

So, isn't 1 - 1/1.25 = 0.2 exactly the juice we calculated, where the sportsbook takes in $100 and pays out $80?

This formula can also be applied to 1X2 (Home, Draw, Away). Using your previous example where the odds for home, draw, and away are all 2, the margin would be 1.5, and 1-1/1.5=0.3333333. This means the online sportsbook takes in $150, pays out $100, and earns $50 as juice (50/150 = 1/3). So it looks like the margin formula is fitting; for us, it should probably be called the "sportsbook's profit ratio," although it's not very intuitive, at least not to me.

Lastly, I have another question. I found that if the home team's odds are 3.6 and the away team's odds are 1.2, and the sportsbook can actually get balanced bets, it can also earn a 10% juice. For example, the home team takes in $100, expected payout is $360; the away team takes in $300, expected payout is $360. The total intake is $400, total payout is $360, earning $40, so the juice is 10%. While sportsbooks might not set odds like this in reality, this suggests that the sum of the odds doesn't necessarily have to be under 4. Is that correct?

**Thank you very much for patiently reading through these discussions, and I'm delighted to have this exchange with the author.**

First of all, I apologize for the delayed response. I've been quite busy with work these past few days and haven't had the time to check my messages. After reviewing your calculations, I believe your conclusion is spot-on: this formula aims to tell gamblers that our "site's profit margin" is the lowest. This interpretation offers the most perfect explanation for this "standard formula."

Therefore, when Pinnaclesports introduced this formula, the message they are trying to convey to all players is that, because Pinnaclesports has a low profit margin that can be easily compared to other betting websites using this formula, savvy players should stick with Pinnaclesports. However, the issue is that the odds available to players are only partially related to the website's profit margin. A significant part depends on the site's current betting status. So, truly savvy players should always compare the current market rates and place bets on the highest odds, rather than focusing solely on the site's profit margin.

Next, you're correct in observing that the total odds don't necessarily have to be under 4. Your example is accurate; even if it exceeds 4, the site still makes money. But you're right in your intuition that websites wouldn't set their odds like this. When we design software systems for these sites, we automatically keep the total odds under 4 to prevent traders from making judgment errors or entering incorrect figures. Because the system has this limitation, you won't see any betting lines with total odds exceeding this number in the market.

Lastly, I appreciate your message. Although I'm no longer in the gaming industry, it remains an interest of mine. So, I welcome anyone interested in this topic to engage in further discussions.

Hello, Teacher. I am a sports betting enthusiast and regularly watch NBA games. I have some questions for you. I learned from your book that online sportsbooks aim to make money by balancing the juice and extracting profits from it. The point spread and odds are determined by computers analyzing large amounts of data. Then, based on the volume of bets, traders adjust the point spread and odds to achieve as balanced a state as possible. Therefore, the sportsbook doesn't really care which team wins or loses; as long as they can balance the juice, they will make money. Before reading your book, I used to analyze the movement of the money line and betting volume an hour before the game started. However, after reading the book, I've become conflicted. If sportsbooks adjust the point spread or odds merely to balance the juice, then watching the money line doesn't seem to make much sense. So, my question is, can you really analyze a game based on changes in the money line?

People say you can discern the sportsbook's confidence level at the opening line. What does that mean? For example, today's game between the Bucks and the Pacers started with a point spread favoring the Bucks by 15 points. Does this indicate that the sportsbook is confident that the Pacers will cover the spread? But if the sportsbook's aim is to make money through balancing the bets, why would they have any subjective confidence level? Isn't it enough to adjust the point spread based on changes in betting volume?


Hello,

This question understandably poses a dilemma, as it arises from looking at the situation from two entirely different perspectives. First, let's consider it from the viewpoint of a sportsbook operator. The core of the sports betting business is to make a profit from the "juice." To achieve that, balance in the odds is crucial. Tools like point spreads and odds are used to maintain this balance. From this perspective, analyzing a game based on odds expressed in dollars makes no sense; it's as absurd as deciding what to have for breakfast based on how someone else's house is built. As a sportsbook operator, you're not concerned with which team wins or loses, nor do you need to predict the outcome of games. In fact, in the computer systems I've been involved in developing, there's nothing of the sort.

But we must also consider this from another angle: that of the trader or the "control desk," as they are commonly called in Taiwan. A trader's job is to constantly observe betting trends and adjust the odds and spreads to maintain balance. Their effectiveness directly affects the balance and, therefore, the risk and potential profitability of a game. Maintaining this balance is an art, and a basic rule is that the team more likely to win will attract more bets, and therefore should have lower odds. Simply put, strong teams have low odds and weak teams have high odds. If this rule is not followed—if, for example, the strong team has high odds and the weak team has low odds—then everyone will bet on the strong team and nobody will bet on the weak one. For the trader, this would result in a severe imbalance, and even quick adjustments might not restore equilibrium.

From the trader's perspective, there's something we might call "confidence level." This isn't a scientific measure of which team is likely to win or lose, but rather how confident the trader feels that, given a certain spread, bettors will divide their bets fairly evenly between the two teams, thereby making it easier to maintain a balanced book.

To use your Bucks vs. Pacers example, does a 15-point spread in favor of the home team indicate that the sportsbook has confidence in the home team? Definitely not. Such a large spread simply suggests that the sportsbook believes this particular handicap will lead to a fairly even distribution of bets between the home and away teams, instead of everyone betting on one side.

So if we were to clearly define "confidence level," for sportsbooks, this confidence refers to the confidence in achieving a balanced book, not confidence in a team's likelihood of winning.

**Thank you for your response, Teacher. I have some additional questions. It turns out that analyzing the odds from the perspective of the U.S. market really doesn't make sense. Thank you for enlightening me! So, besides using arbitrage to make profits, the really smart players focus on in-game betting, also known as "live betting," correct? Besides having a good grasp of team information, are there any other techniques for live betting? In the NBA, it seems that there aren't many opportunities for arbitrage, as the total odds usually are less than 4. However, when I played in Korean or Japanese professional basketball leagues, I found that the strengths and weaknesses between teams are very clear. Typically, weaker teams are suppressed throughout the game, and it's normal for them to lose by**

40 points at the end. One way to bet is on which team will first score 10 or 15 points in a quarter. When there's a strong and weak team, the odds for these bets are usually higher than 4. For example, the odds for the weaker team might start at 6, and the strong team at 1.2. In this case, I would first bet on the weaker team and then wait for the odds on the stronger team to rise before performing arbitrage. However, this approach has risks. Another situation that can occur is that neither team reaches the target score. As you mentioned in your book, one shouldn't play if the odds are less than 50%. So, this is clearly not a good method. Do you have any techniques for live betting?

Hello,

As you've analyzed yourself, your method of Arbitrage in live betting is not only laborious but also carries risks. But let me clarify that Arbitrage is indeed the only risk-free method in sports betting, as it doesn't conflict with the interests of online sportsbooks.

Actually, real Arbitrage players don't operate like you do. The scale of Arbitrage is much larger than you imagine. First, they would search for betting sites accepting wagers globally, at least several dozen if not hundreds. Then they buy or commission software that continuously fetches the lines and odds from these sites. With this, they can compare the lines and odds across all these websites.

Of course, the software also automatically finds Arbitrage opportunities for them. So all Arbitrage players have to do is sit in front of the computer and wait for the system to tell them which team to buy at what odds on which site, and what the profit rate could be. Then they just execute according to the indications.

Frankly speaking, real players, just like online sportsbooks, don't actually care about the outcomes of the games. Their job is to find as many global betting sites as possible and perfect their computer systems. Due to the nature of sports betting, their computers will sooner or later find Arbitrage opportunities. This is how real players operate; it's actually very professional.

**Hello!**

**I read your book "Sports Betting and Lottery Tickets - The Unspoken Rules of the Bookmaker," and found it to be a fascinating read.**

**I have a question about something mentioned in the book. It states that the odds for both teams must be lower than 4. However, I often see such a set of odds:**

**NBA, Heat vs Hornets, 1.05, 5.00.**

**How should this be interpreted?**

**Thank you.**

Hello,

I'm quite curious as to how you came across my book? This book is only available in Taiwan and is only in traditional Chinese, not simplified, so I don't have many readers from mainland China. However, I'm delighted that you found it. I know that China has many players skilled in sports betting, and I hope to release a simplified Chinese version of the book soon.

Regarding your question, why do you often see odds greater than 4.0, especially in the NBA where there are no draws? Firstly, offering odds greater than 4 is risky for online sportsbooks. Let's take your example of the Miami Heat vs. the Bobcats. If the amount wagered on the Heat is $100, and the same is true for the Bobcats, the sportsbook could potentially lose money. The total income from both the Heat and Bobcats is $200. If the Heat win, the payout is $100 x 1.05 odds = $105, and the sportsbook's profit is $200 - $105 = $95. If the Bobcats win, the payout is $100 x 5 odds = $500, and the sportsbook incurs a loss of $200 - $500 = -$300. Hence, the sportsbook would be down $300 if the Bobcats win. That's why we say odds should not exceed 4, as it creates the possibility of losing money.

But sportsbooks have more to consider than just odds. Another crucial factor is "balance." Using your example again, let's say the sportsbook mathematically sets the odds at 1.05 for the Heat and 3.9 for the Bobcats. While this keeps the odds below 4, mathematically it's very unlikely for the sportsbook to lose money. However, if all players one-sidedly bet on the Heat, making the wagers $1 million on the Heat and only $10 on the Bobcats, we find that due to the imbalance in bets, the sportsbook still faces the potential risk of loss.

In this scenario, if you were the sportsbook, your only option would be to significantly increase the odds for the Bobcats. At this point, you could see odds not just of 5.0 but even 10.0, because maintaining "balance" in the betting lines is the real key to this business. This is likely why you often see such odd rates.

Lastly, I would like to hazard a guess. Are you primarily playing on unregulated underground betting sites? Usually, large online sportsbooks will disclose their juice, like 5%~10%, and it will be accurately reflected in the lines. If the juice is 5%, then the sum of the odds for both teams must equal 3.95. This transparency is necessary for the sustainability of the business. Odds higher than 4 are more likely to be found on unregulated or small sites that intentionally go head-to-head with players. I sincerely advise you to stay away from such sites.

Best Regards,

The Relationship Between Sports Betting and Lottery Tickets - Part Two

Dear,

Thank you for taking the time to respond to my email amidst your busy schedule. I'll address each of the questions you've raised.

You're correct that my book is not available in Mainland China. I'm glad to hear you went to the lengths of purchasing it online and waiting a month and a half for its arrival. As for the Traditional Chinese text, I understand that readers from the mainland are generally able to comprehend it or at least grasp the main idea.

Regarding the odds for the Heat vs. Bobcats game that I previously mentioned, those kinds of odds are indeed frequently offered. This isn't limited to underground bookmakers; many legal lottery centers in Mainland China often set their lines this way. However, you can't bet on just one game; you have to parlay at least two games, which you referred to as "1串2." Are you familiar with legal sports lottery issuing companies in Mainland China, such as Oukewang, 500 Million, or China Sports Lottery?

Here are the odds for two NBA games scheduled for tomorrow, set by Oukewang:

- Mavericks vs. Thunder 3.68 1.15

- Warriors vs. Clippers 3.68 1.15

The sum of the odds for each game exceeds 4, and it's not apparent where the bookmaker's juice is accounted for. How would you explain this issue?


Hello, Katie.

It turns out it's China's official sports betting, my apologies. I'm not very familiar with this area, so I didn't think of it at first. The main reason for my unfamiliarity is that China's official sports betting is not strictly sports gambling in the traditional sense. As far as I know, they have so-called "pools" and "parlay" betting methods, neither of which are very fair to the players.

Let's talk about parlays first. As you mentioned, when you place a bet, you can't just bet on one game; you have to parlay, with a minimum of two games. That's what we call a two-leg parlay. You only win money if you guess both games correctly. From this rule, we can immediately see that the odds for an average player to win money have dropped from 1/2 in a single game to 1/4, while the odds for the online sportsbook to win money have risen to 3/4. This changes the juice rules we've previously discussed (including in the book), as those only apply to single-game situations where both the website and the player have a 1/2 chance of winning.

So, how do you calculate the juice for parlays? The simplest way is to list it out. Let's use your example to illustrate:

Mavericks vs. Thunder 3.68 1.15

Warriors vs. Clippers 3.68 1.15

First, let's assume that the online sportsbook has achieved balanced betting on both sides (this assumption is generally accurate, as balancing the books is what the website does every day). So, in a perfect scenario, the projected income and expenditure would be as follows:

For the Mavericks, they collect $115, and because the odds are 3.68, the payout for a single game would be $423.2.

For the Thunder, they collect $368, and because the odds are 1.15, the payout for a single game would be $423.2.

For the Warriors, they collect $115, and because the odds are 3.68, the payout for a single game would be $423.2.

For the Clippers, they collect $368, and because the odds are 1.15, the payout for a single game would be $423.2.

The total income is $966.

From the perspective of the online sportsbook, the total revenue from these four teams is $115 + $368 + $115 + $368 = $966. As for the payouts, since it's a parlay involving two teams, there can only be one of the four possible scenarios:

- Mavericks win and Warriors win, resulting in a parlay payout of $846.4.

- Mavericks win and Clippers win, resulting in a parlay payout of $846.4.

- Thunder win and Warriors win, resulting in a parlay payout of $846.4.

- Thunder win and Clippers win, resulting in a parlay payout of $846.4.

No matter which scenario the player bets on, the expected payout is $846.4. Therefore, we can deduce that the sportsbook's theoretical profit before the game starts is $966 - $846.4 = $119.6. The juice ratio is 119.6 / 966 = 12.38%.

Of course, the actual profit for the sportsbook won't precisely be 12.38% because the acceptance of bets on various lines won't be perfectly balanced. Additionally, the rules of the parlay sometimes also involve using the winnings from the first game to place bets on the second game. So, the actual parlay payouts would be higher than our theoretical calculation here. Regardless, you can rest assured that sportsbooks work very hard to balance their lines every day, aiming to get as close as possible to this theoretical profit of 12.38%.

As for another official type of betting pool, it's even simpler. In this betting pool, there are no odds; those who guess the winner share a prize. The size of the prize depends on the total amount wagered that day, usually a percentage of it. We won't discuss this form of betting here, as it offers no challenge to the sportsbook in terms of balancing the lines.

In conclusion, I hope the above calculations have clarified any doubts you may have about the odds. In the world of parlays, sportsbooks can absolutely offer odds higher than 4, and the more teams you include in your parlay, the higher the odds can go. However, for you or the average player, it's better to steer clear of this type of betting. Compared to many companies offering a juice of 5%, a juice of 12.38% is simply too expensive.


Best Regards,

**The Relationship Between Sports Betting and Lottery Tickets - Part Two Three**

Hello:

Sorry for the delayed response to your email! Your analysis of the odds and the bookmaker's juice was very detailed, and I have gained a lot from it. I haven't finished reading your book yet, and I estimate it will take some time to fully understand it. I will continue studying it.

I'm curious, do you personally buy sports lottery tickets? Is Fubon Bank's sports lottery available for online purchase? I want to thank you for your patience in replying to my emails all this time. Thank you.

Thank you very much for enjoying the book, and feel free to reach out with any questions. Fubon Bank has already lost its license to issue sports lotteries, and it's now being handled by CTBC Bank. They do offer online betting, but you must first open an account with CTBC Bank.

I've only engaged in sports betting once or twice, mainly for fun during the previous FIFA World Cup. Occasionally indulging in sports betting can indeed add some excitement to watching the games. However, I don't recommend it as a regular activity or a profession. In the business of sports lotteries, there are many ways to make a stable income, but none of them involve relying solely on "betting."

Dear Mr. Liu Jianzhi,

Today, I watched the 9:30 a.m. Taiwan Sports Lottery NBA game between the Trail Blazers (away) and the Spurs (home). The pre-game odds for the money line were Trail Blazers: 3.6; Spurs: 1.18. I wanted to ask you why the sum of the odds for both sides is greater than 4. I thought of an example where, let's say, there is $100 on the Trail Blazers and $300 on the Spurs. The total revenue would then be $400, and the expected payouts for both sides would be around $360. Therefore, the juice should be around 10%, in an ideal scenario.

**Is my thinking correct?**

**Looking forward to your guidance.**

**Thank you!**

Dear Zonghua,

Your thinking is indeed correct. Let's examine your example.

If players bet $100 on the Trail Blazers with odds at 3.6, the projected winnings would be $360.

If players bet $300 on the Spurs with odds at 1.18, the projected winnings would be $354.

The total revenue for the online sportsbook would be $400, and the expected payout would be around $360. Thus, the sportsbook's profit would indeed be around 10%. So, even though the sum of the odds for both sides is greater than four, the sportsbook can still make money, and we can consider this a reasonable line. Generally, the sum of the odds should not exceed four, as that would risk the sportsbook losing money.

Normally, sportsbooks wouldn't set odds this way, but there are exceptions, especially when the odds between the two sides are very different. Your situation is one such exception. On my blog, there is a spreadsheet available that allows everyone to calculate their return on investment (ROI). Just input the odds and the betting amount to see the player's ROI and, of course, the sportsbook's profit margin as well.

Please refer to the following website for more information.

http://791088.blogspot.com/2008/07/blog-post_14.html

**Dear Mr. Liu,**

**Hello, Mr. Liu. I'm one of your readers from China and also a sports betting enthusiast. I've had the pleasure of reading your book "The Economics of Sports Betting."**

**I have a question for you. If Pinnacle's pricing is the most sensitive and effectively reflects the true value, how can players make money on Pinnacle?**

Hi Radar,

That's a good question and one that many people have asked before. I believe you already know the answer: the vast majority of players can't make money on Pinnacle. If everyone were winning, Pinnacle would have gone bankrupt a long time ago.

However, I do have a few tips that can certainly lower your chances of losing, thereby increasing your chances of winning.

- Stick to two-way betting markets. For instance, never play on a three-way market. The logic is simple: with three options, your chances of guessing right are only 33%, whereas with a two-way market, it's 50%. If you're serious about winning, you should only play in markets where you have a higher chance of guessing right. Essentially, the more options there are, the more you're just handing money over to the online sportsbook.

- Don't only back the side with higher odds. For example, in a given market, many people would back the team with odds of 2.130, especially those who have been playing for a long time and losing. While it may seem like you win more because the odds are higher, this approach is absolutely wrong. You should be betting on the team that is likely to win, not the one with higher odds. Therefore, extensive research and accurate judgment are necessary.

- Don't play long-term or continuously. Mathematically, the odds are not in the player's favor. With Pinnacle, a typical line is at 1.95. This means that if you bet $100 and win, you'll only win $95. If you lose, you'll lose the full $100.

That's a very bad proposition. If your chance of being correct is 50%, you'd lose $5 for every two bets you place. Unfortunately, the more you play, the closer your performance will align with this statistic—that's just how probability works, and we can't beat math. However, if you play infrequently and with fewer bets, statistics won't have much of a grip on you. When the sample size is small, statistics don't mean much, and your chances of winning are higher.

**Thank you. But what I mean is, if one must gamble, how does one win? I've studied pricing, liquidity, and statistics, and I've found that bookmakers can be categorized into three types.**

**The first type includes companies like Betway and Bet365. Betway uses data from SBTech, while Bet365 is technologically supported by Betradar and Betgenius, in addition to their own proprietary design and pricing. Although Bet365 has its own pricing, it usually doesn't differ much from the reference odds provided by data suppliers. Betway, on the other hand, is entirely managed. The common point between these types of bookmakers is their focus on managing players. If a player wins money and profits over the long term, they'll be subjected to betting limits or even be banned altogether. Although they will pay out the winnings, they won't allow the player to continue playing. They don't welcome winners. Betway and Bet365 are used as examples because they represent the vast majority of bookmakers; most operate in a manner similar or identical to them.**

**The second type follows the model of Pinnacle, which focuses on managing prices rather than players. Marathon is an imitator of Pinnacle but has never really taken off. What I mean is that Marathon lacks liquidity and can't compare with Pinnacle. Pinnacle claims to welcome arbitrage and winners, which fundamentally stems from their confidence in their own price management. Or, to put it another way, at times they are willing to take risks against players and compete on price with their peers. They can do this precisely because of their strategy of not limiting winners; winners' bets help them adjust market prices, increasing price depth (each price level has a higher betting limit than competitors) and acquiring more liquidity. As the start time of the event draws closer, the price depth gradually increases, as does price accuracy. Closing prices can generally reflect the probability of**

an event happening, or its value. Pinnacle is genuinely the bookmaker that fears not your wins but your absence.

The third type involves Asian bookmakers like Singbet Crown, SBO, and IBC Saba. Crown is different from Pinnacle in that they don't welcome arbitrage; in some events, they even "scratch tickets," meaning that the player's confirmed order is considered invalid after the game ends. This behavior is common on other Asian platforms like SBO and WLG. Theoretically, these large Asian bookmakers shouldn't be concerned about whether individual bettors make money because they mainly operate on the Asian lines, including point spread and binary betting. If more money flows into the upper line, they slightly lower its price; if less flows into the lower line, they slightly raise its price. As long as they control the funds well for each accepted bet, they make a profit regardless of the game's outcome. However, the phenomenon of scratching tickets suggests that Crown's operations are not rigorous enough, and other Asian bookmakers are no better. Some even plagiarize from each other; for instance, CMD in Cambodia mostly copies from IBC Saba. These plagiarized platforms are of low quality, providing no valuable signals, only adding noise to the market. Taiwan Baoying's own BB sports line is also plagiarized, piecing together products from various sources, which is quite subpar. Kyushu Sports operates independently but its trading department is also lacking. Moreover, in the past two years, Kyushu has lost all credibility and turned into a scam platform. Winners can't even withdraw their winnings, let alone get back their principal.

I realize I've gone off on a tangent; what I wanted to ask Brother Liu is, from an industry perspective, have you discovered any trading or betting strategies that can efficiently make a profit? (Aside from manipulating games)

Hi Radar,

Haha, after reading your text, I now know not only are you knowledgeable, but you're also an expert in the field. My apologies for the rudimentary response in my last letter. Most of the people who write to me are beginners, so I usually only respond with the most basic ideas to prevent them from having unrealistic expectations.

Your research into the current market is far more in-depth than mine. After all, I've been out of this industry for over a decade and am not as familiar with the current market. So, seeing your commentary on Taiwan's sportsbooks brought a knowing smile to my face. These sportsbooks have been copying others for over a decade and are still doing the same, showing no innovation.

Since you're an expert, I'll follow your line of thinking. If one must gamble, plans to do so long-term, and also intends to make money, then aside from arbitrage, there likely aren't any other options. You certainly know that to employ arbitrage, one needs at least two sportsbooks, or bookmakers, who don't mind you arbitraging. Pinnacle is one option; you'll need to find another. From there, it's a matter of writing software to monitor the lines at both bookmakers, identify arbitrage opportunities, and place bets automatically. But these are just details, and I'm sure you're well versed in them.

Your analysis is already very insightful. The first and third types of bookmakers are definitely out of the question. Even if there's an arbitrage opportunity, the practice of order revision could seriously jeopardize your arbitrage strategy. Once your bet is revised, you're essentially gambling, which could result in significant losses. The bookmakers that ban you after you win long-term are also not an option. Unfortunately, these two types make up the majority, which is why long-term stable arbitrage is so difficult.

Additionally, based on both of your letters, it's clear you hold Pinnacle in high regard, especially their lines at closing time, which may reflect the probability of an event occurring. So naturally, one might wonder if it's possible to leverage these lines for some sort of advantage?

I'm a hands-on person. If I were still in this industry, I would try to collect all the closing prices of Pinnacle's lines for a year and then compare them with the actual game results for the same year. The aim would be to see if there is a positive correlation, and more importantly, what the probability is of accurately predicting outcomes and the average odds. If the calculated results show that the probabilities and odds provide me with a positive return on investment, and that return is higher than a bank deposit, then it's valuable and could actually be used to make money. Otherwise, there's no need to hurry; just put your money in a bank deposit. I recommend you could try calculating it yourself.

However, based solely on my current understanding, I would argue that Pinnacle's prices are not valuable. The reason lies in your statement that closing prices generally reflect the probability of an event occurring or, in other words, its value. But this should be more precisely stated: closing prices generally reflect what bettors think is the probability of an event occurring, or its value. And whether what the bettors think will actually happen is very much up for debate. For example, factors often seen in sports competitions like player injuries, referee mistakes, or even biased officiating can significantly affect the outcome. These are factors that bettors cannot foresee, so they will affect the actual probability of events. Additionally, the odds for teams that most bettors think will win are generally noticeably lower, which affects the return rate. So I believe that these two factors combined make Pinnacle's prices lack any substantial meaning.

I am also very curious; aside from arbitrage, is there a second way to consistently make money? If there are other ideas, feel free to email me anytime.

Thank you. I'm pleased to converse with Brother Liu. The closing price reflected by Pinnacle is indeed reliable, but the issue is that when the market closes, you can't place bets on other platforms even if you know the so-called accurate price. If you're betting in-play, that's actually a different product. In-play odds are priced based on live conditions, so using pre-game odds as a guide would be incorrect at that point.

In pre-game markets, platforms are actually not very concerned with finding the most accurate probabilities. They're focused on balancing their liabilities to ensure profitability. It's different for players; they need to understand the odds for each option very well. Otherwise, how would they determine the value? What price is worth taking? Players' behavior usually has some patterns.

As a result, some people establish strategies similar to financial trading. They take high prices at exchanges like Betfair and Matchbook to hedge against other bookmakers, or complete the hedge directly at the exchange. They use a system to predict players' betting preferences, or predict market price trends. They might build early positions on certain options and complete the hedge when the price of the hedging options rises, or take advantage of time delays to hedge. Didn't we say that some platforms plagiarize odds from other platforms? If you plagiarize, there's inevitably a delay, be it 10 seconds, 2 seconds, or whatever. Any delay creates arbitrage opportunities.

Personally, my research isn't focused on arbitrage but mainly on in-play markets. In these, it's almost impossible for bookmakers to balance liabilities, meaning they have to take on greater risks. They also need to predict the game in order to set reasonable prices. We can see that Pinnacle has far fewer in-play markets than pre-game ones, and their product lines are also far less diverse. That's because the model they use for pre-game markets can't be directly applied to in-play markets. In-play traders are essentially gambling against players. They set a price that they think is favorable for themselves (or the company). If a player accepts this price, it's like starting a Texas Hold'em hand with 3Q against AA. It's not that 3Q is guaranteed to lose against AA, but AA obviously has the advantage.

If players can establish a mathematical model that calculates prices more accurately than the bookmaker, then they would essentially have the equivalent of starting every Texas Hold'em hand with pocket aces. However, the scale of this task is immense, requiring a team of dozens or even hundreds of people, including mathematicians, seasoned programmers, sports analysts, and quantitative analysts, to work together to solve this challenging problem. I failed in this direction and realized that one person is insufficient to complete this monumental project.

Taking a step back and using a "curve-saving-the-country" mindset, I delved into the three key elements mentioned earlier: pricing, liquidity, and statistical data. Platforms like Pinnacle and brokers (various betting brokerage platforms, such as stage8, Asianodds, Molly, bet-ibc, etc.) provide easy access to pricing and liquidity across various platforms like pin, isn, sin, wlg, ibc, sbo, cmd, betfair, matchbook, and more. Meanwhile, statistical data from Sportradar, Fandom (for the eSports LOL project), and HLTV (for the eSports CSGO project), provide valuable references for individual players. This data helps players analyze the capabilities of various teams or even individual athletes.

Statistical data can assist players in determining which options are more likely to translate into cash at a higher frequency, thus minimizing investment drawdowns. Being able to stay in the game without going bankrupt is a prerequisite for discussing profits or the extent of those profits, right? Betting on the low-priced strong players is fundamentally a good approach, but the price must be right for profitability. If the price is wrong, even frequent wins will result in a net

**loss. Moreover, a low price doesn't necessarily indicate a strong player, and not every match shines like the EPL. This ultimately tests a player's ability to gather and analyze information.**

Your insights are very deep. I particularly like the statement that betting on low-priced favorites is generally a good direction, but you must get the price right to make a profit. Betting on teams with low odds is actually the main trading strategy for most players. However, they don't think deeply enough and miss the latter part of your statement, which is why they end up losing money in the long run without understanding why.

It's clear that in-play betting, especially identifying high-priced strong teams, is your main area of research. Strong teams naturally won't have high odds; only weaker teams would. So, you need thorough research and statistical analysis to filter out teams that bookmakers consider weak but are actually strong due to various factors. This way, you can capitalize on these good "high-priced strong" hands.

Your approach is correct, and it doesn't conflict with the bookmakers' strategies, so they won't actively try to block this tactic. I'll mention their perspective later. First, let me praise your strategy. In-play betting is a tough market to make money in. Bookmakers can easily make mistakes here and find it very challenging to balance the bets, often ending up directly gambling against the players. This happens frequently.

Moreover, the mistakes made by the traders on the platforms far exceed a 5 or 10-second delay. Plagiarizing the wrong information, failing to update the odds in real-time, or even falling asleep at the wheel are common occurrences. To expect all of them to be experts on every team in every match is unrealistic, even for major platforms.

Don't overestimate traders; they're salaried employees and cannot match the expertise of players who are putting their own money at stake. I always believe that many veteran players possess more knowledge and insights into matches than traders. Of course, you can also identify these "high-priced strong" teams.

But let me add that this all depends on the line. Essentially, the more important the match or the more popular the team, the less likely the bookmakers are to make a mistake. There's a host of traders at bookmakers, and some are experts assigned to popular lines. Their chances of making errors are low. Furthermore, during significant events, not only traders but all supervisors and even the owners will be watching. Mistakes are hard to come by in such situations.

But when it comes to obscure betting lines or matches between two low-tier teams, it's a different story. The traders in these cases are average and not well-paid, and they don't get much attention from the management. Slow updates on odds—or even incorrect odds—are not uncommon. Therefore, I believe the key to this strategy of betting on high-priced strong teams lies in focusing on these overlooked low-tier teams. In conclusion, the bookmakers know the complexities involved in in-play betting, but we've discussed these issues and our stance is simple: we don't really care.

Firstly, the bookmaker takes at least a 5% commission. So, if you, the player, have $100 to bet, if you win, you can win a maximum of $95; if you lose, you lose $100. This is a significant advantage that the bookmaker holds, making the bets inherently unfair. Given enough time and a sufficient number of bets, the bookmaker will eventually win the money.

Secondly, in-play betting is not entirely peer-to-peer betting. It often starts with laying off bets to achieve a balanced book, and then taking the unbalanced portion to the betting market. That initial balancing act already guarantees a fixed 5% profit. So even if there's a higher likelihood of losing in the short term, the fixed profit can cover those losses. The risk for the bookmaker is actually quite low.

Thirdly, as you mentioned, most bookmakers fall into the first category you described. We regularly study the track records of players. If you're consistently winning more than losing and not contributing to our platform, then the easiest and most cost-effective solution is simply to ask you to leave.


**Thank you for sharing.**

**Liu, you're clearly a veteran in the industry. A few years ago, I began to focus on the key issue of pricing. My mistake was assuming that all betting lines were generated by advanced algorithms, complex mathematical models, and top-notch programming. So, I foolishly relied entirely on the odds of one platform to compare with those of another, looking for significant discrepancies to place bets.**

While this approach isn't entirely wrong, it's fundamentally naive. What I learned later is that the technology in the sports betting industry hasn't reached a level of full automation for pricing and bookmaking. It's unrealistic to think it would be entirely without human intervention since, after all, humans control the switches and logic of the software.

Besides realizing that manual management of betting lines is still the norm, I also understood that not all trading desks are the same. The traders who manage the English Premier League lines are worlds apart from those managing Greek basketball games. No platform would risk sending a rookie to handle high-profile events like the Premier League.

So, the pricing issues in sports betting need to be considered on a case-by-case basis. This led me to pay attention to liquidity issues. For example, in some ITF tennis events, even on a large platform like 365, the limits could be just a few thousand or even a few hundred dollars. Of course, I know that limits vary from account to account. I'm talking about new accounts, what you'd call a "1x account."

Speaking of 365 account issues, it reminds me of another question I'd like to ask you, Liu.

This brings us to the issue of "fixed matches." From what I understand, there are two "lay-off" teams on Hainan Island, and similar organizations exist in Zhejiang, Hubei, and Sichuan. These teams likely get "fixed match" information from countries like Cambodia, Malaysia, and Singapore, meaning they know which matches are rigged before they start. They then acquire negative-balance accounts on platforms like 365, Betway, Crown Credit, Betway, Jiuzhou, and so on for the purpose of laying off. So, from the platform's perspective, how do they view this issue? If there's a significant risk of manipulation in some low-tier matches, why do they still offer lines for them?

From my personal observations, match-fixing is widespread in esports. This is especially true in DOTA2; even clubs that have won world championships have disbanded due to match-fixing scandals. The League of Legends scene is also not clean. In China's LPL, nearly all clubs are intricately familiar with the betting lines, and there have been frequent instances where players collude with betting syndicates to manipulate the outcome of matches for profit. The situation is even worse in secondary competitions like the LDL, which has had to suspend matches for restructuring due to rampant match-fixing. The

LPL has cleaned up its act somewhat in recent years, mainly because players now earn more, but there are still those who "gamble," and because LDL players earn so little, match-fixing is basically an open secret; efforts to reform the scene have been ineffective, only making it harder to detect match-fixing.

What puzzles me is that the odds for some manipulated matches do not experience significant fluctuations. It's as if these bets are being laid off stealthily, and the winnings are collected without arousing suspicion. The reason these individuals avoid laying off at Pinnacle is precisely to prevent significant odds movement. But how can they achieve this "ghost-like" effect elsewhere?

Match-fixing has always been a fascinating topic, especially when viewed from the perspective of a bookmaker's line. Let's start with the approach the industry I was in took years ago, which was to completely avoid it. For example, professional leagues in China or Taiwan from over a decade ago were off-limits. While there were people who wanted to bet on them, the industry generally refrained from offering lines for these events. Most were willing to offer only well-known European and American leagues. At that time, esports hadn't yet become popular; if they had, chances are the industry wouldn't have offered lines for those either.

There are two main reasons for this. First, everyone knows which leagues are more susceptible to match-fixing, and no one likes rigged games. So, the number of people who are truly willing to place substantial bets on these leagues wouldn't be high. Given that the betting volume wouldn't be too great, it naturally makes no sense to develop such a product. To clarify, in our era, the primary revenue for the industry came from major European and American leagues, accounting for over 90% of the total. Even in the case of Chinese football, very few people in China were interested; most were placing bets on European and American games.

Secondly, it's difficult to manage lines that are prone to match-fixing. These lines have significant volatility. Balancing them is hard, and trying to lay off the risk to other bookmakers is equally challenging. Ultimately, you'd either have to cancel individual large bets or shut down the line altogether, refunding the money to the players. Both options would significantly damage the bookmaker's credibility. Moreover, there's no point in going through all this trouble for such small business, so it's best to stay away.

However, we did offer what we called "junk games," which are usually very low-profile matches, like some minor European football leagues or other sporting events. Very few people bet on these, and there are many restrictions, such as lower odds and limitations on individual and total bets. The main purpose of offering these is to kill time when there are no popular events to bet on. These don't pose a risk; if something seems off, you can simply cancel the bets. Canceling bets on these junk games isn't news. In my experience, nobody has ever placed a substantial bet on these, nor have I seen a sudden spike in the total bets for any of these games. They are purely a way for some people to pass the time.

Because my industry refrained from offering lines on leagues prone to match-fixing, it's hard for me to say why some might still want to do it. However, I suspect the mentality surrounding junk games could apply. As long as the betting volume is low and poses no risk to the bookmaker, then it's doable. As long as there is no counter-betting, match-fixing doesn't harm the bookmaker. The only ones who get hurt are the players who aren't privy to the inside information. But if they're willing to play, they probably are prepared for the risks and can't blame the bookmaker's credibility, especially since the bookmaker isn't the one instigating the match-fixing.

Another significant possibility occurs with small bookmakers who dare to accept all sorts of bets. If they lose, they can simply run away, leaving the players with no recourse. Or they could claim there was an issue with the bet and cancel it after the game. I've heard of such situations before, but they aren't major news.

Your idea of a "lay off" team seems to be a challenging business to me. We all know that placing bets is easy; the hard part is claiming the winnings. Buying accounts from major platforms to lay off bets is one option, but it's difficult to do on a large scale. Big platforms are always watching. If a worthless team suddenly becomes worth betting on, they'll definitely take action.

Going to small platforms to lay off is also unreliable. Small platforms can disappear at any moment, so they can't be relied upon for large returns. So even if you have information on fixed games, you can only make small moves on these platforms. That's why you won't see drastic fluctuations in the lines, as there are no large bets being placed.

However, if large bets do come in, the lines will undoubtedly fluctuate. A long time ago, Macau's sportsbook experienced this with a fixed game in the

Chinese football league. The line changed rapidly, made the news, and even prompted an investigation by the club. Adjusting the lines is a cardinal rule for legitimate bookmakers; they must do so whenever there is an imbalance in bets. So if you notice a fixed game but the lines aren't moving, there are only two possibilities: either the bookmaker is illegitimate and takes the bets themselves, or there are no large bets coming in because the lay off teams know they can't collect.

From what I understand, teams that lay off on fixed games generally don't use regular, legitimate platforms—at least not on a large scale. The real money is made by betting against specific individuals, such as those in organized crime, celebrities, or big players in the industry. In this kind of genuine betting, there's no possibility of one-sided cancellations or defaults, making it the true channel for lay off teams to collect their winnings.

**Thank you. Brother Liu, your insights are truly enlightening, and I've learned a lot.**

**I haven't been to Taiwan yet. If the COVID-19 pandemic subsides, I should make a good plan and take a trip to Taiwan.**

**If possible, I'd also like to treat Brother Liu to a meal. What's your favorite local restaurant? Even if we don't get the chance to meet up, I'll still go and try it out. Haha.**

**From a local's perspective, besides Taipei, which other places are highly favored?**

Taiwan is a really fun place to visit, especially because it's not very large, so it doesn't take much time to get around. I highly recommend experiencing it for yourself. You should check out the National Palace Museum and try the snacks at Shilin Night Market. Go to Jiufen for the mountain views and Keelung Night Market for the seafood. Eslite Bookstore in Taipei is also really good; I often grab a book there and spend a whole weekend.

# Appendix

## Profit Calculation Table

Sports betting is a unique game. In this game, being a bookmaker doesn't solely rely on chance to make money. Like the players, a good online sportsbook must simultaneously understand the relationship between odds and probabilities to attract players and profit from the game.

"Juice" is the most unique term in this game, representing the website's profit, or a percentage of the total amount of accepted bets each day. For example, if the website declares that it takes 10% in juice, then assuming it collected a $100 betting ticket today, it would make a $10 profit.

The more juice a site takes, the less favorable it is for the players. Therefore, a savvy player always seeks websites that take the least amount of juice for placing bets. However, websites rarely publicly disclose their profits, so players need to figure it out themselves. In this calculation table, you can reverse-engineer the amount of juice a site takes from its betting lines. All you have to do is enter the betting odds from the website into the table, and you can see how much juice they take, and how the player's return on investment is affected.

Please note that juice is constantly adjusted depending on the particular match or sport, so you can regularly input the observed odds to study a website's pricing strategy.

Additionally, the table also integrates calculations for the return rate of parlays. And we find that by setting up a game mode like a three-game parlay, websites can increase their profit from a single game's 10% to 27.1%. Frankly, this is a very smart move.

Please connect to this URL directly using a browser.

http://791088.50webs.com/Lottery/a.html

## Betting Balance Sheet

In sports betting, it's not easy for an online sportsbook to turn a profit. Many people think that all a bookmaker needs to do is post the lines, let players place their bets, and the profits will naturally roll in. This notion is incorrect. In reality, if the lines are not managed properly after they are posted, the online sportsbook not only has no hope of making a profit but could also lose a significant amount of money.

In this spreadsheet, we present a management tool for an online sportsbook, commonly referred to as a betting balance sheet. By utilizing this sheet, the online sportsbook can keep track of players' betting activities and monitor its own profits. Ultimately, it can decide how to manipulate players so that they place their bets on the intended teams.

The foundation of this sheet is that every time a player places a bet, their betting ticket needs to be entered into the sheet. Then, one can observe whether the total payout for each team exceeds the total income. In the best-case scenario, the expected payouts for both teams are equal; this is what we commonly refer to as a "balanced line," allowing the online sportsbook to achieve the most stable profits.

If the situation is not ideal, with players betting randomly and disrupting the balance of the spreadsheet, then if a particular team wins, the online sportsbook could potentially incur significant losses. At that point, the online sportsbook needs to adjust the odds for the teams, using higher odds to attract players to bet on the team the sportsbook wants them to. This will help restore balance to the sheet.

Please connect to this URL directly using a browser.

http://791088.50webs.com/Lottery/b.html

## Arbitrage Spreadsheet

"Arbitrage" is a specialized term in sports betting, referring to the tactic of purchasing two betting tickets, each placed on different teams, so that the player profits regardless of which team wins. This strategy relies on mathematical principles and the constantly changing odds in sportsbooks. If the timing of the ticket purchases is right, the player can arbitrage the odds.

The spreadsheet above explains the principle behind this tactic. Let's say the sportsbook opens a line for "NBA Team A vs. Team B." The player could first buy a betting ticket for Team A, for example, placing $100 at odds of 2.28. Then, the player continues to monitor the line until the odds for Team B also rise to a high point, such as 1.95. At this point, the player can purchase the second betting ticket, but the amount to be wagered must be raised to $117.

In the end, the table shows that the player will earn $5 regardless of whether Team A or Team B wins. With a total investment of $217, the return on investment (ROI) is 5.07%. And this is the unique risk-free money-making strategy in sports betting known as "Arbitrage."

To execute this strategy, three key factors should be considered: the amount wagered on the first betting ticket, the odds at which it was purchased, and the odds of the second betting ticket. Interested individuals can try altering these three fields in the spreadsheet to see how the ROI changes. By calculating the ROI, it becomes easier to pinpoint the optimal timing for purchasing the second betting ticket.

Please connect to this URL directly using a browser.

http://791088.50webs.com/Lottery/c.html

## Balancing the AB Table

If players want to achieve stable profits in sports betting, they must master the relationship between the probability of guessing correctly and the odds. By either increasing the likelihood of each correct guess or securing higher odds, players can noticeably improve their profits.

The AB Table is a tool for bettors, helping them better understand their betting tendencies and make informed bets in the future. Let's say you place bets based on the recommendations from two different sports publications, one being the "Orange Daily" and the other the "Banana Daily." The AB Table can be used to evaluate the accuracy of these two publications.

Assume you've purchased 10 betting tickets based on the recommendations from these two papers, 5 from the Orange Daily and 5 from the Banana Daily. So, in the AB Table, you fill in '5' under total bets for Group A and also '5' for Group B. Next, you sort out the winning tickets from the Orange Daily; let's say there are only two. The odds for these two winning tickets are then entered under Group A. The same is done for the Banana Daily, where there are three winning tickets.

The final results indicate that within Group A, which followed the Orange Daily, the rate of return is -6%, whereas for the Banana Daily in Group B, it's 4%. The conclusion is straightforward: the Banana Daily's predictions are more accurate. If you plan to continue betting based on the Banana Daily, it's essential to pay attention to the odds, aiming to secure odds higher than the average of 1.73.

Please connect to this URL directly using a browser.

http://791088.50webs.com/Lottery/d.html